The Idealism of Freedom

Critical Studies in German Idealism

Series Editor

Paul G. Cobben

Advisory Board

Simon Critchley – Paul Cruysberghs – Rózsa Erzsébet – Garth Green
Vittorio Hösle – Francesca Menegoni – Martin Moors – Michael Quante
Ludwig Siep – Timo Slootweg – Klaus Vieweg

VOLUME 26

The titles published in this series are listed at *brill.com/csgi*

The Idealism of Freedom

For a Hegelian Turn in Philosophy

By

Klaus Vieweg

BRILL

LEIDEN | BOSTON

Library of Congress Cataloging-in-Publication Data

Names: Vieweg, Klaus, 1953- author.
Title: The idealism of freedom : for a Hegelian turn in philosophy /
   by Klaus Vieweg.
Description: Leiden ; Boston : Brill, 2020. | Series: Critical studies in
   German idealism, 1878-9986 ; volume 26 | Includes bibliographical
   references and index. | Summary: "This volume brings together essays on
   Hegel from various decades of my involvement with the most important
   philosophical thinker of modernity. It is directed against some of the
   misinterpretations, malicious legends, and fairy tales about Hegel that
   are still prevalent today"– Provided by publisher.
Identifiers: LCCN 2020025339 | ISBN 9789004429260 (hardback) |
   ISBN 9789004429277 (ebook)
Subjects: LCSH: Hegel, Georg Wilhelm Friedrich, 1770-1831.
Classification: LCC B2948 .V5758 2020 | DDC 193–dc23
LC record available at https://lccn.loc.gov/2020025339

Typeface for the Latin, Greek, and Cyrillic scripts: "Brill". See and download: brill.com/brill-typeface.

ISSN 1878-9986
ISBN 978-90-04-42926-0 (hardback)
ISBN 978-90-04-42927-7 (e-book)

Copyright 2020 by Koninklijke Brill NV, Leiden, The Netherlands.
Koninklijke Brill NV incorporates the imprints Brill, Brill Hes & De Graaf, Brill Nijhoff, Brill Rodopi,
Brill Sense, Hotei Publishing, mentis Verlag, Verlag Ferdinand Schöningh and Wilhelm Fink Verlag.
All rights reserved. No part of this publication may be reproduced, translated, stored in a retrieval system,
or transmitted in any form or by any means, electronic, mechanical, photocopying, recording or otherwise,
without prior written permission from the publisher. Requests for re-use and/or translations must be
addressed to Koninklijke Brill NV via brill.com or copyright.com.

This book is printed on acid-free paper and produced in a sustainable manner.

Contents

Preface IX
Acknowledgements X

PART 1
On the Fundament of Hegel's Philosophy

1 Hegel's Adventures in Wonderland, or the Beginning of Philosophy 3
   1 With What Must the Science Begin? 3
   2 Mediation or Immediacy 4
   3 The Beginning of Practical Philosophy 8
   4 Conclusion 12

2 Hegel's Sicilian Defence: Beyond Realism and Constructivism 13
   1 The Logic of Essence 14
   2 Immanent Negativity 20
   3 Conclusion 22

3 The "Reversal of Consciousness Itself": Along the Path of the *Phenomenology of Spirit* 23
   1 Reversals 24
   2 Conclusion 37

4 Pyrrho and the Wisdom of the Animals: Hegel on Scepticism 39
   1 Pyrrhonism – Freedom of Character and Freedom of Thought 41
   2 Happy and Unhappy Consciousness 47
   3 The Unity of the Theoretical and Practical Idea 51
   4 Ataraxia and Conscience 55

PART 2
Hegel's Practical Philosophy as a Philosophy of Freedom

5 Hegel's Theory of Free Will 61
   1 The Foundational Structure of the Will – §§5–7 61
   2 Conclusion 72

6   **Inter-Personality and Wrong**   73
     1   The Concept of the Person   73
     2   Personality and Inter-Personality – Recognition of the Person and Legal Capacity   75
     3   Wrong and the Theory of 'Second Coercion'   76
     4   The Logically Grounded Structure in Judgment   81

7   **Care and Forethought: The Idea of Sustainability in Hegel's Practical Philosophy**   84
     1   Property   85
     2   Property and the 'Formation' of the Natural   86
     3   The Appropriation of Elemental Things   89
     4   'Forethought Which Looks to, and Secures, the Future'   90
     5   Natural Sustainability – the Forest as Paradigm   92

8   **Hegel's Philosophical Theory of Action**   96
     1   Crime and Punishment – the Eumenides and Hegel's Grounding of Punishment in the Theory of Action   99
     2   Orestes and Oedipus – Heroic Self-Consciousness and Modernity   105

9   **Beyond Wall Street: Hegel as Founder of the Concept of a Welfare State**   115
     1   Civil Society as Modern Community of Market, Education and Solidarity   116
     2   All-round Dependence in the 'Community of Need and Understanding'   118
     3   Political Economy and the Regulated Market   120
     4   Regulation and Social Organization   121
     5   Oversight and External Regulation   122
     6   Social Care and Forethought – Foundations of Hegel's Conception of a Social State   122

10   **The State and Its Logical Foundations**   125
     1   The State as a Whole Consisting of Three Syllogisms   127
     2   The State as a Triad of Syllogisms   128
     3   The Inner Law of the State or Domestic Right – the Second System of Three Syllogisms   129
     4   A New Conception of the Separation and Interdependence of State Powers   133

- 5 The Constitution as a System of Three Syllogisms – a Reformulation of the *Philosophy of Right* 134
- 6 The State as a System of Three Syllogisms – against the Letter of the *Philosophy of Right* 137
- 7 The Universal, Law-Making Power – the Syllogism of Necessity (P-U-I) 138
- 8 The Categorical Syllogism 140
- 9 The Hypothetical Syllogism 141
- 10 The Disjunctive Syllogism 141

11 **The Right of Resistance** 144
- 1 Considerations on the Right of Necessity 145
- 2 The Concept of Second Coercion 147
- 3 The Stages of the Inversive Right of Resistance 149
- 4 Conclusion: State of Exception and Second Coercion 159

PART 3
Hegel on Art and Religion

12 **Hegel's Conception of the Imagination** 163
- 1 Imagination and Mind 163
- 2 From Intuition to Representation 165
- 3 Representation 167

13 **The World Turned Upside Down** 174
- 1 Reversals as Fantasy Castlings 178
- 2 Narrating Lives and Journeys 'Downhill' 183
- 3 Free *hystera protera*: Scepticism – Music – Carnival – Politics 185
- 4 Closing Remarks, or: Endgame 186

14 **On Hegel's Humour** 188
- 1 Negativity and Humour 193
- 2 The Victory of Subjectivity 196

15 **Religion and Absolute Knowing** 198
- 1 Basic Determinations of the Transition 198
- 2 Core Determinations of the Turning Point of the Transition, the Final Return out of the Realm of Representation 200
- 3 Freedom and Comprehensive Thought 209

16   **The East and Buddhism from Hegel's Perspective**   212
    1   The First 'Translation': That of Antiquity   212
    2   The Second 'Translation': Modernity   215
    3   Religion and Philosophy – Imagination and Concept   215
    4   Buddhism as a Religion of Silent Being-in-itself   216
    5   Freedom from Oneself and the Beautiful Soul   220
    6   The East and Modern Poetry   221
    7   Brief Resumé   221

Bibliography   223

Preface

> Ideas can be superseded,
> not the idea of freedom.
> LUDWIG BÖRNE

This volume brings together essays on Hegel from various decades of my involvement with the most important philosophical thinker of modernity. It is directed against some of the misinterpretations, malicious legends, and fairy tales about Hegel that are still prevalent today.

Hegel's idealism of freedom contains a number of epoch-making ideas that articulate a new understanding of freedom and which still shape contemporary philosophy. Hegel establishes a modern logic and the idea of a social state. With his distinction between civil society and the state he makes an innovative contribution to political philosophy. He defends the idea of freedom for all in a modern society and is a sharp critic of every nationalism and racism. According to Ernst Gombrich, Hegel is the father of the discipline of art history. According to Jacques Derrida, he is the founder of modern semiotics and makes a decisive contribution to the philosophical understanding of language.

The highest praise comes from Hegel's Nuremberg pupil Johann Georg August Wirth, who wrote that Hegel "ignited" in him "the immortal idea of freedom".

A new Hegel biography, published on the occasion of his 250th birthday, offers detailed discussion of the path of his life and thought: Klaus Vieweg, *Hegel – Der Philosoph der Freiheit*.

Klaus Vieweg
Jena, Autumn 2019

Acknowledgements

For translation of the essays comprising this collection I am grateful to:

Henny Blomme (Chapter 11), Elise Frketich (11), Timothy C. Huson (3, 12, 14, 16), Emma Moormann (11), Sebastian Stein (10), Gesa Wellmann (11) Adrian Wilding (1, 5, 6, 7), Nicholas Walker (8), Antonia Wilckens (11) and David W. Wood (11).

Thanks for permission to reprint some articles goes to:

Text 7: In: Readings in the Anthropocene d. by Sabine Wilke and Japhet Johnstone, Bloomsbury; Text 8: Hegel's Theory of Action; In: The Impact of Idealism. Volume III. Ed. by Nicholas Boyle/Liz Disley/Christoph Jamme/Ian Cooper; Cambridge University Press; Text 10: The State as a system of three Syllogisms. In: Hegel's Political Philosophy. Ed. by. Thom Brooks and Sebastian Stein, Oxford University Press; Text 11: In: Hegel and Resistance. Ed. by Rebecca Comay and Bart Zandvoort, Bloomsbury; Text 12: In: Inventions of the Imagination. Ed. by Richard T. Gray, Nicholas Halmi, Gary Handwerk, Michael Rosenthal, Klaus Vieweg, University of Washington Press; Text 13: Literary Castlings and Backward Flights to Heaven, In: Shandean Humour in English and German Literature and Philosophy. Ed. by Klaus Vieweg, James Vigus and Kathleen Wheeler. Legenda.

The revision of the English texts was in the capable hands of Adrian Wilding.

PART 1

On the Fundament of Hegel's Philosophy

∴

CHAPTER 1

Hegel's Adventures in Wonderland, or the Beginning of Philosophy

" 'Where shall I begin, please?' asked the white rabbit. 'Begin at the beginning,' the King said gravely.' " The King's answer in Lewis Carroll's *Alice's Adventures in Wonderland* recalls the answer given by the sovereign of modern philosophy, under the heading "With what must the Science begin?" Hegel's philosophical 'magic trick' is to pull the white rabbit of the beginning out of the hat of wisdom. As is well known, the question of the beginning in Hegel's philosophy is one of the most controversial points in Hegel scholarship – 100 different Hegel researchers will give you a hundred different (sometimes contradictory) answers: a Babylonian babble of voices. What follows is my attempt at an interpretation. Better, what follows represents the building blocks of an interpretation.

1   With What Must the Science Begin?

With this passage and *Introduction* to the *Science of Logic*, Hegel follows on from his Jena reflections, giving them now an argumentatively rounded form. Only now is it sufficiently clear what Hegel intended with the paradoxical dictum of a third philosophy that would be *neither dogmatism nor scepticism, neither realism nor constructivism, but both*. He offers a way out of the fixation on the beginning.

Were philosophy's starting point to be something determinate, something mediated, it would disqualify itself as a beginning, for it would presuppose something that justifies it and so would fall into the inconclusive regress of relativity. Were the beginning to be the indeterminate, the unfounded, the immediate, it would amount to a dogmatism of pure assertion. At the beginning Hegel, relying on arguments he had already developed in Jena, decisively turns against such arbitrary postulations of the beginning, "shot from the gun of inner revelation, of faith, of intellectual intuition" (*Werke* 5: 65–6), turns against Jacobi and Schelling who ignored from the outset the method of logic and thus abandon hope of knowledge. By contrast, Fichte's "more consistent transcendental idealism" is praised for "letting reason itself represent its determinations" (*Werke* 5: 41). In the *Introduction* the elements of the superseded

© KONINKLIJKE BRILL NV, LEIDEN, 2020 | DOI:10.1163/9789004429277_002

opposition of consciousness are emphasized again three times, and Hegel's beginning with pure knowledge – the pure concept – is seen to be no provisional assumption or mere assertion, but is said to have received its justification, its *proof*, in the procedure of the *Phenomenology of Spirit*. The 2nd edition of the *Logic* of 1831 confirms that the Jena *Phenomenology of Spirit* provides the deduction of the concept of pure science, of the beginning of philosophy as such and thus also of the beginning of logic. However, with the *Logic*, the 'ladders' of accomplished scepticism ascended in the *Phenomenology* can be set aside.

It *seems* that the logical beginning can thus be taken in two ways, in a *mediated* or an *immediate* way. Early on in the section "With What Must the Science Begin?" Hegel emphasises these two paths. Drawing upon the *Encyclopedia*, Hegel highlights that "there is nothing, nothing in heaven, or in nature or in mind or anywhere else which does not equally contain both immediacy and mediation, so that these two determinations reveal themselves to be *unseparated* and inseparable and the opposition between them to be a nullity" (*Werke* 5: 68).

To this extent Hegel, like Odysseus, attempts to escape a dilemma. The ancient hero managed to escape the monstrous dilemma of Scylla and Charybdis lurking on both sides of the Strait of Messina. The question of beginning in Hegel's *Logic* recalls in many ways Odysseus' audacious enterprise. Knowledge is to avoid falling victim to both the all-consuming pull of the Scylla called immediacy and the voracious tentacles of the Charybdis mediation. Put another way, the dilemma is that in contemporary philosophy between realism and constructivism. Two equally great evils are to be avoided and, like the Straits of Messina in ancient times, the route between them is narrow and treacherous.

2 Mediation or Immediacy

In §12 of the *Encyclopedia* we read: When both moments, immediacy and mediation, "present themselves as distinct, still neither of them can be absent, nor can one exist apart from the other" (*Werke* 8: 56). §65 of the *Encyclopedia* argues against an either/or of immediate vs. mediated knowledge; according to Hegel it depends on the logic of the opposition of immediacy and mediation. "The whole of the second part of Logic, the Doctrine of Essence, is a discussion of the intrinsic and self-affirming unity of immediacy and mediation" (*Werke* 8: 156).

Here, too, the question of the beginning cannot contravene the basic principles of the method Hegel has outlined, cannot go against the internal structure of the concept – self-relating negativity. Consequently, the possibility of an either/or is excluded; one can begin neither with mere immediacy nor mere mediation. Even if both moments *appear* to be distinct, they must be understood as inseparably connected. Thus, the author provides two 'variations', two 'perspectives' on the one beginning, two logical paths which are two moments in their respective one-sidedness, which at the same time contain their own sublation (*Aufhebung*), which contain negativity within themselves and which thus establish the identity, the *unity* of immediacy and mediation.

In Variation A – the *mediation* version – the result of the *Phenomenology* figures as the logical beginning, a beginning mediated by the proof contained therein of the standpoint of pure knowledge, of *comprehending* thinking. All other possible starting points are excluded – opinions, feelings, beliefs, ideas etc. In this respect, the *Phenomenology* is a presupposition of the *Logic*; it legitimates the beginning by means of the negation of the paradigm of consciousness – by means of the 'sceptical' side – as sublation of relativity, of mediation in pure, comprehending thinking. Thus the 'result' immediately reverts to the 'beginning', the end to the start. The consequence of the path of mediation was the sublation of mediation: pure comprehending knowledge as simple immediacy, *without any further determination*. Mediation involves the sublation of itself in the purely immediate.

In Variation B – the *immediacy* version – the beginning is to be taken immediately, by means of *the decision to want to think purely*, to think thinking as such. This "deciding" (*Ent-Schließen*, literally "de-closing") means 'opening', implies immediate positing, the *is* of incipient thinking, nothing else. Indeed there can be no talk of 'existence' before the decision – Hegel suggests that "what constitutes the beginning" and "the beginning itself" are synonymous (*Werke* 5: 75). Thus pure being as the *first* immediacy is posited, pronounced. Here *nothing* is presupposed, no mediation is called upon. However, pure being *is*, and this *existence* is a determination. The absolutely immediate proves to be just as absolutely mediated. Through the necessary progress of deduction, the beginning loses what it represents in this first determination, namely to be something indeterminate and abstract as such. Even pure knowledge is negative determination, has negativity in itself, thus has the minimal determination of being indefinite – *negatio est determinatio*.

Both roads lead to Rome, to pure being as a determination that must first emerge in knowledge, the Immediate, the Simple, that which is not yet determined, is mere beginning. With this, Hegel declares the argument to be concluded, what remains is mere explication and illustration. The legitimation of the beginning combines one-sided mediatedness with equally one-sided immediacy, combines 'presupposition' with the 'presuppositionless' – both variants lead to the pure *is*, to pure being. Strictly speaking, the *Logic* begins with pure comprehending thinking and the pure *is* of the thinking posited thereby. The *Logic* contains nothing but purely self-comprehending thinking, nothing more; it starts with this thinking in the form of Being. To take an example, whoever decides (*entschließt*) to play chess, whoever *opens themselves up to the game* (*Ent-schließt*), manifests their decision to play chess through their *opening* move, which, however, involves (chess) thinking as a precondition and must comply with the game's principle, its rules.

Being, pure Being articulates the minimum definition of the concept. With this 'first' Being, immediacy, the in-itself defines itself as indefinite, without any further determination (*Bestimmung*), simply as equality with itself (n.b., in German, when one says *"without any further determination"*, it implies that at least one determination is given, while further determinations are excluded).

Hegel insists on this minimum with his use of the superlative: Being is "the very poorest, the most abstract" determination; for thought there can be "nothing less" in terms of content than pure being (*Werke* 8: 136). It is the *least* that can be pointed to in the concept, *the most meagre, most abstract initial determination of all* – here we see precisely the seeming paradox of indeterminacy as determinacy or the determinacy of indeterminacy. This beginning as beginning, in its radical simplicity, its simple determination of *being*, can only be emptiest determination. The *Phenomenology* had likewise begun with the most immediate, poorest, most abstract figure, whose poverty was its only asset and was itself destined to disappear – the simple consciousness of what 'is' and what is 'meant'. The logical beginning can be described as the initial unity of the universal, the particular and the individual, in which these moments are not yet distinguished by their unfolding; though still under-determined they are already in play – equality as the most abstract universality, abstract difference as indeterminate particular, singularity as under-determined individuality (cf. Koch 2014: 62ff). This extreme deficiency demands a corresponding linguistic expression, but there can be no proposition or judgement here, only the simple word *being*, an *exclamatio*, the transformation of a sentence into an exclamation, here an isolated word, the minimalistic linguistic prototypes of the concept. The beginning thus emerges as that which is deficient in itself, the deficit par excellence: the simple beginning is "*posited* as afflicted with a negation" (*Werke* 6: 555) – the scantiest, most meagre definition of negativity – pure negativity – nothingness (non-existence).

Such a first step, such a departure still remains immediate, insofar as being is posited here immediately, "the *nothing* emerges in it only immediately" (*Werke* 5: 104). The superlative is unable to escape the determinacy, the mediation, the relation that is immanent to it. The logical second step, the 'second issue', i.e.

the negative),[1] proves to be an original 'first affliction': pure Being is posited as afflicted with negation, while Nothingness is likewise pure equality with itself. In linguistic terms it is like saying "*Being-nothing*": two opposing, mutually exclusive words in one, an oxymoron, something wittily stupid, something 'unspeakably sayable' (Goethe).

In Hegel's version: being and nothing are the same, absolutely identical, the minimum of unity (identity), yet there is a "wholly abstract difference" between the first word or issue 'being' and the second word or issue 'nothing'. Thus *the minimal form of distinction* (primal form of non-identity: difference) and contradiction (contraposition) is articulated – the logical first and the logical second, nothing more. Each carries negation in itself and so 'disappears' immediately into its opposite: the first abstract, minimal movement as an initial logical movement – what Hegel calls abstract *Becoming*. Thus the beginning necessarily involves the unity of Being and Nothing in becoming and its negative, existence, in which Being and Nothing first make themselves present as moments. This Hegel characterizes as the 'first truth', which now underlies all further things: qua reflexive negativity, Being and Nothing are prototypes of their own other, their radically under-determined logical formation. Negativity relating to itself proves to be the basic constitution of logic, the germ cell of the 'free' concept itself.

This is illustrated in the sections of the *Logic* headed 'Remarks' (*Anmerkungen*) in which Hegel discusses key moments in the history of philosophy, but in logical rather than temporal-historical sequence – firstly Parmenides' Being, secondly the Nothingness of Buddhism, and thirdly the profound Heraclitus, who had sublated the simple and one-sided abstractions of Being and Nothingness in a higher realm – becoming – but had done so in minimal, abstract form: everything as becoming (*panta rhei*).[2] In addition, the author adds examples of blatant, vacuous misinterpretations of the language of Being and Nothing which treat it as the same thing: Being and Nothingness must be taken very strictly in the radical, extreme abstraction mentioned, as abstract 'things of thought', not as anything more specific. The assumption that there is anything more determinate to them is absurd and nonsensical, it would see equivalence in whether this house exists or doesn't, whether 100 thalers belong to me or not.

With this 'first', minimalist unity of opposites the cornerstone is laid for the concept, the foundation for the immanent movement of the further

---

1 Compare Hegel's understanding of scepticism, where the 'second issue' in thinking is 'doubt' (a play on the words *Zweite Fall* and *Zweifel*).
2 This logical sequence does not correspond to their historical sequence.

determinations of thought, for the 'self-constructing path' to knowledge. Anton Koch states: "As the *Science of Logic* progresses, the theoretical understanding of its beginning will gradually expand. In the beginning we know only very superficially what we are doing, we understand only as much as is necessary to begin, and then to proceed in an orderly way" (Koch 2014: 63).

In this way it is possible to avoid illegitimate presuppositions and dogmatic intrusions by uniting 'presupposition' and the 'presuppositionless'. However, the next steps must show, especially in their transitions, logical stringency, another unavoidable challenge to the new logic of the concept.

3   The Beginning of Practical Philosophy

Among the most convincing passages in Hegel's philosophy are paragraphs 5 to 7 of the *Philosophy of Right*, in which the logical anchoring of the philosophical theory of free will and action, of Hegel's practical philosophy, is subtly demonstrated. Here one finds, in addition, a clear exposition of the relation between immediacy and mediation that is essential for Hegel's philosophizing at large. The fundamental definition of the concept of free will as the principle and beginning of the science of right can only be meaningfully and wholly understood by referring back to Hegel's innovative logic.

The fundamental triad of the determinations of the concept of will is as follows:
α)   Universality
Equality, Indifference, Identity
β)   Particularity
Disparity, difference, Non-Identity
γ)   Individuality
Identity of Identity and Non-Identity

The starting point – the universal concept – results from the endpoint of subjective spirit: the ego as the first form of truly free will, the immediate individuality posited by itself, elevated to universality. The immediacy of the ego, emerging from the total renunciation of any particular content, is categorically stated in paragraph 5: the free will as *self-thinking-itself*, the ego as *pure thinking of oneself*. Both the *Philosophy of Right* and the *Logic* present this first moment of the will as a thinking ego in almost identical ways: the ego is "*first*, this pure self-related unity, and it is so not immediately but only as making abstraction from all determinateness and content and withdrawing into the freedom of unrestricted equality with itself. As such it is *universality*" (*Werke* 6: 253). The indeterminacy, the abstract identity is the sole determinacy, the one that is found in the determinacy of identity. In this pure thinking, I want myself to be a universal and to exclude all particularity, I want to have all determinations as possibilities within me. But this first moment is "itself not without determinacy; and to be something abstract and one-sided constitutes its determinacy" (*Werke* 7: 52).[3]

The concept of the will is still under-determined, though – here we should remember the quotation from the *Logic*: "without any further determination". But it is by no means completely indeterminate or purely immediate, rather it has precisely the minimum of one determination. Here we should pause, for we have here nothing less than the fundamental argument of Hegelian logic and the guiding idea of his practical philosophy, the fulcrum of Hegelian philosophizing: immediacy and mediation, universality and particularity, *contain their other in themselves*. We thus have the germ of the contradiction which is to be sublated. Only in this way does the door open to a logical transition from universality as (supposedly total) indeterminacy to particularity. Primarily, it is a question of "this absolute possibility of abstraction from every determination in which I may find myself or which I may have set up in myself" (*Werke* 7: 51). The ego emerges as potential agent, as author, as unconditional and undetermined initiator. Yet this moment *alpha* lacks the dimension of efficacy, it remains in the supposedly purely 'theoretical' realm. Freedom thus remains only absolute possibility. In this first step of thinking for the will, its opposite paradoxically emerges – a motionless, unwanted and inactive thing. This negative, 'theoretical' aspect of freedom remains a necessary but inadequate definition of freedom.

Paragraph 6 of the *Philosophy of Right* deals with the moment *beta* of free will, its particularity. The ego (because of the essential one-sidedness of the first moment of determination) must simultaneously be thought of as the abandoning of indeterminacy, as the unlocking of closedness, as opening, differentiating, primordial dividing (*Ur-Teilen*, i.e. 'judgment'), as the positing of the determinacy of a *content* or *object*. The will emerges in a logically necessary way from its universality into its particularity.[4] Essential attributes of the particular such as attribution, responsibility, authorship rest on this theorem.

---

3 This same cardinal idea of Hegel's philosophy is to be found at the beginning of the *Science of Logic*: The indeterminacy of being itself is what constitutes its determinacy (*Werke* 5: 82–3), nevertheless it remains 'without any further determination' (ibid.) and thus an *under-determined* form of mediation.

4 Judgment, therefore, is the first genuine particularity of the concept" (*Werke* 8: 317), it is the first division of the original Unity, of the concept by itself.

By performing this determining (*Ent-Schließen*, literally 'un-closing'), the ego can be described as an *actor*, as an *acting ego*. By positing itself as a particular – determining (*Entschließen*) as 'unlocking' (*Aufschließen*) – the ego becomes *existence* (*Dasein*), it becomes finitude. The *specificity of the ego* is thereby articulated. "Through this positing of itself as something determinate, the I steps into determinate existence [*Dasein*] in general" (*Werke* 7: 52). This is the absolute moment of the finitude or particularization of the I. The second moment is already contained in the first, it is – as the key passage says – "only something determinate, one-sided; i.e., being abstraction from all determinacy, it is itself not without determinacy; and to be something abstract and one-sided constitutes its determinacy, its defectiveness, and its finitude" (*Werke* 7: 52).[5]

This moment *beta* is not simply added in the sense of 'also'. The negative is not just a supplementary second step but is inherent in the first. Immanent negativity as the core of Hegelian logic must be conceived in terms of free will. The first moment already implies what it excludes, it is not pure, true infinity and universality, not yet the complete concept, but in its status as indeterminate and abstract we find precisely its determinacy. The ego can indeed abstract from everything, but not from thinking, because *abstraction is itself thinking*. Thus it is not without determination, not empty, not eternal indecision, but rather *its indeterminacy constitutes its determinacy*. Pure abstraction has 'the determinacy of indeterminacy' – supposed indeterminacy must be considered a determinacy.

The path to the ground of generality and peculiarity is revealed in paragraph 7 – the logical unity of both moments, in individuality (γ). Immediacy and mediation of knowledge are both one-sided abstractions, one like the other. True speculative thinking – comprehension – does not exclude one or the other but unites both in itself. In individuality, the two conceptual determinations have their ground in that each are only moments which are 'joined together' (*Zusammen-Geschlossene*), the primordial division (*Ur-Teilung*) becomes a con-cluding (*Zusammen-Schluss*), the logical form of judgement (*Urteil*) passes into the logical form of conclusion or inference (*Schluss*). Hegel regards the individual as particularity reflected in itself and thus returned to the universal, the negativity of negativity, the true self-determination of the ego, which determines itself so that it is particular but remains identical

---

5 That there is not just a subject (ego) but a multiplicity of subjects is given a logical ground by Hegel, and this is also one of the strengths of his practical philosophy. The concept of *recognition* as the foundation of the idea of ascending levels of intersubjectivity characteristic of the *Philosophy of Right* is already implicit in paragraphs 5 to 7.

with itself and joins itself only with itself.[6] Hegel's understanding of self-determination is based on this – the "ego determines itself insofar as it is the relating of negativity to itself" (*Werke* 7: 54). And as this relating the I is simultaneously "indifferent to this determination" (ibid.). The ego is determined, but remains just as 'indifferent' to this determination, knows it as its own, as pure possibility. A being that is able to distinguish itself in this way from the specific nature of its existence can be regarded as a free being, as a rational being.

Hegel emphasizes once again that moments *alpha* and *beta* are easily conceded, but not the moment *gamma* as the speculative and true, the individual, the concept par excellence. The concept is the *universal,* which on the one hand negates itself by its own activity into particularization and determinacy, but on the other hand once again sublates this particularity which is the negative of the universal. For the universal does not meet in the *particular* with something absolutely *other;* the particulars are only particular aspects of the universal itself, and therefore the universal restores in the particular its unity with itself as universal. In this returning into itself the concept is infinite negativity; not a negation of something other than itself, but self-determination in which it remains purely and simply a self-relating affirmative unity. Thus it is true *individuality* as universality closing only with itself in its particularizations (*Werke* 13: 148–9).

The will as self-determination of the ego, in which the individual (γ) must be thought of as the unity of the universal (α) and the particular (β), can only be grasped by speculative thinking, the proof of the core idea of self-relating negativity that we owe to the *Science of Logic*. The concept of willing in the form of an individual is regarded by Hegel as the absolute principle of the *Philosophy of Right* and at the same time as the pivot of the modern world: "the absolute principle – the moment of our times" (*Werke* 7: 78). The concept of free will may thus be understood as absolute or 'holy', but by no means as something transcendent, nor as something relativizable, untouchable – it is freedom alone that constitutes the content of the concept of will. The decisive thing is that the ego "in its limitation, this other, is with itself, that by determining itself, it nevertheless abides with itself and does not cease to abide with itself" (*Werke* 7: 57).

---

6 "I as Thinker, as Active Universal and as Immediate Subject are one and the same I, infinite consciousness and finite self-consciousness; I am the relationship of both sides, the unity of antagonism and coherence – the effort of joining the two sides together" (*Werke* 16: 68).

4   Conclusion

After these reflections on the beginning, a very brief conclusion is in order. Hegel clearly insists *on the unity of the opposition immediacy versus mediation*, which in the form of the logical conclusion presuppose each other, each are isolated one-sided abstractions. The ground of mediation is at the same time the ground from which the immediate emerges and vice versa; the ground of immediacy – this is proved in the sceptical tropes – is the ground from which mediation emerges. Thinking, according to Hegel, is the mediation and sublation of mediation, just as it is the immediacy and sublation of the immediate. The inseparability of the opposing determinations must be thought together in their totality; this also applies to the beginning – no exception is possible. A comprehensive substantiation of this argumentation would still have to be worked on in detail, here I have merely introduced the reader to the issue in question. The King in Lewis Carroll's novel ordered: "Read to the end and then stop!" That's exactly what I'm going to do now, stop talking about the beginning.

CHAPTER 2

Hegel's Sicilian Defence: Beyond Realism and Constructivism

An 'unphilosophical spectre' is haunting the academy, a frightful ghost that shifts shape and takes many forms. One is the logical-mathematical axiomatic that inspires so-called analytical philosophy, which calls itself philosophical science yet cultivates lifeless and colourless formalisms and analytical schemata that resemble what Hegel called a "skeleton covered with labels" (cf. *Werke* 3: 50). Following Gottlob Frege, most analytical philosophies of logic today ignore Hegel's *Logic* and his understanding of contradiction and employ a series of empty, barren calculations borrowed from the natural sciences to give their philosophy the cloak of scientificity. The unphilosophical spectre is also present in recent attempts – grotesque and ultimately futile – to revive realist and constructivist philosophies. Each of these undertakings is something of a disrespectful 'waking the dead': in reanimating past ideas the history of philosophy in general and Hegel in particular – the most important thinker of modernity – is often traduced or maligned.

Hegel would be dismayed were he to meet these dreadful revenants. In his own time he had to face up to a series of philosophical monsters. His *Science of Logic* confronts one particular monstrous dilemma, a double bind that recalls that faced by Odysseus as he sailed into the Strait of Messina in Homer's great epic. By using his wits the ancient hero sought to escape the monsters Scylla and Charybdis lurking on either side of the Strait. Hegel's *Logic*, especially its Logic of Essence, undertakes something no less daring for modern philosophy. As Hegel explains, logical knowledge must outwit the all-consuming maelstrom of the Scylla called *immediacy* and the Charybdis tentacles of voracious *mediation* (*Werke* 8: 165). Hegel's task in the *Logic* is to nothing less than to escape the dilemma of *realism* versus *constructivism*. Like the Strait of Messina in Homer's tale with its stormy, angry surf and deadly whirlpools the route between these philosophical poles is narrow, difficult and treacherous.

In the structure of the dilemma an ancient philosophical motif appears, that of Pyrrhonian *isosthenia*, the antinomy. It is no coincidence that Fichte compared the sceptics with sea monsters and Goethe linked doubt to the devil and his treachery: the etymology of the word 'doubt' (*duo-habeo*; *Zweifel*) lies in the idea of 'two circumstances' (*zwei Fällen*), the two-fold (*das Zwei-Fällige*), duality (*Zwei-heit*) and ambivalence (*Zwiespältigkeit*); 'reflection' in the strict

© KONINKLIJKE BRILL NV, LEIDEN, 2020 | DOI:10.1163/9789004429277_003

sense points to this same double structure. Incidentally, the Logic of *Essence*, where immediacy and mediation are discussed, forms the *second* of the two parts of the *Science of Logic*, and Hegel viewed it as the more difficult and hazardous. On this more will be said later, but for now the core thesis must preoccupy us, of which only a few facets can be explored here: The whole of the second part of the *Logic*, the Doctrine of Essence, is a discussion of the "intrinsic and self-affirming unity of immediacy and mediation" (*Werke* 8: 156). The two monsters – immediacy and mediation – are to be tamed and domesticated. First, they are to be thought of as an "intrinsic unity", in "*inseparable* connection" (*Werke* 8: 56); there is nothing between heaven and earth that does not fulfil this symbiosis. And secondly, this identity is to be understood as a "self-affirming unity". Can such a taming succeed? What role does the spectre of scepticism play? What are the relevant relationships between the Logic of Essence, metaphysics and transcendental philosophy? In what follows I give some preliminary answers.

1   The Logic of Essence

Hegel views essence in a thoroughly critical sense, not as dead, empty indeterminacy, nor as something absolutely immediate that excludes the mediated, excludes all determination. By contrast the protagonists of immediate knowledge affirm that they ultimately take immediacy in isolation from all else, from all mediation, and thus propound an either-or and fall back into the metaphysical understanding. According to Hegel, however, the immediacy of knowledge not only does not exclude mediation, but is so intimately linked to it that immediate knowledge can and must even be regarded as the *result* of mediation, just as, conversely, the logic of immediate being flows into the logic of mediation. A textbook example of this is already offered by the section of the *Phenomenology* titled 'Sense Certainty': sense perception appears as direct knowledge, as knowledge of the immediate or of what plainly exists, but at the same time proves to be mediated; this differentiation and interrelation of the immediate and the mediated is – according to Hegel – inherent in sense certainty itself.

The typically abstract understanding, on the other hand, which regards one of the two sides as absolute, courts the myth of incompatibility or requires a *salto mortale* between them, a philosophical 'oath of disclosure'. Hegel presents convincing arguments against each of these one-sided positions. Being, which seems to represent immediacy, leads through its own inherent negativity, its own dynamics, to its own sublation. Essence cannot be regarded as something dead, empty, indeterminate, certainly not as wholly indeterminate being, as empty content, as measureless 'embodiment of all realities' to which predicates are then simply added. Pure, immediate being cannot escape mediation. But unlike the standard process of predication in the form of the mere ungrounded addition or attribution of predicates, Hegel rightly demands the logically stringent derivation of these determinations: *proof* is required, in the clear logical sense of the term.

A great merit of Fichte lies in his demand that we derive the rules of thought from their necessity, not simply record or enumerate them, that we provide a logical deduction of the categories. We should dwell on this claim, especially with regard to the problem of the immediate and the mediated. Already the fact that pure being as absolute pure immediacy proves to be mediated implies that all logical stages and forms need to be seen as forms of this unity. The argumentation required for this is provided in the section 'The Particular Concept' with the derivation of particularity (*Werke* 6: 280ff). Metaphorically put, it is the logical bedrock of Hegel's idealism at large.

The particular results from the very first stage of the self-determination of the universal, the universal is first of all the particular itself. The immediate, abstract universality, this initial indeterminacy of the concept, is its only quality. To be particular, this absolute negativity is first of all its sole determination – in a reversal of Spinoza, *omnis negatio est determinatio*. But, Hegel adds, this absolute, pure abstraction is not completely empty. It too is afflicted by *horror vacui*, it exhibits "the determinacy of indeterminacy" (*Werke* 6: 285). This initial quality, namely to be indeterminate, is the inescapable minimal endowment, the absolutely minimal and sole determination, though it is by no means a total emptiness or dead indeterminacy, rather it is merely a *radically under-determined determination*. This determination is not simply added to the universal, not simply attributed to it, but is the result of a logical process. An instructive presentation of this core idea of Hegelian idealism is provided by §§5 to 7 of the *Philosophy of Right*.[1]

The Logic of Essence can be considered the result of the Logic of Being, Essence as the truth of Being. Thus, the Logic of Being must necessarily confront the thought of immediacy and indeterminacy with the thought of determinacy and the mediacy of the understanding, must bring both into relation. However, the sphere of essence achieves a 'still imperfect connection of immediacy and mediation'. Essence is the indispensable force of differentiation

---

1 See 'Hegel in Wonderland', in this volume, and for more thorough discussion Vieweg 2012a: 57–67.

and particularization but it is not yet the actual *quintessence* – comprehending thinking.

According to its author, the Logic of Essence – the 'most difficult part of the *Logic*' – comprises first and foremost the categories of metaphysics and the sciences as products of the reflective understanding. It is an understanding which a) fixes distinctions as independent ones, which finds its legitimacy in differentiating the concrete into abstract determinacy and which b) at the same time establishes the interrelatedness of distinctions, but connects them only by setting them side-by-side or one after the other, linking them linguistically with 'and' or 'too' and by fixing a rigid, ultimately indissoluble duality (for example, God as the Being of countless names, God minus all the particular qualities that are inappropriate to him, substance as having two or an infinite number of attributes). Thus it constitutes only an identity of the understanding, not a speculative unity of the concept. In this process of self-determination no genuine self-determination takes place, because the object is not understood as *freely* self-determining. The infinite is taken as something given or found, with the products of the representation merely added or ascribed to it, and we are asked to take this dry assertion on trust.

Traditional metaphysics, which experiences its sublation, transformation and further education in the Logic of Essence, rightly regards the determinations of thought as basic qualities of things – to this extent Hegel's logic as a system of pure determinations of thought is genuine metaphysics – but modern metaphysics in particular draws these abstract determinations from the representation, making it highly partial. The representation, for example, strings together simple predicates – God as Creator, as Omniscient, as Almighty – which, however, necessarily remain mutually exclusive. The understanding follows this procedure, but asserts the necessary relatedness of the isolated determinations of the representation (*Werke* 8: 73–4). In both – representation and understanding – the characteristics are assumed to be given, to be immediately established, their discovery making them valid. Thus Hegel speaks of "ready-made facts" (*Werke* 8: 96) such as 'world' or 'God', to which are then attributed – as Hegel ironically notes – predicates of excellence, 'existence' being the highest and ultimate of these. We learn from these that God *is*, but we do not learn *what* he is; we learn that the world *is* not *what* it is. Secondly, this list of predicates is arbitrary or extends into a 'bad infinity'. And thirdly, in isosthenic-antinomic cases, the proposition is sought via the excluded middle, implying an either-or. Inescapably, this procedure falls into the five terrible tentacles of the Pyrrhonian monster *The Five Tropes of Agrippa*, specifically into the tropus of *progressus in infinitum*, and into the tropus of relativity. Against the one-sided positivity of such metaphysics, combined with the insistence on the validity of the logical forms of proposition and judgement, the Pyrrhonian tropes prove to be the chief weapons against dogmatism with its exclusion of indifferent counter-theses, against the understanding's insistence on isolation. For Hegel, the sceptical method of transcendental philosophy stands in this Pyrrhonian tradition. It is no coincidence that at the beginning of the Logic of Essence this connection is explicitly established – between the terms 'phenomenon' (*phainomenon*) used in scepticism and the term 'appearance' employed in transcendental idealism. The idea of mediation, of duality thus comes radically into play: both – *phainomenon and appearance* – do not represent anything, no indifferent immediate being, but rather exist only in their relationship to the subject, abstractly said, to a self. Thus a necessary reversal takes place, of being into what *appears*. The way out of the extreme of the Myth of the Given is into the other extreme of the Myth of the Construction. On this topic we must make a brief excursus.

In Sextus Empiricus the following critical passage can be found concerning the sceptical *suspens*, the renunciation of assertion: "that I do not assert the certainty of any of the things I will say, that they are exactly as I say they are, but that I report each and every one of them only according to what appears to me here and now" (Sextus Empiricus 1985: 93). Here several important Pyrrhonian keywords are connected: 1) the ego and the particular individual, 2) the here and now, the moment, 3) that which appears and 4) the narrative reporting of this appearance, of one's own experience. In the first German version of Empiricus' text, Niethammer summarises the above passage as follows: "The Sceptical School has as its criterion *appearance*, by which they actually understand *the representation (Vorstellung) of appearance*" (Niethammer 1792: 209). Appearance and representation belong to the indispensable vocabulary of this scepticism. The Pyrrhonist inquires into statements about what appears, whereby appearances are regarded as facts in the form of "an experiential representation" (Sextus Empiricus 1985: 98). The Pyrrhonist is concerned with the "communication of a *human experience*", with what "*appears* to the experiencer" (ibid. 141, my emphasis). With this strategy, the Pyrrhonist wants to avoid premature judgement and at the same time evade the validity claims made in metaphysics.

It is a matter of a temporary attitude of leaving-undecided, by no means of a fundamental exclusion of knowledge – the sceptic admits that perhaps in the future she will be able to acquire knowledge. She communicates her experiences in the form of the narration of what appears to her. Every assertion must be preceded by the phrase 'as it appears to me here and now'. Appearing (*phainomenon*), imagining (*phantasia*), negativity and pure subjectivity merge in this approach. What appears, according to Sextus in his writing 'Against the Dogmatists', is "individual and momentary", such a negative position merely seeks to remain at the level of particular subjectivity and appearance (*Werke* 2: 249).

The criterion of scepticism – in Hegel's profound insight – is what appears, it is the 'subjective' (*phantasia auton*), it is *phainesthai* and *phantasia* (ibid.: 224). This is the idea of subjectivity as independence from any given, it is impartiality – subjectivity and negativity as the free element of philosophy, exemplified by a tradition that stretches from Plato's Parmenides to Kant's sceptical method, an essential part of transcendental philosophy. According to Friedrich Schlegel's apt description, the sceptic seeks to represent *purely* the *subjective* element of philosophy, which, however, comes at the price of a loss of objectivity – Sextus understands appearance as my representation (*Vorstellung*), the *phainomenon* as pure subjectivity (free from any objectivity), as merely subjective, *phantasia, imaginatio*, as *my inner image*.

An obsolete metaphysics persists in the dogmatism of the given, a metaphysics which is challenged by Pyrrhonian scepticism and its modern sister, transcendental philosophy; these latter represent, according to Hegel, the 'free subjective dimension' of philosophy, the second philosophy. Hegel illustrates the solipsistic-constructivist moment indispensable for philosophizing with two characteristic passages: The *Encyclopedia* speaks of the departure of the ship called 'thinking' into open seas, leaving *terra firma* behind; as on Odysseus' raft, we are alone with ourselves. He expresses it even more strikingly in his *Berlin Inaugural Speech*: thinking is an essentially lonely undertaking, it launches us into an boundless ocean with nowhere to drop anchor, the lonely I is haunted by the depths of uncertainty, only the one star, the inner pole star of the spirit, can guide us (*Werke* 10: 416).

Thought as subject – as §20 of the *Encyclopedia* shows – is something thinking, the simple expression of the existing subject as something thinking is *I*. Insofar as *I am* simultaneously in all my sensations, ideas, etc., thought is present everywhere and permeates all these determinations as a category. What is posited in this unity of ego-identity is infected or contaminated by it, pure apperception as the "activity of making one's own [*Vermeinigens*]". It is the "free act of thinking" that "hereby *produces* and *gives itself its object itself*" (*Werke* 8: 63). An indispensable dimension of logic as the self-determination of thinking consists in the continued determination of this self, of the thought of subjectivity, of the free – the concept is the free. The thinking of thinking is as much about the thing itself as it is about pure thought. Hegel attempts the Herculean endeavour of overcoming conceptions of the *given* and the *constructed* – the matter of logic is the logic of matter and vice versa (contrary to the blatant misinterpretation by Marx, who himself reanimates a kind of metaphysical empiricism in the form of materialism).

In absolute idealism, on the other hand, what is finite – whether the supposedly immediate or the supposedly mediated – is not regarded as truly existent. The ideality of the finite can be regarded as the principle of philosophy par excellence. According to Hegel, the immediate or external object has no true reality, it has merely apparent independence (*Werke* 10: 215–6). According to Hegel, scepticism and transcendental idealism successfully undermine the myth of the given, of dogmatic realism or the dogmatism of innate ideas or its recent equivalent – flickering neurons. He sees scepticism as a negative science that can be applied to all forms of cognition, showing up the nullity of mere presuppositions and dry assurances (*Werke* 8: 167). In the wake of scepticism and transcendental philosophy, the phrase 'it is' can no longer be taken for granted.

With his conception of an essence that appears, a core moment of the Logic of Essence, Hegel accepts the challenge of scepticism and transcendental philosophy while also offering a new understanding of existence and reality. However, in both Pyrrhonism and in transcendental idealism, Hegel notes, the baby is thrown out with the bathwater: the appearing thing has no ground at all for being, the thing-in-itself is actually an empty 'beyond', an empty name, a *caput mortuum* cut off from knowledge. These philosophies have "an excess of tenderness for the things of the world" (*Werke* 8: 126), things that are not supposed to contradict each other – the finite is considered not to contradict itself. What appears, however, contains the manifold determinations of what is given, contains all the diverse riches of the world. The translation from Being to Appearance succeeds in eradicating the myth of absolutely immediate Being, the idea of mediated, reflected immediacy, but fails to overcome the paradigm of the given, since the content is not established for itself and no new absolute immediacy is created. As a result there is no adequate unity of immediacy and mediation. The *phainomenon* of the Pyrrhonist remains as what immediately appears to me and which I then narrate. Even with Kant, according to Hegel, this immediacy is not completely overcome, since the content of experience and perception is still regarded as given, and there is no logical derivation of how and to what extent these are self-determined by thinking. In Fichte's *Wissenschaftslehre* of 1794, the infamous 'impulse' (*Anstoß*) is contained directly in the subject, the I, but negativity is merely an addition, not immanent in the strict sense, the negativity of the identical is not immanently conceived. Of course, this cannot be further examined here. In the Logic of Essence, Hegel views Fichte's subjective idealism as a consistent *constructivism*; he speaks of the *systematic idealism of subjectivity*. Any content is rightly regarded as a 'making one's own' in the sense of subjecthood – this principle, Hegel makes clear, can no longer be abandoned by philosophy, contra all the variants of realism and materialism that still abound today. Fichte, however, wants to assert the *exclusivity* of this subjecthood vis-à-vis any objectivity or external existence of content, thus downgrading the positive achievements of the reflective, discriminating understanding, i.e., experience.

Here it becomes clear what a difficult route Hegel takes between the philosophical Scylla and Charybdis, how carefully these antinomies are to be navigated: overcoming the dualism of dogmatism and scepticism in a third philosophy which is neither dogmatic nor sceptic and yet both at the same time; overcoming the dualism of a realism of being and a subjective idealism, of the Myth of the Given and the Myth of the Construction in a speculative thinking of absolute idealism.

2   Immanent Negativity

Scepticism and idealism, isosthenics and antinomics are able to show the nullity of all finite things, and to call into question the alleged strength of the understanding. Reflection puts isolated determinations into relation, but leaves them in their isolated validity. For Hegel, the task is now to understand the sphere of reflection as the sphere of posited contradiction, to demonstrate an immanent, logically necessary superseding of the determinations of understanding, to conceive negation as the self-sublation of the finite. Crucially, Hegel's route through the dilemma makes use of *the argumentative strategy of scepticism itself*, specifically the centrepiece of Pyrrhonism, Agrippa's 3rd trope, the theorem of *isosthenia*, which cannot be attacked from the outside or with other arguments but only immanently, through a retorsion, a *turning of the tables* – here in the form of the application of the trope of relativity to itself. Hegel shows that the proposition '*All knowledge is relative*' itself falls into relativity – the understanding errs. Scepticism is revealed as dialectical: isolated on its own by the understanding and claiming to be a science it leads inevitably to its own negation. According to Hegel, the truly dialectical moves immanently – via its own dynamic – *beyond* reflection and one-sided immediacy and mediation. Thus the famous §82 of the *Encyclopedia* formulates the core provisions of the highest stage of philosophy: comprehending, speculative thought, a type of thinking that is clearly distinguished from the understanding and the dialectical moment of the logical. Hegel already refutes the ubiquitous cliché that he is a dialectician.[2]

---

2   *Encyclopedia* §48 speaks of a "dialectical *moment* of the logical" (*Werke* 8: 128, my emphasis). Cf *Encyclopedia* §82 concerning *speculative* logic.

This transition, too, can only be briefly addressed here, suffice to say it is the hardest transition, according to Hegel, that from necessity to freedom, from the real to the concept. As is well known, a decisive moment here is 'independence' as an under-determined determination of freedom. As unity pushed to the extreme of being for itself, this is the abstract, formal independence that manifests itself in such phenomena as abstract freedom, arbitrariness, pure duty, evil, each of which is discussed in the *Philosophy of Right*. But independence does not remain in such one-sidedness; it also exhibits the structure of the previously described relationship between universality and particularity, especially with regard to the fundamental transition from the universal to the particular. It can be regarded as the infinitely negative relationship to itself, an independence which "though self-repulsive into distinct elements, yet in that repulsion is self-identical, and in the movement of reciprocity still at home and conversant only with itself" (*Werke* 8: 303). In this kind of thinking of necessity, the structure of freedom is already essentially fulfilled and the transition to the Logic of the Concept is signalled – the merging of the concept with itself in its Other. Already here Hegel speaks emphatically of liberation, of the concept as the free, of the concept as free mediation with itself, and when existing for itself this liberation is called 'I', in which again a recourse to scepticism and idealism is visible. Here, too, the *Science of Logic* proves to be a theory of the self-determination of the concept, a logical theory of freedom, capable of transcending the common antinomy of necessity and freedom. Hegel illustrates this at one point with his example of injustice as a peculiarity of law in which the appearance of law merges into semblance. The truth of this semblance shows itself as its nullity, in which the power of essence expresses itself in the act of punishment, which the criminal views as a foreign, subjugating power and restriction of his freedom – in punishment the free comes upon the criminal with the semblance of something alien. Yet his punishment represents merely the manifestation of his own action, the consequence and law of his own will, as something inherent in his action itself, the necessary result and completion of his own action – punishment as the rational moment in the deed as misdeed.

The above-mentioned difficulty of the transition to the Logic of the Concept must, of course, be explored more thoroughly. One of the core moments is no doubt the category of contingency (*Zufälligkeit*), which in practice represents the moment of arbitrariness (*Willkür*). The transition to the realm of the Concept as the realm of subjectivity and freedom is also about enlightening the talk of the absolute randomness of distinctions and a transformation from randomness to freedom, it is about an understanding of the individual as being identical with itself, which does not arise as a completely empty nothingness – it is about the sublation of the Logic of Essence into the 'infinite freedom of comprehending thought'.

3   Conclusion

The good Odysseus escaped the two fearsome monsters only with great difficulty and with much ingenuity. Only with great philosophical insight and wisdom was Hegel able to overcome the dilemma of one-sided immediacy and one-sided mediation via an understanding of the paradox of mediated immediacy, the determinacy of indeterminacy. Nevertheless, shedding light on the transition from the Logic of Essence to the Logic of Concepts remains one of the great challenges in the interpretation of Hegel's *Logic*, one that has not yet been sufficiently addressed. What Hegel sets forth as the *logical code of the relationship between universal and particular*, along with his unique understanding of *freedom*, could form the basis for clarifying this key transition. Today's academic 'emperors' of analytic philosophy tend to overlook this, indeed tend to overlook Hegel's logic as a whole. It is to their loss, since Hegel's project already shows the way to overcome the one-sided positions of constructivism (subjective idealism) and realism, the Myth of Construction and the Myth of the Given, shows a way to unite and overcome both conceptions. The Logic of Essence is a key step along this path. It becomes clearer to what extent Hegel's innovative logic, a revolution in the history of logic itself, can be regarded as a new metaphysics.

CHAPTER 3

The "Reversal of Consciousness Itself": Along the Path of the *Phenomenology of Spirit*

When Hegel introduces the motif of *'reversal'* (*Umkehrung*) in the Introduction to the *Phenomenology of Spirit*, it is with the intention of examining this notion "more closely, in order to shed new light on the scientific side of the subsequent presentation" (*Werke* 3: 79). The phenomenon of reversal, Hegel notes straight afterwards, is "in fact, however, the same circumstance spoken of above in terms of the relationship of this presentation to scepticism" (*Werke* 3: 79). This revealing remark will guide my discussion here. In what follows I take seriously Hegel's reference to scepticism and show how it allows us to comprehend the notion of 'reversal' that is so crucial to Hegel's *Phenomenology of Spirit*. This internal reconstruction of one key facet of Hegel's train of thought thus focuses on the connection between the *"reversal of consciousness"* and *scepticism*.

As is well known, Hegel understands his *Phenomenology* as a 'journey through the appearances of knowledge' (*das erscheinende Wissen*), a voyage of discovery into knowing. The singular forms of spirit (*Geist*) constitute way stations. Conceptually construed, the *Phenomenology* can be seen as the science of the experience of consciousness. The science of this journey is the "presentation of the appearances of knowledge", the science of the appearances of spirit, the "science of the experience that consciousness makes" (*Werke* 3: 72, 38). Understanding the entire path of this journey as what Hegel himself calls "self-perfecting scepticism" (*sich vollbringender Skeptizismus*) (*Werke* 3: 72) opens up new insights onto the fundamental structure of the *Phenomenology*, requiring a study of the connection between "what appears" (*Erscheinen*) and scepticism.

Science in its emergence – as Hegel sees it – is itself an appearance, and freeing itself from this appearance is the path towards secure knowledge. Mere claims or 'empty assurances' are not suitable for attaining this. With the presentation of the appearances of knowledge a justification of knowledge is to be attained and this by means of a testing process, one Hegel describes as "the way of doubt" (*Werke* 3: 72), as a scepticism directed at the whole expanse of the appearances of consciousness. To make this clear, I will need to explain Hegel's use of the word 'doubt'.

Natural consciousness naively takes itself to be actual, real knowledge, and in this way it is clearly positive or dogmatic, since it expects that this *one* actual case has unconditional validity. But one basic component of testing, whatever kind of test it may be, requires that we accept the possibility of at least one more case, a second variant, an otherness. With the second case it would be *double*, and hence in *doubt* – for the Latin origin, *dubitare* (to doubt), goes back to *duo* (two), just as Hegel similarly plays on "*Zweifel*" (doubt) which contains the word "*zwei*" (two). With the concept of two at its origin, doubt thus contains the possibility of distinguishing *an other*, otherness, and it implies the negation of the first case, the overcoming of the singularity of the dogmatic, and the constitution of relation, of relativity.

Hegel sees in scepticism the paradigmatic agent of this test, the absolute questioner who makes the second case valid, thus establishing the negation of the first case and introducing otherness and relativity. In principle, testing in the sense of this notion of doubt as negativity must be done thoroughly, and that means it must be applied to all appearances of knowledge. If not, there is the danger of unreflectively and dogmatically "standing by the truth". Along this "way of doubt", two decisive reversals and hence three main stages occur. I will sketch the correspondence between the conceptual structure in three of Hegel's texts: his early Jena-period essay on scepticism, the *Phenomenology*, and the *Encyclopedia*).

1   Reversals

1) The first stage encompasses the completion of the structure of consciousness in which, corresponding to the principle of consciousness, that which appears (*das Erscheinende*) is seen as other, as external – knowledge should be *knowledge of an other*. Along this first stretch of the journey are found the three forms of consciousness – sense certainty, perception, and understanding (I will describe this stage by stage: the first stage of experience, the first reversal, and a hint at the way of setting out again.) In all these forms the reversal has already been carried out, but in a still incomplete form. We will come back to this point later. The first immediacy, the one imputed by natural consciousness, that is, a truth as it should be 'in' the object, this initial positivity and pure objectivity, is experienced as what is to be reversed, that is, as the first reversal of consciousness. The immediate shows itself to be mediated, positivity shows itself to be negativity, and pure objectivity shows itself to be pure subjectivity. *Knowing of an other* falls back into a *knowing of oneself*, and being-in-itself is transformed into being-for-consciousness.

Instead of apprehending what appears as an other, as ob-ject (*Gegen-Stand*, i.e. what stands opposed), what appears is now taken as representation (*Vorstellung*, also 'image'), as something internal, as fantasy; consciousness experiences itself as self-consciousness.

2) In self-consciousness, in knowing oneself as result, we have the identity of certainty and truth: "consciousness is itself the true" (*Werke* 3: 137) and self-consciousness is thus the truth of the preceding ways. Now in the form of scepticism there occurs the absolute reversal, the radical transformation of the object insofar as what appears completely loses the status of being in the sense of other, i.e., of an external object. The object is now exclusively my representation and thus it is taken precisely the way that Sextus Empiricus understood it. The object has become completely mine (*Meinigkeit*); in the object I know only myself. The originally pure objectivity has reversed into pure subjectivity with solipsistic consequences. Instead of knowing, there is the *epochē*, the assumption that x is true; instead of language there is a new language, or keeping silent.

The core, the truth, of the structure of consciousness – namely to be the appearance of mind, relativity, absolute negativity, and pure subjectivity – this enters the scene in the unique form of the doctrinal scepticism of the Pyrrhonist, a form that can be seen as the ideal type for what appears, for the phenomenal, the model for the experience of what is in itself negative, the model for freedom of thought. In its development, consciousness shows its true face. It distinguishes something – to which at the same time it is related – as a form of knowing that takes for its very essence this one-sidedness of the negative, a form of the incomplete consciousness that is detained in the course of the journey and presents itself. In the strict sense, this self enters the process of "self-perfecting scepticism" as a unique form that reveals the fundamental constitution of consciousness and thus represents its first fundamental reversal. This scepticism is absolute self-consciousness, the self (*das Ich*) as absolute negativity; the freedom of self-consciousness constitutes the turning point.

3) For a comprehensive application of doubt – one without exceptions – to be valid in the strict sense, it must be also be applied to scepticism itself. This is the *second reversal*, the negation of the negation, a sublation of the structure of consciousness into the conception of reason as spirit.

The following reflections concentrate on the first reversal. Before a more precise treatment of the theoretical content, some connotations of the German word '*Umkehrung*' (reversal) must first be mentioned to help our understanding of this idea. At least eight of these can be listed.

a) *Umkehren* as *turning around*, as turning point in the sense of a turning back, the start of a going back, one that might renounce the goal originally aimed at.

b) *Umkehr* as *a stopping off*: the movement shows itself to be one-sided and is replaced by rest, by a pause (*Inne-Halten*) – holding to oneself. The "double-ness" of movement and rest enters the scene.
c) *Umkehrung* in the sense of *opening up a new view*, indeed a new view of that which, while walking forward, must always remain to one's back. This would include the sense of a re-collecting (*Er-Innerung*) of one's path from a new perspective, in the sense of a re-vision, a seeing and testing of what one has traversed from the point at which one turns back.
d) *The renunciation of any particular goal*, the transformation of a traveler into a vagabond, one who supposedly goes along without any real resolve or purpose.
e) *Umkehrung* in the sense of *turning the tables on someone*.
f) *Umkehrung* in the sense of *perverting, falsifying,* "turning wrong-side up".
g) *Umkehren* as *turning up-side down*, overturning, fundamentally changing, whereby there is no continuing with the previous way but rather a setting-out on a completely new, different way.
h) *Going home*, back to the point of departure.

In simply enumerating these interconnected associations with their pictorial and metaphorical meanings, the difficulty of a suitable interpretation becomes clear.

In the Hegelian notion of sublation, which perfects scepticism by subjecting scepticism itself to doubt, these diverse meanings of *Umkehrung* achieve conceptual clarity. The remaining discussion is divided into six sections, following the different but interconnected ways in which scepticism enters the scene in the form of a reversal, that is, as the principle of absolute negativity.

1) At one station along the path a radical reversal occurs in the form of "the liberation from the opposition of consciousness" (*Werke* 3: 180). Consciousness experiences a reversal, a turning from objectivity to subjectivity, a "pushing back into consciousness". Here this can only be briefly sketched:

Consciousness's belief that it merely the unreflective recording (*Aufnehmen*) or apprehending (*Auffassen*) of the world reveals itself to be mere opining. The object, what should be the essential thing, mutates into something inessential; sense-certainty changes into the attempt to access the singular, which can only be done by means of universal terms; language subverts opining. In perception (*Wahr-nehmen*, literally, taking to be true) of a concrete object, opining is transformed into a thing of thought, into an object. It comes to a play of reflection, to the steady oscillation between determining and resolving the determining, to the conflict between the individual and the universal, that of being-for-itself and being-for-another, to seeking the connection between the sensual and what is thought. Finally, in the third form, the finite, the sensual world as what appears, reverts to clarifying, understanding, to the supersensible world of representation, to the thought of the infinite; the *"inverted world"* (*verkehrte Welt*) comes into being. In law, for example, all moments of external appearance are recorded internally (*Werke* 3: 131, 128). Understanding shows itself to be *appearance itself*; meanwhile what was taken to be objectivity changes into subjectivity. What were at first fixed ways or types of objectivity or standing-opposed (*Gegen-Stehenden*) – a) something existing externally, b) thing, c) sensual world – are transformed into ways of being-for-consciousness. In this educative process, consciousness can already gradually perceive itself as self-consciousness. Consciousness already contains the determination of *being-for-itself*, since it *imagines* the object, but it still remains within the dualism of the ideality and reality of the object.

2) Scepticism paradigmatically represents what is substantial in the reversal – free self-consciousness. At this way station, the otherness that is initially certain to consciousness is *radically annihilated*. Consciousness no longer refers to an other in the former sense, but rather now refers *purely to itself*; it shows itself to be pure self-consciousness, pure subjectivity, self-certainty. Certainty is now itself consciousness's object; consciousness is *itself* what is true (*Werke* 3: 131, 128). At this point, the previous way of proceeding cannot be justified, since it is based on the principle of otherness in the form of an external being or the object's reality.

Let us briefly consider the precise transition point here, namely the bridge from understanding to self-consciousness. The transition from consciousness as knowledge *of an other* to knowledge *of oneself* has its point of departure in the antinomy of understanding in the form of the opposition between appearance (of the sensual world) and the 'inverted', super-sensual world of the infinite. The absolute concept of distinction – the domain of Pyrrhonism – must be understood in terms of this opposition-in-itself, this contradiction, this equipollence (two arguments possessing equal validity). Distinction must be understood as the opposite in-and-for-itself – that is, not as one of two but rather as internal opposition, absolute negativity itself. The appearance would present this infinity, the super-sensual, the representation, *image*, fantasy itself. Appearance "already represents itself, but as an explanation it first appears freely; and by finally being an object for consciousness, as what it is, consciousness is *self-consciousness*" (*Werke* 3: 133). Understanding as philosophical reflection is an "act of absolute freedom".

With absolute freedom, reflection raises itself out of the sphere of the given. According to Hegel, the highest and final level of understanding consists in consciousness of one's negativity (*Werke* 2: 66, 34). In self-consciousness we have as distinguished what is not distinguished, the being-one of what is divided. Hegel speaks of knowledge of self-reference, of self-certainty of consciousness. Self-consciousness is "essentially the return from *other-being*" (*Werke* 3: 137) – the reversal of consciousness as return to oneself.

In the scepticism passage of the *Phenomenology*, what is held fast for consciousness is "the complete non-essentiality and non-autonomy, ontological dependence of the other", the thought of the negation of the other in an extreme, radical way, the annihilation of otherness in the form of external objectivity. In scepticism, expression is given to the quintessence of the reversal, *the negative itself*, the experience of the *negative in itself*, i.e. absolute negativity (*Werke* 3: 159). The reversal of consciousness is thus manifested in a unique form of consciousness.

In sceptical self-consciousness, being-for-itself, being free, has been achieved and has posited its *pure* form. In immediate being-for-itself we have the subjective representation of the one of the self as singular (*Werke* 5: 174–175).

At this stage of the path, self-consciousness reveals itself as the truth of the previous forms. The new object – and so a further parallel between the introduction and the passage on scepticism – contains the *nothingness* of the first object; it reveals itself to be the experience it had of that first object. In scepticism, in *ataraxia*, we have the truth of the path of consciousness to itself, moving from mere language to self-discussion and quiet being for-itself and in-itself, that is, from certainty to self-certainty.

All lack of autonomy, all heteronomy in the form of determinateness in respect to an other, has at this point been swept away. In scepticism we have "*actual experience, what freedom of thought is*", the certainty of absolute autonomy (*Werke* 3: 159, my emphasis). Consciousness is no longer in an other, no longer slave, but is now *with itself* and *free*. This negative side, the absolute negativity through which every enslaving other is shaken off and every necessity is nothing, is held by Hegel to be the "*free dimension*" of philosophy in the sense of free thought and free will.

In the *Phenomenology*, scepticism is given a characteristic *double function*: First it presents "conscious insight into the untruth of the appearance of knowledge" (*Werke* 3: 72) by applying the "sceptical method" (Kant), the principle of absolute negativity. But secondly, since scepticism makes this "one-sided" view of absolute negativity into its own knowledge, this scepticism itself enters the scene as one of the forms of incomplete consciousness (*Werke* 3: 73–74). The unity of self-consciousness is held to be "an entity which is only an *appearance*, with no being in itself" (*Werke* 3: 139). But scepticism must equally be applied to this sceptical assumption itself, to what *simply appears*. The supposedly indeterminate negation reveals itself to be determinate; on one side of the indeterminateness there emerges its *reversed* side, determinateness.

With the first arrival of radical freedom, of pure being-for-itself, consciousness reverses itself. It "has *its turning point* only in consciousness" (*Werke* 3: 145). Scepticism represents this transformation point; it enters into the midst of its self-perfecting as a unique form, as the negative, free, subjective side of philosophy in its purity. Scepticism, according to Friedrich Schlegel, seeks to present in pure form the subjective element of philosophy (Schlegel 1958 Bd. 18: 387). In Hegel's words: "Scepticism completes the view of the subjectivity of all knowledge" (*Werke* 19: 514).

3) In the Introduction to the *Phenomenology*, Hegel also speaks of experience as a movement "in which what is immediate, what is *inexperienced*, that is, what is abstract [...] *is alienated* and then *returns* out of this alienation" (*Werke* 3: 39, my emphasis). At the beginning there is pure immediacy, pure objectivity, a knowing that takes the object as it is, the in-itself as *pure recording* of the object to which *apparently nothing* of consciousness itself, nothing active, free, or subjective is added. Yet this immediate, inexperienced, natural consciousness is inverted into its opposite. Hegel calls it the "for-it-being of this in-itself"; the *pure objectivity* transformed into its opposite, *pure subjectivity*. The point of turning back is represented by absolute indifference, absolute negativity as absolute being-for-itself: none of the previous thoughts of objectivity and determinateness are able to hold out against sceptical objections; none of the understanding's thoughts can resist the chief Pyrrhonian weapon – the argument of the trope of relativity, the idea that everything depends on everything else. In antinomy, understanding has its fundamental structure and its highest form. As scepticism shows, absolute determinateness proves to be negativity – *determinatio est negatio.*

This turning inside-out culminates in *pure negativity* and *pure subjectivity*, and precisely these are, in Hegel's eyes, the two chief signatures of consistent, radical scepticism. Knowing in the intended sense is *inverted*; maintaining something to be the case based on the authority of what is objective is inverted into maintaining something to be the case based on subjective conviction. Objectivity is renounced; every proposition must necessarily be preceded by the qualification: 'as it appears to me here and now'. Objects are transformed into phenomena of mineness, i.e. my subjective representations – the "being-for-consciousness of the first in-itself" (*Werke* 3: 79).

In paying attention to *appearances*, the Pyrrhonist lives without attaching any claim at all to them (*Werke* 2: 224). But in the case of dogmatic beliefs, they withhold judgment, and an objectivity of values remained in place. The Pyrrhonist's measure is what appears, the *phenomenon*, by which is understood the representation (*Vorstellung*) in consciousness, *fantasy, the subjective element of representation,* representation as "what is experienced or suffered without being willed", an appearance as something held to be true subjectively (Sextus Empiricus 1985: 22; Hegel *Werke* 2: 224). The Pyrrhonist gives notice of his representations (images) and reports experiences or remains silent. Then, as soon as he speaks, he embraces the "new" language, distinguishing himself from the "normal language" and, with this distinction, falls into the determining that he forbids.) Here we can see that the development of the ancient conception of the *phainomenon* from that of a sensual, objective appearance (a thing) to Sextus' idea of a subjective "being-appeared-to" runs parallel to the development in Hegel's *Phenomenology* from sense certainty to represented self-certainty.

In holding fast to absolute indifference (Kant justly describes sceptics as indifferentists) and to absolute negativity or nothingness, being is transformed and emerges now – as Hegel tells us in the *Logic* – but still in the determinateness of subjectivity and in relation to subjectivity. The content is transformed from the "language of being" into the "language of seeming" (*des Scheins*), into the language of appearance. The sceptic doesn't allow himself to say 'it is', only 'it seems to me that'.[1] From the sceptical standpoint, the supposed journey towards objective knowledge is seen to be on the wrong track. Instead of the demand for knowledge, the credo is suspension of judgment.[2] Everything that appears is indeed tested, but is then thrown into the same abyss of nothingness. But the achievement of knowledge cannot in principle be ruled out, since this would amount to dogmatism.

The reversal can here be taken as a return to the point of departure. The first step – natural consciousness, pure objectivity – was a contingent recording and finding, an aimless wandering or vagrancy in being. Now, in spite of the reversal, only a single word is changed, no longer *a* discovery, but *my* discovery and *my* contingent recording – no longer the object as it is presented, but rather as it seems to me to be presented. The *supposedly other* object shows itself indeed to be not an *other*, but rather precisely the "knowing of the *first* object".

---

1 Modern idealism, the scepticism of modernity, does not view knowledge as knowledge of the thing-in-itself, but pretends to know only appearances. This idealism has the same ambiguity as scepticism, except that the former expresses this in a positive way, the latter in a negative way. The idea that pure consciousness constitutes all reality has no connection with the idea of stimuli coming from outside (sensual stimulation and imaging). These ideas cannot be unified, leading to the subject being cast from one extreme to another, in the dualism of the bad infinity (*Werke* 6: 20).

2 Historically, the sceptical attitude emerged in diverse forms, both authentic and inauthentic. It was dressed out in various ways and to various degrees, for example as an appeal to discretion and modesty in knowledge, as an attack on presumptive knowledge, or as the idea of infinite approximation. All these are affirmative variations of relativity based on the tropes of Agrippa.

At the turn from being to essence in the *Science of Logic*, Hegel emphatically states that with this transition the content remains the same. Even *appearance and representation* have as content the whole expanse or circle of the manifold wealth of the world, of determinateness. After the initial attempt to avoid every form of subjectivity, we now have the attempt to shut off every form of objectivity. Scepticism is like a vampire – it shuns the objective light of day and wants to remain in the dark of free, pure subjectivity, in the Transylvanian night of opining, of non-knowing, while sucking out all content from the other, living from the blood of the other, and thus eternally suffering the curse of determinateness. With this a new and unavoidable stage in the resolution of the problem of determinateness is conceived.

4) The sceptical notion of *ataraxia* means an end of the journey; the tipping over into peace, into the opposite of movement, Here inversion means *holding within* [*Inne-Halten*] as a reverse into oneself, Pyrrhonian *ataraxia* as the "stillness of the sea in the soul", the "stillness of being-in-itself", the quiet being-for-itself. Sceptical self-consciousness "is itself this *ataraxia* of thinking within oneself, the changeless and *true certainty of oneself*" (*Werke* 3: 161). And indeed Hegel is not opposed to this notion: he speaks of something that cannot be foreign to any true philosopher: the "freedom of character" and "freedom of thought", the free dimension of every philosophy, the free choice and the "passionless stillness of knowledge based only on thought" (See *Werke* 2: 228, 229, 242ff; *Werke* 5: 34). To this extent, scepticism, in its tendency towards the height of unity in being-for-itself, towards the extreme of pure subjectivity, towards theoretical and practical solipsism, shows itself to be a transit station that cannot be avoided on the road towards knowledge, towards a philosophy of subjectivity and freedom (See Vieweg 2004).

Considering that appearances have a different form than sceptical diagnosis, the sceptic withholds judgment as to whether something in its nature is good or should be done at all. But other assumptions or ways of behaving are deemed by the sceptic to be evil on the basis of the argument that they cause irritation to the soul. If he holds that the things around him are naturally evil, he might fear persecution by goddesses of vengeance; or should he attain these things that seem good to him, he might suffer the anguish of conceit or fear of losing them. The sceptic understands himself to be independent or 'free' from all supposedly 'objective values'. But happiness (*Glückseligkeit*) is deemed by him to be an objective, indeed absolute value (Sextus Empiricus 1985: 35–6). The Pyrrhonist ascribes to *his happiness* an absolute validity and celebrates peace and 'noble abstention' (exclusively for himself, however, and only for the here and now). But this 'withholding of judgment' – whether one explicitly articulates it or merely follows its rule silently – does not avoid judging. Acting as though something were true and refraining from judgment already involve a value judgment, for here the self acts in accordance with self-certainty and self-identity.

Consciousness is absolutely free in being certain of its freedom; its freedom is there by means of consciousness itself. All determination, all difference, has its essence in this indifference of the self-identity of self-consciousness, in this pure identity with itself in the form of *ataraxia*, the peace of changeless and true *certainty* of itself (*Werke* 3: 161). For a Pyrrhonist there is *happiness* in this *ataraxia*, in not being disturbed, in changelessness, in this free peace. Hegel is therefore right when he refers in the *Phenomenology* to the practical core of Pyrrhonism as a "happy consciousness". He means the extreme unity in being-for-itself, the freedom that in this being-with-itself flatters itself that it has been achieved purely (*Werke* 5: 192).

In Pyrrhonian consciousness, there occurs, however – and this is a central idea of Hegel – a doubling of consciousness in itself into a free consciousness and one that is not free, a happy consciousness and an unhappy one; as self-consciousness, consciousness is *doubled in itself*. In its self-understanding consciousness oscillates between the extremes of free, self-identical self-consciousness and contingent, lost self-consciousness: Consciousness "does not unite these two thoughts of itself, but *at one point* knows its freedom as being exalted above all worry and contingence of being and nonetheless *at another point* professes itself again to have fallen back into irrelevance and carousing about" (*Werke* 3: 162).

All determinations of the will are deemed contingent; they merely *happen* to the individual. While the image presented to the sceptic can have this or that content, he does not determine this content, but rather the content is given without mediation. The Pyrrhonist maintains that he is affected arbitrarily. Sextus Empiricus speaks of experiences which, as impressions, are like fantasies, and he argues that they are immediate, "[s]ince the experience which occurs to us indicates nothing more than itself" (Sextus Empiricus 1998: 1, §193–197). Thus, "as regards actual experiences, I am without error", and what is found as a representation in consciousness is individual and momentary (ibid.).

Thus happy consciousness, which constantly emphasizes mediation, is plunged into the pure immediacy and objectivity of a natural consciousness that announces its own annihilation. In this sense, happy consciousness involves a loss of selfhood and freedom; it is a "lost", "animalistic" self-consciousness (*Werke* 3: 162). ("Animalistic" thus has a double meaning: first, in the sense of 'practical' sceptics or empirical idealists, who go to the finite and annihilate it; secondly, as merely practical, as an act that would be completely without a theoretical component.)

Along with singularity's universality, pure self-consciousness also contains the moment of excluding itself from the singular and excluding all otherness, that is, the tarrying of subjectivity in the empty space of inwardness, the moment of *solipsistic independence*. The highest abstraction of negativity and subjectivity take place in absolute egoism. Being-for-itself is at first immediate – as unity, as singularity, *solus ipse* (itself only). As Kant also argues, alongside rational self-love or self-recognition there exists *arrogance* in the form of vain self-love, haughtiness, the pure selfishness of the will, freedom in its complete unrestraint, loneliness as the 'vanity' of self-conversation. The determinateness of this arbitrary act remains contingent; it happens to the individual by chance, is given to him, is experienced by him and indeed is not freely posited by him.

When arbitrary freedom (*Willkür*) in the sense of one-sided subjectivity is brought together with contingency (*Zufall*) in the sense of a one-sided objectivity (as being affected without willing it) we are in the presence of an unresolved antinomy of freedom and necessity.[3] With this complete indifference and lack of involvement, *purposelessness* advances *as the purpose of the will*. A purpose is posited everywhere, but one that should not count as purpose (not as one's own decision). This self-established universality of the singular, the free being-for-itself, is confounded and the determination of will and action turns into blind necessity. The two moments involved in conceptualizing free will – pure indeterminacy and determinacy – are divided into two extremes. The dividing in two marks sceptical consciousness; here, simple rest and freedom, the liberation from *tarachē* and worry, the side of changelessness and identity – there the falling into worry and constant disruption, the plunge from the essentiality of 'phenomena' into multiplicity, difference, and non-identity. The mixture reveals itself to be a continuous and disquieting carousing here and there.

Along with the *free non-conformity* born of radical abstraction and a disregard for everything, there is an *unscrutinized conformity*. On the one hand there is selfish positing, free determining, while on the other hand there is the unquestioned reception of the foreign 'command' – theoretical and practical freedom and philosophical and political apathy are united. The quiescence as continuous rest and resignation, the sovereignty vis-à-vis all here and now and this, is contrasted with an indifference in the form of total quietism and bowing down before what has only now and here been discovered, a deification of the 'this'. Since the sceptic does not decide between good and evil, he remains without a perspective on the given order of things, the traditional customs and practices,

---

3 A sensual image of the mixture of freedom and necessity can be found in the parable of the painter Apelles, where freedom is experienced as arbitrary will and necessity as contingency.

and so he aligns his action according to them. How does the Pyrrhonist act if the tradition is a tyranny? As a strict conventionalist who has renounced leading an independent style of life and pays homage to traditional habits, he must put up with the given existence of tyranny, including its rules, even if these demand the killing of children. At any moment he could meet with something unsettling to him, whether or not he is true to the conventions and even if many conventions and habits cause him unrest (Ricken 1994: 145–6, 151; on page 161, Ricken speaks of a "decisionistic traditionalism incapable of reform"). In one breath we have the recognition of free individuality and the renunciation of genuine republicanism – as formulated in the sense of a rational form to deal with public matters (*res publica*) and truly critical political institutions.

Self-consciousness holds within itself the division into master and slave; it combines an independent and masterly consciousness with a dependent and slavish one. The Buddha, resting within himself, has a second face; he shows himself at the same time to be a restless and unstable vagabond, a 'rolling stone', a restless wanderer – indeed, in an allusion to Montaigne, Hegel speaks of "carousing about" (*Werke* 3: 162).[4] The *autonomous monad* reveals itself to be precisely the *heteronomous nomad*, the unchangeable equanimity plunges into permanent adventurousness. As the most impressive protagonist of this free character, the combination of *self-certain unreflective repose* and *unbridled, adventuresome carousing about*, Hegel shows us a literary figure: the *happy-unhappy* Don Quixote.

5) We can 'look behind the back' of the experience of this negativity, indeed negativity in general; indeed we *must* and *can* go behind the very curtain of that which we have now experienced as selfhood, as self-consciousness. We thus look back, as it were, at the road we have mastered and remind ourselves of what we have under-gone (*er-fahren*: Hegel plays on the word *fahren* – to travel). And when we do so we can show the sceptic who is tarrying at the point of reversal what he has negated and what he doesn't want to admit. We show him his one-sidedness and inner turmoil, exactly as he does with the dogmatist, and we do it with the very means we have borrowed from him, namely the results of his most personal experience. The thesis *determinatio est negatio* is reversed. Now with equal force – according to the sceptical trope

---

4   The apparently aimless carousing about in fact also has a determinate aim. To supposedly have no aim is indeed itself a determination. Montaigne's maxim, that I well know what I flee, but don't know what I seek, is questionable. The knowledge of that which I flee shows a determination of what is sought. It provides at least one single determination: the avoidance of what one flees. (According to Pascal, Montaigne, the first modern carousing Pyrrhonist, also allowed himself to be determined by what merely occurred to him. For Hume, custom then takes over this role as another form of Pyrrhonian traditional convention).

of *isostheny* (that for every argument there is an equal opposing argument) – we can say that *negatio est determinatio*. Thus by means of this reversal a new perspective is opened up and a *re-vision* in the double sense of the word is possible. The pure, absolute negativity as indeterminateness is unmasked as determinateness. As Hegel puts it in the *Logic*, "the abstract independence, the unity of being-for-itself in its extreme form represents the error of seeing its own essence as negative and behaving negatively towards it. Thus [this independence] is a negative behaviour towards oneself, which, in trying to attain its own being, actually destroys it, and thus this action only makes manifest of the nothingness of such action" (*Werke* 5: 192).

The nothing is determined as the nothing of that from which it results; it has determinateness as its very result. In the well-known principle of determinate negation the transformation is manifest; here is the completion of the turnaround within which the "turning point" is revealed as an unconditional way marker and which even proves to be a necessary "path of departure", the overcoming of rest (*Werke* 3: 74).

The central sceptical thesis of relativity and indifference is applied to itself, and the reversal is seen to be a reversal of the Pyrrhonist's own weapon, now turned against himself. Yet nothing else been assumed: no other experiences or philosophical arguments have been introduced (that would not have been cogent). The only thing introduced was *the result of experience itself*, the experience that sceptical self-consciousness itself conceded, including the reversal. Negativity is demonstrated through negativity itself.

In strict keeping with the renunciation of judgment, retaining pure negativity and subjectivity, such an 'excessive' scepticism would become something completely other than itself, namely something that would not be relevant for thought. Scepticism 'inverts' itself by speaking without any claim to validity and so is no longer a concern of philosophy. Philosophizing is indifferent to such a Pyrrhonian indifference. Philosophy completes this reversal by turning its back on the sceptic who turns his back on knowledge. Whoever thinks only on the basis of what occurs to him, to his feelings, his internal oracle, is at a loss to oppose anyone who disagrees (*Werke* 2: 249, *Werke* 3: 64). Pyrrho can always be silent, laugh, and turn his back; he cannot complain when he suffers the same treatment at the hands of philosophy.[5]

---

[5] If a 'mitigated scepticism' were to be defended, it would act contrary to its own intention, contrary to absolute indifference, immediate being-for-itself, and negativity, and thus it would itself become dogmatic. According to Sextus Empiricus, the rashness of the dogmatists should be cured by means of argumentation. Thus 'dogmatic scepticism' (K.L. Reinhold) mutates into the form that it fights against and goes public as understanding.

The form of communication of this scepticism is not argumentation and theory, but rather description, narration, reproduction of my representations, the telling of what is subjectively experienced, of what seems so to me. The corresponding slogan of Montaigne reads: "I don't give an argument, I tell, I narrate". In Lawrence Sterne's *Tristram Shandy*, the sceptical cat is ironically let out of the bag, and indeed with the following statement: the stories told in the book "are all true; for they are about myself" (Sterne 1985: 533).

This equivocation, the sphinx nature of Pyrrhonism, this hybrid form, this mixture of philosophy and literature, is manifested in the emphasis on imagination and fantasy – whereby the affinity to poetry is clear – as well as in its characteristic forms of presentation in the hybrid of hypotyposes and tropes.

6) The path left behind – scepticism's path – doesn't lead to knowledge, but it does reveal the sceptical *epochē* as itself problematic. Consciousness arrives at the sceptic's destination as doubled in itself, hybridized, divided, two-fold, as a dubious being. The dualism of consciousness is overcome in self-consciousness, but it continues to exist internally. This requires a further change of direction, a *third* way, a *third philosophy*, one that, according to Hegel, is neither dogmatic nor sceptical, but must be both at the same time (*Werke* 2: 227). This further reversal back to what is rational in a positive way is thematised in the *Phenomenology* as the transition from self-consciousness – which is already reason – to reason in the form of *spirit*. In this reversal, the "previously *negative* relation [of self-consciousness] to other-being changes into a *positive* [relation]. In idealism [self-consciousness] gains *peace* in relation to the world the world and discloses this world now as its new, actual world . ... Consciousness *annihilates the annihilation of its reality* and is certain of experiencing only itself in the world" (*Werke* 3: 178–9) – a reversal of the reversal.

This turning point refers to a completely new experience, to a completely new type of necessity to go further. Now, with the presence of spirit's concept or fundamental structure, the process is carried out in native realm of spirit. With self-consciousness we have "entered the native realm of truth" (*Werke* 3: 138)

As the protagonist of what appears to him, the sceptic cannot achieve self-negation by himself; what simply appears to him does not lead him to negate himself and return to essence. The sceptical position only indicates that appearance, as the determinateness of essence, is negated and preserved in a higher form in essence itself (*Werke* 6: 21). No other philosophy than scepticism, no other way of thinking, can hold out against scepticism. Indeed scepticism cannot be attacked 'from outside', but can only be 'reversed' – *in the many ways discussed here*. The sceptic must be shown that the determinations that distinguish his thought from speculative thinking are *determinations of speculative philosophizing itself.* Scepticism's role vis-à-vis speculative philosophy parallels the role of appearance vis-à-vis essence. In advocating mere appearance, the sceptic does not represent another philosophy; rather, the determinations of thinking that emerge as scepticism are transformed into the determinations of the idealism of freedom (as the phenomenon changes into essence, representation into the concept, and *ataraxia* into free spirit). This is the meaning of Hegel's conception of implicit, immanent scepticism, the incorporation of scepticism into idealism, a scepticism that essentially belongs only to speculative philosophy.

2 Conclusion

Hegel understands his *Phenomenology of Spirit* to be the presentation of the very experience of consciousness. The fundamental principle of the structure and motion of consciousness, taken as the "*appearance* of spirit", as "spirit that appears", is absolute negativity, the "duality" of self and object, of subjectivity and objectivity, the "opposition of consciousness". As radical protagonist of this absolute negative, of what appears, Hegel counts as a sceptic. The path of the appearance of knowledge, from natural consciousness to spirit as absolute knowledge, the logic of the phenomenal side of spirit, can in this sense be described as self-perfecting scepticism, as the achieving of absolute negativity.

The first function of scepticism, of the principle of negativity, consists in the production of conscious insight into the one-sidedness of all forms of appearance of knowledge. This insight is attained by means of the sceptical testing of the forms of consciousness and their "reversal".

But insofar as scepticism takes this one-sided principle of negativity as its fundamental principle, it too proves to be one of the forms of incomplete consciousness as appearance. Consciousness reveals itself as self-consciousness, and certainty as self-certainty. At one station along the path through the formations of consciousness, through the particular constellations of subjectivity and objectivity, there occurs a special reversal, the reversal of consciousness itself. This results from a key transformation in the constitution of consciousness as regards the relation between self and object, whereby the object no longer has the character of an external being, an external objectivity or reality but comes to be seen as an *appearance*. This object is transformed into the self's representation, precisely into what Sextus Empiricus called "that which appears": an image, a fantasy. It is precisely in this that the self finds certainty of the self, freedom as *pure*, immediate being-for-itself, *pure* subjectivity without objectivity. What is essential in consciousness, being a self in the form of absolute negativity, self-consciousness, the appearance of spirit, emerges in a unique and extreme version, self-certainty expressed in the manner of the representation. On the road through the appearances of spirit, through self-perfecting scepticism, through absolute negativity, what appears – pure negativity and pure subjectivity – represents a turning point: the departure point of pure subjectivity, *absolute negativity itself*. This is an essential step in the liberation from consciousness. (In the "Spirit" chapter of the *Phenomenology of Spirit*, scepticism will appear once again as the principle of the negative in the form of subjective idealism and then as the reversal within the sphere of spirit itself.)

Here the different moments or aspects of the reversal of consciousness – turning point, change of perspective, re-vision, and return – have been expounded and shown to be inseparably linked, and the fundamental internal connection between the reversal of consciousness and scepticism has been underlined.

CHAPTER 4

Pyrrho and the Wisdom of the Animals: Hegel on Scepticism

Wisdom is not a basic concept in Hegel's thought. To him philosophy as such is wisdom. As a consequence, wisdom is not situated above reason, it is rationality itself or, as Hegel calls it, thinking-for-oneself. Behind this lies the thought that two hitherto opposed dimensions in philosophy – theoretical and practical reason – are in fact one.

Against the clichés and malevolent interpretations which we unfortunately find even today – for instance the tired thesis that Hegel is an absolute logicist and a forerunner of totalitarianism (the state is everything, the individual nothing) – I think some reflections on Hegel's 'wisdom' by means of his idealism of reason, his idealism of freedom are in order. Even to this day, on the one hand, the predominant world view is a scientifically determined, empirico-positivistic one, sceptical of the absolute; on the other hand, superficiality is rampant, combined with a recourse to belief, feeling and intuition – in other words an appeal to immediacy which goes hand in hand with a rejection of foundation and argumentation. Therefore I would like to present Hegel as a modern thinker, in whose concept the individual's emancipation is at the centre and whose thinking ought to influence once again our philosophical discourse as well as our academic curriculum. I find signs for hope in the current Hegel renaissance in the U.S.A and in the engagement of prominent analytic philosophers such as John McDowell and Robert Brandon with the previously unpopular Hegel. An essential aspect of Hegel's concept of a modern culture of freedom and autonomy is to be found in his understanding of scepticism as 'the free dimension of all philosophy', in his idea of incorporating scepticism into philosophy's search for absolute knowledge.

Our starting-points are two of Hegel's references to Greek Antiquity in which *the wise man* and *wisdom* are thematised. In one of the most penetrating and important works of modern philosophy, the *Phenomenology of Spirit*, written in Jena 200 years ago, we read: "I would recommend all dogmatic thinkers like the protagonists of the so-called common sense, the philosophical realists and empiricists to 'visit the lowermost school of wisdom', to learn the Eleusinian Mysteries of Ceres and Bacchus, the Mystery of the Eating of the Bread and the Drinking of the Wine" (*Werke* 3: 91). "Animals too", according to Hegel in this astonishing remark, "are not excluded from *this wisdom*, they rather prove to be utterly initiated in it, since they do not stop before sensible things as if they were things in themselves, but [...] in the full certainty of their nothingness they seize them and eat them" (ibid.).

A second 'animal' example can be found in an anecdote about Pyrrho, the ancient forefather of scepticism, which Hegel frequently recounted. On a boat during a fierce storm, Pyrrho shows his troubled and fearful companions a pig that keeps on eating undisturbed, and says: "Such *ataraxia* the wise man should possess". Hegel immediately adds: "but this wise peace of mind should not be merely 'piggish', but born of reason" (*Werke* 19: 370). In what follows I hope to illuminate the importance of both these 'animal' principles and to point out the topicality of Hegel's understanding of wisdom – wisdom needs genuine scepticism as a corrective to dogmatism and fundamentalism, as an inclusive part of philosophy.

Hegel's pupil, Eduard Gans, repeatedly emphasised that Hegel's thought consists of one sole component: *freedom*. Later interpretations likewise see Hegel's philosophy as an *idealism of freedom*. This view cogently describes the nerve-centre of his philosophy. One foundational aspect of this evaluation deserves closer scrutiny: in the context of his reflections on scepticism Hegel refers to a *real* scepticism as the "free dimension of *any* philosophy" (*Werke* 2: 229, my emphasis).

Accounts of Hegel's understanding of scepticism are dominated by a disproportion between the value attributed to the *theoretical* and the *practical* dimension. Any convincing explanation of Hegel's view of scepticism must take into account his *incorporation of real scepticism into his own philosophy*,[1] the integration of the truly sceptical – "speculative philosophy contains scepticism within itself as an essential element" (*Werke* 19, 371). Such an explanation must provide proof of the inseparability of the theoretical-epistemic and the practical-ethical, proof of the sublation of *isostheneia* and *epoche*, of *ataraxia* and *adiaphoria*.

To provide just such an explanation I must now focus on Hegel's important distinction between what is 'really' sceptical and the different forms in which sceptical thoughts arise as independent doctrines, and on the distinction between 'sceptical method' and scepticism. Hegel writes that "those notions of scepticism which appear merely in a specific form as pure, unadulterated scepticism, disappear when faced with a philosophical viewpoint which would allow scepticism as real scepticism to be found" (*Werke* 2: 227). This real, authentic, true scepticism – Kant calls it the 'sceptical method' and takes it up in

---

1 For more on this idea see Vieweg 1999.

his transcendental philosophy – is to be found "*implicitly* in every real philosophical system", as "the *free* dimension of *any* philosophy" (*Werke* 2: 229). The question remains however as to how we are to understand the word '*free*'.

1 Pyrrhonism – Freedom of Character and Freedom of Thought

Hegel starts from a certain vagueness or ambiguity in Sextus Empiricus' definition of Pyrrhonism. Sextus understands scepticism as an art, as an ability to create *isostheneia* and the suspension of judgement which results from it, but at the same time as the "choice of a way of life or acting" imbued with happiness (*Glückseligkeit*) in the shape of inner peace: *ataraxia*. The motivating principle here is the hope for "a mind like a tranquil sea"; the key principle of proof here is *isostheneia*: each argument can be countered by an equivalent one (Sextus Empiricus 1985: 94–96). Due to this ambiguity Hegel distinguishes two varieties of Pyrrhonism: the archetypical form in Pyrrho which he calls "subjectivity of character" and the 'thinking' Pyrrhonism which he terms "subjectivity of knowledge", the latter being a consequence of the former.

1.1 *"Subjectivity of Character" – Practical Scepticism as a Way of Life*

In its archetypical form, the 'positive' essential element in Pyrrhonism lies "solely in the character and in its complete indifference towards nature's necessity" (*Werke* 2: 239). At this stage the *relativity,* the *relation,* the uncertainty with regard to finitude and the acknowledgement of finitude is exposed – "the entire scope of reality and certainty is raised to the power of uncertainty" (*Werke* 2: 241). In this revolt against nature's necessity, in which the Pyrrhonist perceives nature as 'a nothing', Hegel sees a first stage of the *"freedom of reason"* (ibid.).

In our character we have this positive side, in our *way of life*, in our attitude of indifference, of letting-things-be, in our *adiaphoria* as a *practical* indifferentism, a fundamental 'non-conformity' to everything. "The Pyrrhonists perceived happiness in *ataraxia*, peace of mind, and the way in which they understood this is the actual moving and determining factor of their scepticism" (Sextus Empiricus 1985: 31). Happiness in the figure of a soul like a tranquil sea, of serenity, of abstinence, imperturbability and indifference forms the highest practical-ethical principle; a kind of practical-philosophical axiom is at the core of Pyrrhonism.

Ataraxia consists in the fact that a sceptic cannot fear any disturbance, any external determination. Starting from this 'positive' side it is clear to Hegel that "this scepticism is not alien to any philosophy" and here we see one *practical* dimension of his incorporation of scepticism. In *ataraxia* we recognise "the general indifference of the philosopher" (*Werke* 2: 242). In this plea for an original indifferentism, in this rejection of every outside 'intrusion', of every presupposition, of every prejudice, the radical negation of 'difference' and determinateness is aligned with *freedom*, in the sense of free *potentiality* of willing. Pyrrho's individuality, his way of life was "his philosophy itself and his philosophy was nothing but freedom of character. How could any philosophy be opposed to such scepticism?" (*Werke* 2: 243). Individuality and freedom of character – being *free* – means being only with oneself, means the fundamental negation of any other independent otherness. I am not determined by others, by the outside, by a 'world', but only by myself; I am autonomous. In this 'self-constitution' I *rest* within myself. All determinateness is utterly annihilated; we are dealing with a setting free, a free oneself of any kind of determination outside my determinate resolve, my choice of a determinate way of life. In his Jena period, Hegel pictured this moment of indifferentism, of nonconformism in striking terms – "the terrors of the objective world as well as all manacles of the ethical world and with them all extraneous pillars [...] must tumble down" (Hegel 1968 Bd. 5: 270). Everything that seems to be objective, to be fact or certainty, falls prey to annihilation, disappears in this viewpoint of absolute negativity. What is essential is the resolve to rely on one's self.

Hegel understands this principle of pure subjectivity as a *purely practical* relation to the world; on the level of its immediateness, self-consciousness is understood as a *desiring* self-consciousness, as a *purely practical behaviour without any theoretical or objective determination.* Whereas the 'theoretical' is understood to mean the contemplation of all *positive* existence, the letting be and acknowledgment of being as it is, the 'practical' consists of the *negative*, of what is independent, of what is self-constituted, of what is resolved and decided upon, of what is self-substantiated, of autonomy.

The correlation between the theoretical and practical relation to the world is further elucidated in the *Phenomenology of Spirit* and in the reflections on the subjective spirit in the *Encyclopaedia*. In the beginning of the *Phenomenology* we find sense certainty as an immediate, pure, theoretical involvement, as a natural consciousness, a pure 'taking in' – the first stage in the figure of pure objectivity. As a result of the 'inversion of consciousness itself' sense certainty changes into self-certainty, pure objectivity changes into pure subjectivity, *immediate, natural, individual* consciousness changes into *immediate, natural, individual self*-consciousness; consequently the purely theoretical (the immediately certain) changes into the purely practical, into a mere way of life in its immediateness and individuality, into the 'freedom of character'. Pyrrho himself is the perfect embodiment of this type: his philosophy wants to be nothing more than his way of life; he never wrote a single word; the 'theoretical' seems to disappear in this silence of being within oneself.

In his *Encyclopaedia* too Hegel describes this first stage of self-consciousness as a *purely* practical behaviour, as a *desiring self-consciousness*, shaped by individuality and desire. All objects *seem* to have independence; they have no genuine reality. They have been transformed into mere representations, and are therefore null and void with regard to the subject. Finite things count not *for themselves*, they are 'selfless' or 'slaves'. As a result of this 'mastery' of the subjective – desire is "destructive and selfish" (*Werke* 10: 218) – things are changed and annihilated. Through this absolute negativity of the practical the objects are *consumed* and *presented as imaginary*. In this purely practical relation lies a kind of *natural idealism* in the sense of an initial, elementary approach to the finite as something which has to be sublated. In this respect the un-theoretical or a-theoretical behaviour of animals, who consume finite things without qualms, mirrors the attitude of idealism. Even in the "lowermost school of wisdom", in the Eleusinian Mysteries, early scepticism and idealism unite in "doubting the being of sensible things" (*Werke* 3: 91). Need, desire, inclination is typical of the empirical sceptic as of the 'empirical idealist'. Hegel characterizes the practical side of the Pyrrhonist consciousness in its pure form of genuine being-for-oneself as 'animal consciousness'. This is the scepticism and idealism of Empiricus. All objectivity has to be wiped out; the objects are transformed into I-phenomena, into my representations. The originally pure objectivity in the form of contingent observation and detection is turned around: now we are dealing with *my* discovery and *my* contingent observation. But the attempted elimination of objectivity completely fails: negativity itself is determinateness. The content remains, only the form has changed, that is to say it is translated from the language of being into the language of appearance. Such a consciousness no longer says 'what a particular thing is here and now' but 'how that particular thing *appears to me* here and now'.

The Pyrrhonist may prefer the pure way of life as a dumb or silent certainty, but even their silence is a statement, and their passivity an act, a choice between inclinations or desires. What one mistakes for letting-things-be in the form of doing nothing is actually a *determinate action*. Even when this sceptic declares (whether in words or not) that he is 'without will', that he rules out every moral valuation, that he does not want to be free, that he wants to remain 'uninvolved', this first of all means that he must have a definite idea of what 'his own free decision' or 'being involved' means. Secondly, he cannot escape from the choice of contents and inclinations, from the choice of a determinateness (even if it is transformed into appearance as representation), from the necessity of willing and acting. The Pyrrhonist *desires* his abstention, *chooses* his not-choosing. Letting-things-be (*Gelassenheit*) or neutrality are always nothing but a delusion, a fallacy. 'Selecting' one's determinate course of action, deciding and acting upon it remain inevitable.[2] The individual sets an end which, however, ought not to spring from their own decision. That is the dilemma of the Pyrrhonists: having no end should count as an end. In §§478 to 480 of the *Encyclopaedia* the contradictory nature of the Pyrrhonists' purely practical relation to the world is further elaborated: the contrast between purely one-sided subjectivity as arbitrariness and purely one-sided objectivity as contingency. "As arbitrariness the will is free for itself insofar as it is reflected into itself as the negativity of its merely immediate self-determination. To the extent, however, that the content, in which the will's formal universality towards reality lies contained, is still nothing but urges and inclinations, it is only real as a subjective and contingent will" (*Werke* 10: 299).

Thus the will comes into view as a pure, abstract subjectivity, as arbitrariness, while the unavoidable determination of subjectivity remains contingent, something that befalls the subject, an *experience* or an *involuntary stimulus*, as Sextus formulates it. The essential elements of free will – indeterminateness and determinateness, voluntary choice and involuntariness – are disunited, are merely intermingled as arbitrariness and contingency, not synthesised. Insofar as the I is active and renounces itself, it determines itself. "The truth of a particular satisfaction is the universal truth, which the thinking will sets as his end as happiness" (*Werke* 10: 299). Pyrrhonist arbitrariness manifests itself as 'necessity in its universality'. Happiness is posited as an end in the form of a representation (of an 'as if') and in one and the same breath it is rejected. With the presumed pure subjectivity in Pyrrhonism we enter the stage of the *representing* and *desiring* self-consciousness (cf. Vieweg 2004).

As far as the dissimilarity of things is concerned, the sceptic is to refrain from saying whether something is by nature good or practicable. This assumption, however, he evaluates as evil by means of the argument that it causes agony of the soul.[3] On the one hand he self-confidently makes a valuation, independent or 'free' from all 'objectivity', from all presumed 'objective values', from 'duty'. On the other hand he holds happiness (*Glückseligkeit*) to be an objective and absolute value,[4] even if only for himself and for this moment. He loves 'to feast

---

2 In the absolute freedom of subjectivity (of which only humans are capable) this can culminate in the absolute abandon of self to suicide. Here we are dealing not with a way of *life* but with a way of *death*.

3 Sextus Empiricus 1985: 186. Should someone take his surroundings to be threatening, he will think himself pursued by avenging goddesses; should he obtain things that he deems valuable, he will suffer agony of the soul for fear of losing them.

4 See also Sextus Empiricus 1985: 36.

on his virtue of honourable abstinence' (Nietzsche). Nevertheless abstinence or reticence do not avoid valuation; they are themselves a fixation of value through an I, a constitution of an I, which in doing so becomes sure of itself, creates its 'identity', coincides with itself.

Consciousness is "absolutely free in knowing its freedom", it has its freedom as if it were 'given by itself', self-constituted (*Werke* 3: 442). All determination, every difference derives its essence from this indifference of the self-consciousness which coincides with itself, in this pure identity with oneself as *ataraxia*, as serenity, as inalterable and genuine certainty of oneself (*Werke* 3: 161). For the Pyrrhonist, happiness is to be found in this *ataraxia*, this undisturbedness, this inalterability, this free serenity. This is why Hegel, in his *Phenomenology of Spirit*, talks of the practical-philosophical essence of Pyrrhonism as 'happy consciousness'.

In the chapter on subjectivity of his *Science of Logic* Hegel thematises this element and invokes it as one side of the I, of the pure self-consciousness, viz. as a "pure unity, involved with itself only, which is not immediate but has emerged from the *abstraction* (the 'renouncing') of all determinateness and all content, and which returns in the freedom of unbridled identity with itself" (*Werke* 6: 253). The *ataraxia* forms a first articulation of the '*universality of individuality*' and a necessary condition, a foundation of thinking about freedom. In the same way, Pyrrhonism is discussed as freedom of self-consciousness in Hegel's *Lectures on the History of Philosophy*. Essential in *ataraxia* is not the truth, but *certainty of oneself*, serenity and resolution of mind, a consciousness of happiness, of liberation from fickle finitude, by no means the a purely *practical* non-theoretical position but rather an indifference towards the world and towards necessity, an indifference born in *thought* (*Werke* 19: 362).

1.2 'Thinking' Pyrrhonism – 'Subjectivity of Knowledge'

In a second version of Pyrrhonism – a logical continuation of the first, and one which clearly highlights its problems – Hegel deals with *thinking* scepticism, which leads to a 'subjectivity of knowledge'. *Ataraxia*, imperturbability, indifference do not spring from a mere immediacy but from recognition; equanimity is 'acquired through reason'. Education, study, exercise and *ascesis* are required in order to climb to this high position (Hegel 2004, 157–158; *Werke* 2: 238–9). In the universality of individuality there is a unity, which is only unity with itself through negative behaviour appearing as an *abstraction*, and which therefore contains all determinateness dissolved within itself (*Werke* 6: 253). Originally, scepticism means observing and searching without prejudice. This investigative dimension was already present in the original version of Pyrrho; its form, though, was no mere 'animal' way of life. In his *Scepticism Essay* from his Jena period as well as in the Berlin Lectures Hegel recollects the story of Pyrrho's sea travel with his restless and shaken companions. Pyrrho shows them a pig, eating nonchalantly despite the storm: that is how *a wise man* ought to live. But this *ataraxia* towards world and necessity is not to remain 'piggish' but is a product of reflection (*Werke* 2: 238–239 and *Werke* 19: 359). Insofar as the Pyrrhonist rises above necessity, he *recognises* it as a nonentity and at the same time *acknowledges* it in its universality. From the very beginning, Pyrrhonism was not only a 'guide to how to *live* right' but also 'to *think* right': an interesting amalgam of practice and theory which is given due honour in Hegel's strategy of incorporating and sublating scepticism.

This later variant of thinking scepticism, which developed into the extreme of mere subjectivity of knowledge, was compelled to take up a position against rival concepts of *ataraxia* (Epicureanism, stoicism) and claimed it wanted to redress the rashness of the dogmatists through *argumentation*. At the same time, however, in accordance with the original impulses and due to the problem of self-inclusion, an asserting, argumentative attitude and discourse ought to be avoided. To every proposition, the caveat '*as it appears to me here and now*' should be added, which deprives it of its claim to validity. This way the predications of the Pyrrhonists remain merely subjective and can never be attributed the status of objectivity in thinking and judging. Consequently this 'excessive' scepticism of pure negativity and subjectivity leaves the domain of philosophy and remains a *story of one specific, individual way of life*.[5] If, however, the sceptic lays the emphasis on argumentation understood as *mitigated scepticism*, he counteracts the original stating point of pure subjectivity, and becomes a dogmatist himself.

The dilemma which doggedly follows the Pyrronist is apparent in his self-understanding of his basic thoughts – Agrippa's five tropes. As tropes they represent both arguments and non-arguments, which makes them hybrids of philosophical argumentation and literary description. Pyrrhonist statements (*hypotyposes*, tropes) are intermediary forms between argument and narrative, they are forms of representation (*phantasia*) which are situated between perception and concept. Hegel takes them in their argument form and

---

5 Philosophy takes an equally indifferent stance towards this indifference, which has nothing philosophical about it. In a certain sense this indifference is 'impregnable' since it is not situated on the level of argumentation. Pyrrho can always keep silent, laugh or *turn round*, and will then remain uninteresting as a philosopher for Hegel. One who invokes his 'inner oracle', Hegel says "has finished with one who does not agree" (*Werke* 3: 64). Hegel describes this typical 'turning round' as "*inversion* of consciousness" at the "culmination of pure subjectivity". See also: Vieweg 'The Inversion of Consciousness Itself', in this volume.

understands them as the paradigmatic weapon of *investigating, free thought*, capable of defeating any dogmatism. Only by means of its sublation in speculative thought can philosophy obtain immunity against these objections.

Sceptic negativity exists in the simple coincidence of the self with itself, in the self-attributing of identity in the sense of a first and necessary step towards recognition and acknowledgment of oneself as I, in a first stage of self-consciousness, of the certainty of free resolve and free thought. Hegel understands sceptical indifference in both theoretical terms – *isostheneia* as theoretical indifference – and in practical terms – *adiaphoria* as practical-ethical indifference, the "ataraxia of thinking oneself" (*Werke* 3: 161) – as constitutive of the I, as the non-negotiable side of freedom, as a first step in the constitution of the concept of freedom. The immediate being-for-oneself as one, *the principle of solipsism, forms the first stage of the thinking of subjectivity before every intersubjectivity*.

In modernity the tendency towards *theoretical* and *practical solipsism* takes shape specifically in the subjective idealism of transcendental philosophy ('I-ism'), in which the higher form of *morality*, the unity of the individual and pure consciousness, takes the place of character. Hegel sees this element of individuality, of subjective individuality, of an I, which is at the same time indifferent universality, as an insufficient but necessary requirement: this thought is 'truly central', the *free* side of all philosophy.

2   Happy and Unhappy Consciousness

The next step in the Pyrrhonist consciousness – according to Hegel's already mentioned idea – is a doubling of consciousness within itself into a free and an unfree consciousness, a happy and an unhappy consciousness; as a self-consciousness it is *disunited within itself*. In its self-understanding it oscillates between the extremes of a *free consciousness coinciding with itself* and a *contingent, lost one*. "It does not bring together these two ideas of itself: *sometimes* it recognises its freedom as its elevation above all confusion and contingency; *sometimes* it admits to having fallen into *insignificance*" (*Werke* 3: 162). Being is transformed into seeming, into the subjective of representation.[6] The old sceptic was far from raising his consciousness of every day life objects that were forced upon him to the level of understanding in the sense of an

---

6   In scepticism what 'seems' is termed 'phenomenon'; in idealism it is 'appearance'. "The sceptic did not allow himself to say "it is"; the more recent idealist did not allow himself to consider his recognition as a knowledge of the Thing Itself" (*Werke* 6: 20).

objective assertion. According to Sextus we live, paying attention to *what appears* without linking it to any assertion whatsoever. In matters supported by dogmatic assertions, one can demur and let objectivity be. What appears is the standard by which its appearing – the subjective – is to be understood; the object 'seems' in the sense of a subjective taking it for truth (*Werke* 2: 224). All determinations of willing count as contingent, they merely befall the individual. Hegel speaks here of an 'involuntary stimulus' (ibid.). The sceptic's representation can have this or that content, but whatever content it has, it has not been constituted by himself, it is an immediate content which arises involuntarily. Sextus speaks of 'experiences' that are seen as appearances. "As to my own experiences I cannot be mistaken" (Sextus Empiricus 1998: §§193–197). But whether the cause of the experience is so or so (white or sweet) cannot possibly be ascertained (Sextus Empiricus 1998: §191). The Pyrrhonistic consciousness openly and explicitly admits that it is an entirely *contingent, individual, empirical* consciousness, a consciousness which "is guided by something that has no reality, which obeys something it does not perceive as a being, which acts and brings to reality something that has no truth for it" (*Werke* 3: 161). Such an individual and contingent consciousness resembles 'animal life' and in this reduction it stands for the loss of selfhood and freedom; it is a '*lost*' self-consciousness (*Werke* 3: 162).

Apart from the universality of individuality the pure self-consciousness also contains the individual's exclusion of all otherness, the persistence of subjectivity in 'the empty room of its inner self'. The highest abstraction of negativity is to be found in 'absolute egoity'. As in Kant, *philauta*, rational self-love or acknowledgement of the self, stands side by side with *arrogantia* in the sense of conceited *philautia*, self-importance, pure selfishness of the will, mere particular subjectivity of the 'single'. The determination of this arbitrary action remains contingent, it befalls the individual, is given to him and is not constituted freely by him. The entwining of arbitrariness in the sense of one-sided subjectivity and contingency as one-sided objectivity forms an indication of the unsolved antinomy of freedom and necessity.

With the perfect indifference and disinterestedness, having no end becomes the end of the will. There is always an end, which nevertheless should not be considered an end (as a proper decision). This results in a random behaviour towards issues based on dogmatic belief. The self-installed universality of individuality is thwarted and all determination of willing and acting changes into 'blind necessity'. Both moments of understanding of the free will are disunited in their extremes. The disunion shapes the sceptical consciousness: here plain serenity and freedom, liberation from confusion; there the fall into confusion and constant disturbance, the fall from reality into 'phenomena', into diversity, difference, non-identity. In this constant swaying to and fro every attempt to reconcile the polarities fails.

The voluntary non-conformity which renounces everything stands opposed to untried conformity. On the one hand there is the egoistical constitution or free determination, on the other hand the unquestioned acceptance of external 'commands'; theoretical and practical freedom as opposed to 'philosophical' and 'political' *apragmosyne* or idleness. The *quiesco* as permanent serenity and imperturbability, the sovereignty over every here and now, over every this, is contrasted with an indifferentism that is *total quietism*, as a prostration before the very things that are found here and now, as an apotheosis of the 'this'. Since he does not decide upon good and bad, the sceptic stands 'opinionless' before the given order, before existing customs and practices, and attunes his actions to them. Every safe pillar of consciousness, every traditional habit is dropped and immediately reinstated as a criterion of behaviour. The question arises as to how the Pyrrhonist behaves in a world that puts considerable limits on his free and individual way of life, for instance a tyranny. As a conventionalist and traditionalist he has to affirm the existing order (cf. Ricken 1994: 114–151). As in later versions of scepticism, the Pyrrhonist puts his trust in the undifferentiated and insufficient instance of *habit*.

The acknowledgement of free individuality is formulated in one and the same breath as the denial of genuine republicanism – in the sense of a rational configuration of the 'res republica' and genuine critical political engagement. An 'indifference *against* the world' comes into being, a mixture of 'intellectual freedom' and 'cold indifference' (E. Gibbon). The resting Buddha has two faces: he appears as both as peripatetic and as disoriented vagabond. With an allusion to Montaigne, Hegel speaks of the sceptic's freedom as mere "carousing about" (*Werke* 3: 162). Thus the *autonomous monad* shows himself as a *heteronomous nomad*, steadfast equanimity turns into permanent adventure, into the 'squirrel-soul', incessantly jumping from tree to tree (F. Nietzsche). Hegel sees the happy-unhappy Don Quixote as the most impressive protagonist of *reflectionless serenity* and *boundless adventurous wandering*. In Hegel's concept of the modern humoristic novel (in the form of a poetic representation) lies the return of the *freedom of character*; the heroes of these novels, such as Don Quixote and Walter Shandy, represent the modern poetic Pyrrhonist par excellence.[7]

The Pyrrhonist anticipates the principle of free consciousness and of solipsism. He pronounces the insignificance of ethical essentials (the *res publica*)

---

7   Cf. Vieweg, 'Freedom and Humour', in this volume.

but then uncritically makes these same insignificant things into authorities for his actions. Arbitrariness as a subjective and contingent will manifests itself as a contradiction in terms – the sceptic should try to realise himself in a specificity which is at the same time an insignificance to him. Abstract individuality wants to set happiness as an end in itself and at the same time deny it (*Werke* 10: 299–300). Like his modern brother the romantic ironist, the Pyrrhonist finds himself in the eternal oscillation between self-creation and self-destruction.

Hegel sees all these disunions as the intrinsic Achilles' heel of scepticism, which is to be confronted with these incoherencies and self-deceptions, these inner conflicts, which has to be criticized as a way of thinking and living, by answering indifference with indifference, thus fighting it with its own weapons.[8] Particularity and universality, indetermination and determination, freedom and necessity, subjectivity and objectivity, individuality and community spirit, morality and ethical practice are split, *disunited, two-edged, two-fold*, in *two minds*, in dubio.

According to Hegel, a prototype of such indifferent way of thinking and living is to be found in the late Roman world; *ataraxia, isosthenia* and *adiaphoria* are the concepts of a world of 'real, universal, factual scepticism'. Indeed, for him the 'arid world of reason' of his own times bears much resemblance to the late Roman world: a condition where the modern individual has been frightened into their own inner world and who intends to stay there. This individual's consciousness is happy-unhappy, their way of life resembles 'ongoing death', it is a way of life as well as of death. In Athens, political *apragmosyne* led to a death sentence; in modernity political lethargy and pretended neutrality can endanger and destroy the free self; self-determination can easily turn to dictatorship and barbarity.

Hegel's purpose seems to be to build a moral I, which neither loses itself in the unreal and unworldly 'virtuous soul', nor is so unthinking as to resign itself to everyday natural constraints and conventions (cf. Fulda 1996: 24). Subjectivity as a virtuous soul and objectivity as a contingent fact, tradition and habit are one-sided, inadequate positions. What Hegel tries to conceive is a *third* philosophy that unites the theoretical and practical aspects, a sublation of the poles of pure, one-sided subjectivity and narrow-minded objectivity, of scepticism (negativity) and dogmatism (positivity), of conformity and nonconformity, of freedom and necessity. He wants to lay the foundations of a philosophy of self-determination, of freedom.

---

8 See Vieweg, 'The Inversion of Consciousness Itself' in this volume.

3 The Unity of the Theoretical and Practical Idea

An excellent example of Hegel's thoughts on the identity of the theoretical and practical idea is the correspondence between the beginnings of the *Logic* and the *Philosophy of Right*. The sublation of scepticism has fundamental relevance for the question of the beginning of the *Logic* and for that of the beginning of practical philosophy (cf. Vieweg 2003). I can only point out the basic lines of Hegel's thought here. A first indication is that in well-known passages of the *Science of Logic* and the *Encyclopaedia* the 'resolve to want to think purely' and 'resolving' (which can also be understood as *arbitrariness*) are emphatic themes. In the *Philosophy of Right* he metaphorically claims that 'the *primal germ* of every human existence' lies in self-resolution, in the indeterminateness of the will, in this 'neutral' indifference (*Werke* 7: 63).

The key to the beginning of practical philosophy is to be found in the final part of the section 'Subjective Spirit' in the *Encyclopaedia* (in the foundation of the notion of free will) and in the explanatory paragraphs 5, 6 and 7 of the *Philosophy of Right*. Within the scope of these preliminary considerations it is necessary to pay special attention to some passages which clearly refer to scepticism (of both Pyrrhonistic and modern subjective-idealistic form) and which highlighting in particular the 'highest' thoughts of this scepticism: absolute negativity, indifference, the identity of the I in the first sentence of Fichte's first *Wissenschaftslehre*.

Freedom as foundation of the will forms the starting point. The sublation of the sceptical principle is explained in three steps:

3.1 *The First Moment (§5)*

In the first element of the will, the pure indeterminateness, the pure reflection of the I within itself comes to the fore. In a sceptical sense, every determinateness, every specific content dissolves. With an apparent change into 'theoretical' language Hegel labels this as "absolute abstraction", as "pure thinking of oneself" (*Werke* 7: 49). Within the context of the will as 'free intelligence' the unity of theoretical and practical spirit, of theoretical and practical reason is confirmed (*Werke* 10: 300–301). Without thinking this indeterminateness, this indifference, this 'waning of all determinateness', this melting away of the difference into universality cannot be accomplished. Whatever its actual shape, the 'renunciation' is a thought-shaped procedure. Only the thinking I can "set itself free from everything, can abandon every end" (*Werke* 7: 51). Here radical non-conformity, fundamental indeterminacy, *ataraxia* and indifference are clearly labelled as negative freedom. "Whosoever considers thinking as a special ability separated from the will, as an equally idiosyncratic capacity [...]

shows from the very beginning that he knows nothing about the nature of the will" (*Werke* 7: 49–50). The distinction between thinking and willing is merely that between theoretical and practical behaviour, which are inseparable. In every human achievement both moments are of necessity present; it is only in *representation*, i.e. in what Hegel calls "the viewpoint of consciousness", that thinking and will fall apart (*Werke* 10: 288). When this undifferentiated indeterminateness, this indifference, this abstract self-consciousness of identity are given their due in their one-sidedness, the need to annihilate every determinateness, the abolition of every difference, leads to the merging of the individual into the universal. This first moment consequently counts as a restricted but necessary transition. With an allusion to the sceptical, abstract negativity one could say: the formal universality of the self-consciousness is the will's 'abstract certainty' of its freedom, but not the 'truth' of it (cf. *Werke* 7: 66).

In the "viewpoint of consciousness", in the philosophy of consciousness (which stagnates with the *appearing* spirit[9]) the identity of the I only comes to the fore as an abstract, formal identity. The I is only involved with what is negative to it, with what is *beyond* it and *obscure*. Consciousness, therefore, just like the relation, is the contradiction of the independence of both sides and of their identity, in which they are sublated. This concerns the contradiction that the 'ground' within me and the 'ground' without me have an equally independent existence. This 'ground', which has to be assumed necessarily, thus remains as a ground that is not posited by the I, that is withheld from knowledge, is *merely immediate,* and in no way resistant to scepticism (*Werke* 10: 201–2). Therefore Hegel wants the transition from *certainty of oneself* to *knowledge of oneself*. Through this '*last negation of immediateness*', of the ground as an obscure ground inaccessible to knowledge, comprehending thinking determines its own content; thinking as *free* notion becomes free as to its content (*Werke* 10: 287).

3.2   *The Second Moment (§6)*

In §6 a second element is shown to be already implicit in the first; Hegel shows the deceit involved in the presumed indeterminacy and the 'ground' to which knowledge ostensibly has no access. Hegel here inverts the proposition "*determinatio est negatio*" and shows "*negatio est determinatio*" to be equally true. The abstraction from every determinateness is not itself without determination; indeterminacy should be seen as a determination, for "being something

---

9   *Werke* 10: 202: Kant's thinking "conceived spirit as consciousness, and comprised mere *stipulations* of phenomenology, not a phenomenological *philosophy*. It sees the I as a relation to what lies beyond, which in its abstract determination is called the thing-in-itself".

abstract is in itself the determinateness". The immediateness which is putatively closed off from knowledge turns out to be mediated at the same time. The I is the transition from undistinguishing indeterminateness to distinction and determination, to the specific (*Werke* 7: 52).

3.3   *The Unity of Both Moments (§7)*

Both elements – indeterminateness and determination, immediateness and mediation, identity and non-identity – prove to be abstractions. "The undetermined will is as one-sided as that which merely stands in determination" (*Werke* 7: 54). In Pyrrhonism as well as in subjective idealism (as the major variant of modern scepticism) both sides remain disunited: they are only brought into relation by being added together arbitrarily. The negativity which is immanent in both moments is not conceived consistently. In Fichte's early idealism the principle of freedom, and more particularly the distinction and determination of both moments a) and b) are at the centre. This principle, however, is not built into a system; freedom cannot succeed in *producing itself*. The I's theoretical and practical abilities are conditioned by an 'impulse' which cannot be derived from the I *as a fact*. The disunion remains as an antinomy (this time as one immanent to the I) and is expressed in ambition, as 'ought' which is how duty appears. The presumed overcoming of the disunion, the synthesis, manifests itself as a mere demand, as a postulate, as a self-destroying demand, that is to say a demand for a re-union on the Greek calends (*Werke* 2: 66–72). The "never ending impulse" is a determination immanent to the I, a determination however which as *immediate determination* "shows a side of indifference, because, although situated within the I, it contains an *immediate not-being*" (*Werke* 6: 21). Scepticism as well as Fichte's idealism are unable to surmount this *immediateness* and are thus unable to overcome the antinomy of freedom and necessity. Only one side of the will – the absolute indeterminateness, the unlimitedness – is positively acknowledged; freedom counts as "that which sublates all limitations" (*Werke* 2: 82). The other side – the determinateness or negativity – is viewed solely as limitation, as shortcoming. A community which enables the freedom of all rational beings must then be seen as a restricting or an abandoning of freedom. Hegel's diagnosis: freedom has to annihilate itself in order to be freedom; it has to base self-determination on an indefinable ground. Human beings, in Fichte's system of *Naturrecht*, become atoms, atomistic quantities, controlled by an alien law. Universality is fragmentised into the atoms of a host of individuals; we are faced with a 'deceased spirit', a dead ethics (*Werke* 3: 355). The way of life turns into a way of death. Fichte's thoughts on such a society, on such a moral community do not describe a free organisation of individuals but mark the outline of an authoritarian police state.

According to Hegel, when society is understood as a limitation of genuine freedom, it results in "the highest tyranny" (*Werke* 2: 84–85).[10] Fichte's ideal state is shaped by a never ending determination and domination: "so that the police pretty well know where every citizen is at every hour of the day and what he is doing" (*Werke* 2: 85). As a result of this "ruling by the commanding reflection" the *indeterminateness as a potentiality*, a fundamental constituent of freedom, is destroyed. The Pyrrhonistic 'befalling' mutates into the contingency of 'pure insight': the modern equivalent of sceptical negativity (*Werke* 2: 90; cf. *Werke* 3: 391–397). With this turn nothing is achieved; the immutable polarity of freedom and necessity is merely continued.

In both scepticisms – in Pyrrhonism as well as in subjective idealism, the modern form of *thinking* scepticism – a fundamental non-identity ('I' and 'not I') is created; man is *at the same time master and slave*. If "commandment is invested within man himself and within himself commandment and submission are absolutely opposed", the final result can only be the "*absolute disunion*" (*Werke* 2: 88).

Reason easily admits both dimensions – a) that the will can renounce everything and b) that the will is determined – but it cannot manage the conclusive step which characterises the 'third' philosophy – thinking the speculative unity of both elements. The will is sure of itself, knows itself to be 'decided within itself' (*Werke* 10: 288). It has to be understood as the unity of both moments – as self-determination of the I, which constitutes itself as the negation of its self, as determined, limited, and in doing so nevertheless is with itself, remains with itself in the other.[11] The I knows the determination to be its own, as a mere *potentiality* by which it is not bound, but in which it merely is because it constitutes itself in it (*Werke* 7: 54). The proof of this innermost speculation – "infinity as a negativity which refers to itself, as the 'last source of consciousness and activity" (*Werke* 7: 55) – is to be found in the *Science of Logic*.

The unthought unity of both moments gives rise to 'reductionisms' such as voluntarism and subjectivism as well as determinism and fatalism. Pure arbitrariness as narrow-minded subjectivity and befalling determination as narrow-minded objectivity 'change into one another', are two sides of one medal. In the one-sided view of arbitrariness there is the contingency as will. "In the arbitrary will (*Willkür*), the content is not determined by the nature of my will to be mine, but by contingency; thus I am dependent on this content, and

---

10   Fichte makes a theoretical design of what the Pyrrhonist simply had to accept.
11   "It is the advantage of self-consciousness that, unlike the inflexible animal instincts, it is arbitrary and contingent in its determinations while limiting this arbitrariness through its own will" (*Werke*: 4: 346).

this is the contradiction which lies in arbitrariness" (*Werke* 7: 67). This shows the dilemma of practical solipsism as a way of life of indifference and nihilism. From arbitrariness as mere subjective and contingent will, from the unmediated antithesis between objectivity and subjectivity originates the disunion, a "master's" self-determining and a "slave's" externally-determined consciousness as one entity, the "contradiction between the independence and dependence of consciousness" (*Werke* 3: 356). Sceptics, like transcendental-poetical ironists, want to realise themselves in a specific way of life, which nevertheless represents a nothingness to them. They take happiness as an end, and disclaim it at the same time. They represent a *happy-unhappy* consciousness. The free, nomadic monad wanders 'shapelessly' from one contingency to the next. Sometimes he takes himself for God, at other times for an insignificant grain of sand. He finds no determination, but is swayed by changing moods.[12]

4 Ataraxia and Conscience

Hegel further develops this issue of free self-determination and determinateness in the section on morality in the *Phenomenology of Spirit* and in the well-known 'Transition from Morality to Ethical Life' of his *Philosophy of Right*. This is relevant for the question of the sublation of scepticism, since Hegel sees in the modern understanding of morality the subjective-idealistic version of scepticism put into practice – the identity of pure and individual consciousness, the *transcendental solipsism as 'I-ism'.* Two ideas should be looked at briefly:

a) For Hegel *conscience* is the subjectivity in the shape of abstract self-determination and 'pure certainty of oneself'. He understands it as a modern form of *ataraxia* – self-consciousness of the futility of all other determinations, and pure introversion of the will (*Werke* 7: 259–265). The pure immediate truth is "the immediate certainty of oneself represented as content, i.e. the *arbitrariness* of the individual and the *contingency* of his unconscious natural being" (*Werke* 3: 473). On the strength of his certainty of himself "he has the majesty of absolute autarchy". Self-determination immediately counts as duty; duty is knowledge itself (*Werke* 3: 476). In contrast to the Pyrrhonist consciousness – as the immediate resting point, which stands united and unrelated *vis-à-vis* the universal, which contains the universal without difference within itself – the

---

12   Cf. Kierkegaard 2004: Abt., 291 and Hegel *Werke* 3: 356 and *Werke* 20: 416: "Inside himself the subject knows himself to be the Absolute…by right he can destroy all determinations he has fixed for himself".

necessary universality of the self as a pure knowledge-of-oneself and willing appears in I = I, which is every essence and existence. Whereas at first the moral consciousness is still mute, conscience has its reality in speech. Speaking is the genuine reality of doing and the justification of acting. This I is a self, which as such is real in *speech as the centre of autonomous and acknowledged self-consciousness*, which "pronounces itself to be the truth, and in doing so acknowledges every self and is acknowledged by it" (*Werke* 3: 479–480). In the description of its extreme form (the lonely-virtuous soul) Hegel makes the link with the Pyrrhonist consciousness. In this submerging within itself, consciousness achieves its most abstract, its 'poorest' shape. Consciousness of the self is only knowledge of the self. "Every living thing and every spiritual essence has returned within this self and has lost its difference from the I-myself" (*Werke* 3: 483). The moving forces of this seemingly resting consciousness are the extreme abstractions, which are not fixed, but are in perpetual unrest, in alternating constitution and destruction (this may be an allusion to the romantic characterisation of irony as a persistent oscillation between self-constitution and self-negation). Hegel speaks about an "exchange between the unhappy consciousness and itself" which never gets round to expression, to the reality outside its own speech but remains mere passionate yearning (*Werke* 3: 483).

As a foundation for 'choice', for deciding upon a determinateness ('every content has its stigma of determinateness) the corresponding passage of the *Philosophy of Right* advances a knowledge and conscience that are 'ever mine'. Following on from that, in the much discussed §140 Hegel deals with the subjectivity's becoming one-sided, its excesses and perversions. The final step proposes once again that romantic irony is a key form of modern scepticism which developed from Fichte's philosophy and which, with its absorption of the Pyrrhonist ideas of fundamental relativity, the permanent alteration of self-building and self-annihilating, provided a striking description of the disunion and its never-ending progression. The ultimate 'ground' counts as an *immediate* one, inaccessible to knowledge; it can only be guessed at, believed or *poetically* represented.[13]

---

13   In the same way the romantic concept of transcendental poetry "wavers between the universality of the concept and the determinacy and indifference of the form (*Gestalt*), is neither fish nor flesh, neither poetry nor philosophy" (*Werke* 20: 417). Romantic irony pretends to 'know' the unity of counteracting forces immediately from within itself and to represent this immediateness poetically. One's own life and one's self-consciousness remains within oneself; what is spoken poetically is the contemplation of one's own way of life. What is described in the 'transcendental poetry', in the 'philosophical poems' and the 'poetical philosophemes' is the romantic character of the 'virtuous soul'.

The aforementioned paragraphs offer a cogent diagnosis of the sceptical-relativistic trends of modern (and contemporary) philosophy (from a theoretical as well as practical point of view), of the 'degradation of philosophy': such sceptical philosophy takes representation as its criterion of truth, it declares "knowledge of truth to be empty vanity, pays only fleeting attention to the realm of knowledge (which it takes as mere *seeming* and thus *what seems* becomes the principle of action)" and ends up making "the individual's particular worldview and specific convictions into the principle of ethics" (*Werke* 7: 273). When I rule out the knowledge of truth, it does not matter how I think and act.

b) The game of caprice and absolute self-complacency, which the virtuous soul demonstrates, leads to a practical atomism. Autonomy changes into a political autism, into indifference to the world. According to Hegel, genuine freedom can only be thought and realised by means of the transition from morality to ethical life, that is, to a concrete identity of subjectivity and objectivity, of the subjective will and of the realised good. In the idea of freedom, *ataraxia*, conscience as free self-consciousness and the 'notion of freedom which has become the concrete world', have to interconnect in the sense of an institutionalisation of what is rationally free. What is at stake for Hegel is the foundation of individual freedom, which is invaluable in itself, and of society built on the notion of freedom. What is at stake is the speculatively conceived unity of *autonomia* and *res publica*, as clearly opposed to *sceptical atomism* and *disunion*.

With these ideas Hegel's practical philosophy manifests itself as a cardinal point in his wider project of the sublation of scepticism, as an attempt – to be studied in depth and elaborated – to overcome the dualism of theory and practice, as a protection of the 'free dimension of philosophy', as a modern philosophy with 'one' component – *freedom*. Such idealism of freedom today unfortunately is all too often ascribed the status of museum-piece, and is too seldom understood as an important intellectual resource in the organisation of the modern world as a culture of freedom. Hegel, along with the animals-as-true-idealists and good old Pyrrho, may be able to guide us along the path of wisdom.

PART 2

*Hegel's Practical Philosophy as a
Philosophy of Freedom*

∵

CHAPTER 5

Hegel's Theory of Free Will

Hegel's practical philosophy, which he terms the *Philosophy of Right*, represents a philosophy of free will and action. The *Philosophy of Right* delineates the architectonic of free will, from the 'granite foundations' via the cornerstones and load-bearing walls, up to the roof and the keystones. It sets out the 'basic outline' (*Grundlinien*) of steps in the gradual determination of *the idea of freedom and of free will*, the building blocks of a philosophical theory of action. In three key chapters of the *Philosophy of Right* the philosophical theory of free will and action is unfolded in its three stages: a) the personal, b) the moral, and c) the ethical. These present the progressive self-determination of the willing and acting subject, from the person via the moral subject to the ethical subject.

The following reflections refer to and restrict themselves to expounding the core determinations of the concept of free will that precede the actual systematics. It deals primarily with *Philosophy of Right* §§5–33. What are developed here are the basic principles of the spiritual-practical universe, of free will and of action, the core determinations of what, deep down, holds the practical, ethical-cultural world together – *freedom*. Hegel's practical philosophy can thus be described as a modern philosophy of freedom, as an idealism of freedom.

1 The Foundational Structure of the Will – §§5–7

The fundamental determinateness of the *concept* of free will as "the principle and beginning of the science of right" (Hegel 1973 Bd. 3: 213) can only be made meaningful and clear by reference to Hegel's innovative logic. The *Philosophy of Right* rests essentially on the Doctrine of the Concept (subjective logic) expounded in the *Science of Logic*, where Hegel unfolds the *self-determination of the concept* into the Idea. This categorial instrumentation, derived from the doctrine of the concept, is an unavoidable condition for any appropriate interpretation of Hegel's *Philosophy of Right*; disregarding or underestimating this logical dimension of practical philosophy prevents any advance into the core of Hegel's thinking of freedom. The attempt to read Hegel's 'integral theory' as a series of brilliant individual ideas is like using a cathedral as a quarry; one may certainly turn up treasures and usable parts, but the 'spirit' of the whole disappears.

In §7 of the *Philosophy of Right* (*Werke* 7: 54–57) the basic logical pattern (Universal-Particular-Individual) which Hegel had already sketched is reiterated and the notion of free will is developed.

The determinations of the will are as follows:
1. Universality (U)
   Equality, Indifference
   Identity
   The universal concept (*Science of Logic*)
2. Particularity (P)
   Distinction, Difference
   Non-Identity
   The particular concept (*Science of Logic*)
3. Individuality (I)
   Reason
   Identity of identity and non-identity
   The individual (*Science of Logic*)

1.1 §5 – *The First Moment of the Concept of Free Will (Universality – U)*

This starting-point – the universal concept – resulted from the end-point of subjective spirit: the self (*das Ich*), the self-positing immediate individual, which was raised (or 'purified') to universality – the pure immediacy of the ego (selfhood), arising from a total abstraction, the ignoring of any definite content, of any 'limitation', as a pure self-relation, as thinking self-reference, in categorical terms: free will as the self *thinking itself*, the self as the *pure thought of itself*.[1] Elsewhere, this 'theoretical moment in the will' is described as the universal, as 'right' (*das Rechte*) (*Werke* 16: 277). This first moment of the will as a free intellect, as a thinking ego, is characterized in almost exactly the same terms in §5 of Hegel's *Logic* – the self is "first of all this pure self-related unity, and is so not directly but insofar as it is abstracted from all determinateness and content and retreats into the freedom of boundless equality with itself" – the first stage of freedom as identity with itself – "contains all determinateness dissolved within in itself" (*Werke* 6: 253). Herein lies the 'primal possession', the primal ownness of thinking selfhood.[2] This indeterminacy is

---

[1] "We must, therefore, abandon the ordinary conception, according to which will and intelligence are two different subjects, and the will without thinking ... can be rational. Even God remembers that this content belongs to the mind as well" (*Werke* 16: 133–134).

[2] Selfhood includes the being of the self. The self is 'doubt itself', as Hegel puts it in a quite Cartesian line: "I can doubt everything, but not my own being, because I am that which is doubting [...], The self is [here] the immediate relation to itself; in the self is being" (*Werke* 16: 122–3). In a passage corresponding to one of the additions (*Zusätze*) in the *Philosophy of*

the sole (abstract) determinacy and it excludes all particularity and includes all determinations as a possibility. The first moment is however "not without determinacy" since "to be something abstract and one-sided constitutes its determinacy" (*Werke* 7: 52). The will is here 'undetermined', all content remains open, the will is unbound, free, uncoerced. Such a self can want anything and everything, even what it is not itself. One could speak here of a treasure chamber of existence waiting to be unlocked. The self is the potential 'Author' (*dynamis, potentia*), the undetermined 'impulse', it is free, insofar as it alone is able to initiate a chain of conditions (Kant). Such a self can also negate itself: indeed only a being with this possibility (this applies to all possible rational, thinking beings)[3] can be regarded as free, and only in such a case can one speak of free will.

This being-self is a question of pure indecision, akin to the 'emptiness' of Buddhism, the 'ataraxia' of Pyrrhonism, it is negativity as being-still-undecided brought to the level of the (Fichtean) I. In some of the connotations of §5, one can see references to scepticism and particularly its modern variant, subjective idealism as 'egoism'. Just as at the origins of philosophy as such, so here at the origins of practical philosophy, the relevance of Pyrrhonism and transcendental idealism for the problem of philosophical beginning emerges clearly.[4]

With regard to these philosophies, Hegel insists on the (intended but not yet fully established) unity of theoretical and practical reason. Willing and thinking cannot be separated and a strict concept of the will necessarily includes thinking – "the will is only rational insofar as it is thinking" (*Werke* 16: 133). The will is thinking in the form of the free concept (*Werke* 10: 287). Hegel uses the same characteristics of the self, its 'solipsistic' side (cf. Vieweg 2007: 69–84), to describe Indian-Buddhist, Pyrrhonian and Fichtean ways of thinking: abstract generality, the all-unity, 'alone-ness', the pure certainty of self, absolute abstraction and negativity, pure indeterminacy and emptiness, neutrality and indecision, atomism, solitude of the self as perfection of 'acts of absolute negation'. Thinking is willed in its purity, everything else disappears in the abyss of nothingness. This first moment thereby lacks the dimension of efficacy, it remains in the purely theoretical realm, as a form of willing it is not *posited* by the will, freedom is here purely negative and empty, mere

---

Right, we read: "I can abstract from everything, but I cannot abstract from thinking, for abstraction is thought itself, it is the activity of the universal, which simply refers to itself. Being is in the abstracting itself. [...] I am: in the 'I' an 'am' is already entailed" (*Werke* 16: 123).

3 To speak of rational beings is not the same as to speak of humans, although humans are – as yet – the only beings known to fit this description.
4 Cf. Vieweg, 'Beyond Realism and Constructivism' in this volume.

absolute possibility without further determinacy, which defers and destroys every (further) determinateness.

1.2 **§6 – The Second Moment of the Free Will – the Particular Concept (Particularity– P)**

Because of the fundamental one-sidedness of the first moment of determination, the self must at the same time be conceived as the abandonment of such indeterminacy, as the unlocking of closure, as opening, distinguishing, judging (*Ur-Teilen*, literally 'primal-dividing'), as determining and as the positing of determinacy in the form of content or object. The will emerges from its universality into particularity. In particular acts of the will, a closure is removed (*aufgehoben*) and the self as author can be regarded as a genuine 'prime-mover' (*Ur-Heber*) and initiator (*energeia, actus*). Empirical phenomena such as authorship, attribution, responsibility, etc. follow from this. Through this positing of itself as a particular – determining as unlocking (*Ent-Schließen als Auf-Schließen*) – the self becomes something existent, something finite: the particularising of the self (the logical form of judgement, of distinction, of separation, of division).

This second moment, the moment of negativity – to which Hegel attaches extraordinary value – is not simply additional in the sense of an 'also'. Nothing more is added, he says, the negative does not appear in some second, extrinsic proposition but follows logically from the first, is already contained within it. What has already emerged as the core theme of Hegelian logic, namely immanent negativity, must also be conceived in the self. The first moment represents precisely that which it excludes, it is not pure, true infinity and universality, nor the whole concept, but its determinateness consists precisely in its status as undetermined and abstract. The self is able to abstract from everything but not from thinking, since abstraction is itself thinking. Thus it is not without determination, not empty, not colourless light nor eternal indecision. Rather, its 'indeterminateness' provokes determinateness; it gives rise to infinity and finiteness as two unilateral, logically linked moments, the second following logically from the first.

Merely expounding these first two elements (without their logical derivation) would entail nothing metaphysical in itself; they are thoroughly familiar notions. But if, for the sake of imagination, i.e., not for the sake of philosophical reasoning, one appeals to the self-consciousness of every self, the duality of the self's speech becomes clear: to self-consciousness it is evident that as self it can will everything and can relinquish all bonds. The self can even abstract from its mineness (being-ness, self-ness). At the same time, the self adds its own particular being-ness (mine-ness), wherein, as something particular, it wills, and it is thus unique and distinctive: it is indeterminacy plus determinateness, identity and also difference, universality and particularity. Out of this juxtaposition or mere addition of the two terms, where one term 'befalls' the other, there results a dualism of infinity and finitude, unconditionality and conditionality, and the mere understanding (*Verstand*) overlooks the one-sidedness and logical connection of these moments. The understanding (*Verstand*) thus has to be brought to reason (*Vernunft*), to the logical thought of the unity of both moments, to the ground of universality and particularity, of identity and non-identity.

1.3 *§7 The Logical Unity of Both Moments, the Determination of Both Concepts – Individuality (I) as Reason, as the Concept Itself*

In individuality (Hegel also uses the word 'subjectivity') the two definitions have their unity, their ground, of which they are only moments. The primal division (*Ur-Teilung*) becomes con-cluding (*Zusammen-Schluß*), the judgment (*Urteil*) passes into the conclusion, the inference (*Schluß*). It is a question of the particularity that is reflected into itself and thus reduced to the universal, the negativity of negativity, the true self-determinateness of the ego which determines and limits itself but which thereby remains identical with itself, merely joins itself with itself (the logical form of the deduction). The self determines itself but remains 'indifferent' to this determination, knows it as its own, as a mere possibility that does not bind it, which it can always dissolve. A being that distinguishes itself from the particularity of its existence in this way can be regarded as free, as a rational being, this freedom is conceived as the *only* determinateness of the will. Hegel emphasizes once again that while the first and second moments of the will are easily acknowledged, this is not the case for the third moment which is the speculative and true moment – *individuality*, the concept par excellence (*Werke* 8: 307–8).

The will as self-determination of the ego in which the individual (I) represents the unity of the universal (U) and the particular (P) can only be grasped by speculative thinking; the proof of this core idea of infinity as a self-related negativity belongs to the *Science of Logic*. The self is the universal. As will, I exist in my freedom, in my universality itself ... my self-determination; and if my will is rational then self-determination is a determining in general, something universal, a determining according to the pure concept. Rational will is sharply distinct from contingent willing or willing according to contingent impulses and inclinations, for it determines itself *in accord with its concept*, and the concept or substance of the will is pure freedom. All rational determinations of the will are developments of freedom (*Werke* 16: 133).

Individuality or subjectivity so conceived – the concept – is for Hegel the absolute principle of the *Philosophy of Right*, and the fulcrum of the modern world. The free will in this sense is absolute or 'holy', but by no means transcendent, all-knowing: it is no philosophers' stone. Rather, it exists as the determinateness of truth and to the extent that the self is here brought to the concept, the standpoint of the concept is that of absolute idealism in general (*Werke* 8: 307). The insistent and absolute insistence on the freedom of the will, on freely conceptualised knowledge, on a modern thinking of freedom, must be maintained. Freedom constitutes the concept of will.[5]

1.4   §§8–28 *Further Determination of the Basic Pattern*

The caesura and the necessary transition from §7 to §8 of the *Philosophy of Right* – "the further determination of the particular" – can be explained only by recourse to logic. After laying the foundation stone with the conceptual structure, the concept of judgement is further defined (cf. *Werke* 8: 311–322). In judgment we have the posited *particularity* of the concept, namely as determination of the object. To understand an object, according to Hegel, is to be conscious of its concept, which inheres in the object itself.[6] In judgment lies the distinction between moments, which as being-for-themselves are identical, yet are not identical with each another (*Werke* 8: 316–8). When we make a judgment (*Be-Urteilung*) concerning an object, we consider it in the determinateness posited by its concept; in this sense all objects as things are a judgment.[7] They are (as something individual) universal or they are a universal which has become individualized. Hegel speaks of the "Fall"[8] of the finiteness of life and of spirit "into their judgment," in which "the contrary which is separated from them they also have as a negative in them, and thus they are the contradiction called evil" (*Werke* 10: 293).

In religious worldviews, evil is often summoned up by knowledge, for instance in the Christian story of original sin. Here knowledge, *consciousness* is the act

---

5   What is decisive in the unity that individuality (I) presents is that the self is "at one with itself in this limitation, in this other, in that it determines itself while remaining itself and doesn't cease to be at one with itself nor to hold fast to the universal" (*Werke* 7: 57).

6   As he writes in §167 of the *Encyclopaedia*, "Gold is a metal" counts as a judgment whereas "Caesar was in France" is merely a statement (*Werke* 8: 319).

7   Hegel considers all things as objects for judgments, because these 'primal divisions' (*Ur-Teile*) concern the identity and the determinateness of things themselves. Objects are, in this sense, 'differentiations' of the primal ground. Hegel is here drawing upon Jakob Böhme (see e.g. Böhme 1958: 209).

8   Alluding to Lucifer's fall from Heaven and Adam's banishment – the creation of the distinction between good and evil.

through which *division* is *posited*, the negative, *judgment* (*Ur-Teilung*). In eating of the Tree of Knowledge, Adam does something which is essentially forbidden and which makes him divine: God says, "The man has become as one of Us" (Genesis: 3:22).[9] This 'sinful' character of knowledge lives on in the spirit: "negativity, subjectivity, ego, freedom, are the principles of evil and pain" (*Werke* 10: 293).

1.4.1 Purpose

Beginning with §8 of the *Philosophy of Right*, the moments of judgment are asserted – finiteness, particularity of content, structure of subject-predicate identity and the question of the copula (cf. *Werke* 8: 319–322). What merits special attention is the further explication of particularity, especially in answering the question of whether and how the self, in its particularisation, can remain at one with itself, how it can retain its universality in particularity.

What is at first the merely formally determined will involves the contradiction of discovering a world and translating subjective purposes into objectivity via the mediation of activity and means (*Mittel*). At the same time, the determinations of the will are taken as the individual's own will, are the *content of the will*, *purpose*, both internal and to be realized.

1.4.2 Will and Nature

The content of the different determinations of the will has to be grasped at its first, initial stage as *immediate, in itself, natural*, since it first refers to something other, thus falling into the contradiction of free and non-free being. The will can be truly free only when it has itself as object, as purpose, only when it is fully *for itself* what it was at first *in itself*. This path, the movement from *in itself* to *for itself*, is inherent in the determination of the will; it is by no means the application of a property to a given substance. For the sake of illustration, let us use Hegel's example: the child is already 'in itself' a rational human, in accordance with the concept, but it must first become a human being 'for itself' – a complete I, fully mature, with full legal capacity, civil rights, etc., and must do so "by working to create themselves, not only by going outside themselves but also by developing themselves internally" (*Werke* 7: 62).

The different determinations of this natural will arise as a direct, naturally existent content for the self – its drives and inclinations, in which it finds itself

---

9 "The animal, the stone, the plant, are not evil; evil first appears within the circle of knowledge" (*Werke* 17: 257) – knowledge, distinction, contemplation are themselves evil, freedom has an essential moment of division, diremption (into good and evil) in itself, it is the source of possible evil ('sickness', 'damage') and of possible reconciliation ('health', 'healing'). Indeed Hegel refers to the idea that Christ is the second Adam, the second God-resembling man.

determined by first nature, which is not annihilated in this respect. But this content must be ascribed to me as my own; the mine-ness of my desires and inclinations comes about only via the mediation of my willing. But the will is here still in the status of immediacy – the given and the found – not yet in the mode of rationality. The inclinations are thus natural, but are also posited by me, dependent on my will (*Werke* 7: 49–52), I am not necessarily inclined to do such and such, but I am "responsible" for the particular ascription (such as when my neurons fire) and can postpone or pass on this responsibility. By producing out of the 'doubled indeterminacy' a definite decision, the will as individual is liberating (*auf-schließend*), resolute (*beschließend*), decisive (*entschließend*).

1.4.3   Resolution and Decision – the Will as Will of a Determinate Individual

The self in its individuality advances to the status of author (*Ur-Heber*) of its actions, and the neutrality, the indeterminateness, the indecisiveness, are left behind. The moment of individuality posits first the moments of the concept as differences – thus Hegel's recourse to logic. With this *distinction*, 'separation', positing of difference, we have the judgment in the sense of a first, original division (*Ur-Teilung*), the *logical form of the judgment*, the "true *particularity* of the concept, for it is the determinateness or distinction of the same, which however remains universality" (*Werke* 8: 317). Here lies the "primordial germ of all existence" (*Werke* 7: 63), the prime movement (*Ur-Heberschaft*), the ground of the possibilities to come, the closedness (*Geschlossenheit*) is now opened (*aufgeschlossen*), and we are dealing now with decision, with resolve (*Entschlossenheit*).

First of all, the issue concerns resolve (*Werke* 7: 52–54, 63–65). As a result of its determination, the will of a particular ego distinguishes itself as something finite from what is other, and in this sense its indeterminacy and possibility are translated into determinateness and reality. Thinking reason is thus the will to resolve to finiteness. A will which tries to avoid this – the so-called 'beautiful soul' or 'beautiful temper' – disparages finitude while longing to be infinite, thus unwittingly restoring the dualism between the finite and the infinite here already overcome. Such beautiful souls are not true wills, they remain finite, mere empty longing and striving.

1.4.4   Doing What One Wants – the Arbitrary Will as a Necessary and Insufficient Moment of Free Will, as Formal, Irrational Will

In the finite will we have the infinite ego (*Werke* 7: 49), which stands above any content and at the same time remains merely formally infinite, in that it is bound to the internal and external determinations of nature (*Werke* 7: 52, 62). It is the self's will to choose sovereignly for this or that content; the self is no falling stone obeying the law of gravity, it is not a magnet drawn in only one direction (*Werke* 7: 65). The indispensable moment of free will, which is an integral part of the whole sphere of objective spirit, is *the arbitrary will* (*Willkür*), the sovereign act of arbitrary will – the will as a contradiction. With the arbitrary will a definite mechanism is instigated which proceeds from the function belonging to the formal self, that which comes solely from selfhood (from the 'indeterminacy of the self') and which secures the moment of choice, an indispensable determinant of the will. While stones or plants or celestial bodies cannot deviate from the necessity of their nature or their truth, rational beings are able to intervene in the realm of necessity of universal spiritual nature, to deviate from it, and to maintain a peculiarly stubborn point of view, even to remain in a position of untruth. Herein lies the freedom of the subject – freedom "carries the arbitrary will within itself, and it can detach itself from its necessity, from its law, and work towards its own determination" (*Werke* 16: 14). This formal element of any free self-determination can, however, be regarded as 'irrational freedom,' since such self-determination does not arise from a reasoning will (*Werke* 13: 136). Only a will determined by thought can be regarded as free; the arbitrary will lacks precisely *thought*.

In contrast to actual, content-rich freedom, the arbitrary will is still contentless and merely potentially free (*Werke* 8: 304). As immediate, natural will (desire or inclination) it remains 'uneducated'. We can speak of a free will only when a resolve to thinking and to truth is formed. In Hegel's words, "freedom is precisely thought itself, whoever rejects thought and speaks of freedom doesn't know what he is saying. The unity of thought with itself is freedom, the free will … The will is only free as thinking will" (*Werke* 20: 307).

The merely possible, undetermined freedom of the self stands antinomically opposed to objective determination by internal and external content. The arbitrary will thus appears as the "means of reflection between the will as determined merely by natural drives and the will that it free in and for itself" (*Werke* 7: 66). Since the content fixed as purpose is conceived merely as possibility, the arbitrary will appears as "*contingency manifesting itself as will*" (ibid.). And it is because a particular purpose is undertaken 'at my pleasure' (*Belieben*) that the randomness (*Beliebigkeit*) arises; the determinations are accidentally produced by the senses, imagination, reflection, and reason. The insufficiency consists in the fact that freedom is here equated with the pure particularity of arbitrariness, and the concept of freedom thus remains unfulfilled. Freedom is taken to mean exclusively doing what one wants. "It is true that one often equates freedom with arbitrary will; yet the arbitrary will is merely irrational freedom, choice and self-determination not from a reasoning of the will but from accidental drives and their dependence on the senses and the external world" (*Werke* 13: 136). The arbitrary will is 'deficient freedom' (cf. Honneth 2007: 407) in so far as voluntary self-determination consists here merely in preferring one of several predetermined inclinations and impulses and the subject fails to relate to something that it can understand as a moment of itself. Each 'limitation' of the arbitrary will, of supposed freedom, is (dis)qualified as coercion, condescension, restriction, interference or repression. Where there is a persistent separation of the subjective side (of abstract certainty – not yet knowledge – of the will of freedom) and the objective side (of the given content), two philosophical positions unfold, namely subjectivism (voluntarism) and determinism (fatalism). Both are correct, but both are one-sided.

The former, subjectivism, rightly insists on formal self-activity, on formal distinction and ability to choose. But this, as already indicated, lacks the objective, content-appropriate determination, whether that which the self chooses is actually appropriate for them. "If immediate knowledge and feeling as such are made into principles […] the determination of the content is arbitrary" (*Werke* 17: 374). Individuality (*Selbstigkeit*), the freedom of the self, could turn out to be pure self-seeking, pure egoism, which, nevertheless, can be quite detrimental to the self. Because of the lack of determinateness, extreme subjectivism threatens to turn into extreme objectivism (determinism, tyranny).

The latter position, determinism, confines itself to the moment of what is given, the non-self, what is 'implanted by nature'. The concept of determinism elevates our natural determinations to a principle of heteronomy. A deterministic naturalism which absolutizes the internal and external impulses of nature, natural presuppositions, must declare freedom (which it mistakenly identifies with arbitrariness) to be illusory.

Today (as always) the philosophical empiricists battle, in their own naturalistic and materialistic way, the principle of thought and thus the principle of freedom.[10] All deterministic doctrines rest on the assumption of necessity, they take the rational being to be a marionette, a mere cog in the great machinery of natural laws, a servant of cosmic powers, a living particle at the edge of the universe.

The sleep of reason produces philosophical monsters: on the one hand an extreme 'anthropism',[11] a practical solipsism (an arrogant view of the human being) on the one hand and, on the other, determinism's dissolution of the

---

10   "Materialism, naturalism, is the consistent system of empiricism" (*Werke* 8: 145).
11   Cf. Wolfgang Welsch's perceptive critique of the anthropic principle, in e.g. Welsch 2012.

will and its concomitants – responsibility, guilt or remorse – such that the acting individual is degraded to a puppet, a mere plaything of external powers (a position of total humility), the fatalistic farewell to freedom as such. The lack of thought consists here in raising a justified and necessary determination to the status of the single and highest, in not conceiving the logical unity of both moments. While fatalistic determinism one-sidedly construes our determination by nature and ultimately takes freedom for an illusion, the subjectivist-voluntaristic conception reduces freedom to arbitrary will (and thus cannot fix an adequate concept of the will). It construes nature as something epiphenomenal, to be controlled and dominated, takes the infinite progress of natural purposes as a pattern for an eternal striving for freedom and comforts itself with the hope that this will one day be attained.[12]

In both variants freedom becomes like a rock covered by eternal snow, which no amount of digging can hope to uncover – freedom as mere illusion. Both extremes are intertwined, interdependent – the arbitrary will and randomness turn out to be their own opposites, as chance impulses or natural impulses and vice versa. Both determinism and subjectivism or voluntarism fail to provide an adequate concept of free will, fail to provide an adequate conception of human action.

With regard to judging and appraising action, Hegel discusses two basic models which still dominate the ethical debate: the position of inclinations, of happiness, exclusive focus on the results of action (eudemonism, utilitarianism, consequentialism) and the position of deontology, of duty, the 'ought' (*Sollen*), the good in itself regardless of consequences. In both patterns, however, the production of a logical unity – either 'being happy without doing one's duty' or 'not being happy but following one's duty' fails. For an adequate judgment of actions we must go beyond both positions – we must focus neither exclusively on intentions nor exclusively on consequences.

1.4.5 The Truly Universal Will

To bring the understanding to reason as well as to bring duty and happiness to freedom are two sides of the same coin, are reached in the same step. True universality is based on *comprehending thinking*, "the thought which is carried through in the will". The will exists only "as a thinking intelligence of truly free will." In the interest of an adequate interpretation of each station of the argument, this must necessarily be taken into account. Thought must always be

---

[12] The principle behind the 'regulative ideas' in Kant's practical philosophy.

taken as a *work*. This shows the true philosophical content of Hegel's doctrine of right: "Thinking is the foundation of right (*Recht*) and constitution as such".

In a concentrated form, §23 of the *Philosophy of Right* (*Werke* 7: 74–5) expresses the content of the comprehended will, the will which has been brought to the concept, which has itself as its own object in its genuine, pure universality, the will which no longer finds itself in a relation of dependence. Here again we find the Archimedean point of Hegelian logic, of his philosophizing as such – the comprehending thought as a self-relation, as a dynamic of self-determination. In such a free will, we have the double self-referentiality of self-knowledge and self-will.

Following this, with explicit reference to the *Logic*, Hegel once more expounds the difference between the universality of the understanding (*Verstand*) – where the universal appears as mere communality or all-ness – and the truly universal. Rousseau, in the most striking manner, had already described this difference with regard to the state, in making a distinction between *volonté de tous* (the will of all) and *volonté générale* (the general will) (*Werke* 8: 312–3). The concrete universality, the concept of free will, lies precisely in the sublation (*Aufhebung*) of its two moments; it is that which transcends its object, elevates it to its own, and which makes it into a thing in which the will itself dwells, in which it can be with itself – the rational, which can be grasped only speculatively.

2   Conclusion

In §27 of the *Philosophy of Right* (*Werke* 7: 79), Hegel draws the conclusion from the concept of the will developed so far, the free will which wants to be free will. The free will which is imputed to rational beings cannot be denied, but the capacity entailed by this imputing can be lost or revoked. The free will must therefore also *will itself*; it doesn't just exist, I must *know* it.

Right (*das Recht*) can thus be regarded as the realization of the concept of free will, as the existence (*Dasein*) of free will, the *existence of all determinations of freedom* (*Werke* 1: 304). It is the idea of freedom in which the succession of concepts is manifested as a succession of forms (*Gestalten*). The principal forms of right (or modes of freedom) which are then logically unfolded in Hegel's great work and which space forbids discussing here – *abstract right, morality, and ethical life* – represent unique manifestations of right, each make their own claim to validity, are ideal-types of performed action, rational determinations of freedom, of free will.

CHAPTER 6

Inter-Personality and Wrong

Hegel's innovative theory of personality testifies to the continuing and enduring modernity of his conception of Objective Spirit as a philosophy of the practical. The cornerstone of the entire building of this philosophy of freedom will be erected here. An array of problematics contained therein ranges from the concept of the person, personality and inter-personality, fundamental rights, property, the formation of the natural as self-formation and formation of external nature, sustainability, appropriation, intellectual property to contract, wrong (*Unrecht*), 'second coercion' (*zweiten Zwang*) and punishment. In the following discussion the problematic of wrong and Hegel's concept of 'second coercion' will take centre stage.

1 The Concept of the Person

The beginning, the first determination, consists in immediacy and indeterminacy. Here we find a fundamental idea of Hegel's, already made explicit in §§5 and 6 of the *Philosophy of Right*: this first indeterminacy itself represents a certainty, namely an abstract identity. Accordingly §5 starts with the universal and abstract, the infinitely self-relating, simple self-reference of the will, the 'I' as immediate relationship to itself (*Werke* 7; 49).[1] With this negative determination and the merely abstract, not yet determinate relationship to itself – "I can abstract from everything, but not from thinking, because abstracting is itself thinking"[2] – the will is now *inherently individual will*: "The will which is free in and for itself, as it is in its *abstract* concept, is in the determinate condition of immediacy" [...] "inherently individual will of a subject" (*Werke* 7: 92). "Spirit in the immediacy of its self-secured freedom is *individual*, but one which knows its individuality as absolutely free will" (*Werke* 10: 306). In this formal, self-conscious and otherwise empty, simple relation to itself, in its exclusive

---

[1] Cf. *Werke* 7: 92: "Such a thing also exists – it is Being that doesn't yet move or relate to what is different, is therefore immediate".
[2] "Abstraction is the *determinateness* of this standpoint." – "Still lacking determination or opposition, in itself [*in sich selbst*]" (*Werke* 7: 92). I can behave 'negatively' to all further particular determinations (drives, needs, qualities), can disregard them. Therein lies the fundamental equality of persons.

individuality, the subject is a *person* (*Werke* 7: 93).[3] Personality entails "that, as *this* person, I am completely determined in all respects ... determinate and finite, yet simply pure self-reference, and thus I know myself in my finitude as *infinite, universal,* and *free*" (*Werke* 7: 93).[4]

With personality the concept as such is expressed; the person however gives the concept the determinacy of reality (*Werke* 7: 444). The beginning of Hegel's practical philosophy, its foundation, finds its ground with this new concept of the person, upon which the further development of the theory of freedom rests.

As this first stage of the work, abstract right and the determination of personality are logically underpinned by the *doctrine of the concept* and the transition to the doctrine of judgment, here in the form of *qualitative judgment*, as judgment of immediacy and abstract universality. The finite person can know themselves as universal, infinite, free. Regardless of the above-mentioned *particularity* of the will in the determination of the abstract person, this is initially something indifferent for the personality: "my universality – the absolute justification, from which all else follows" (*Werke* 7: 95). The first chapter turns on the logical principle of individuality (Individuality – I) that is immediate universality (Universality – U). The (free) will is at first *immediate* and its concept therefore abstract – simply personality. It is "first *immediate*, and hence as a single being" (*Werke* 10: 306), as the abstract formal universality of willing. The concept of the person (personality) demands a knowledge of oneself as abstract I, a thinking knowledge of oneself, the I (re)cognizes itself (cf. Siep 1992: 98–115). Every self-reflecting and willing I which (re)cognizes itself as such, is a person: the individual is the universal.

As this pure being-for-myself I am simply related to myself, I attribute this to myself and recognize myself. My will, my right, the right of the individual, thereby count as universal, infinite. "Indeed law [*Recht*] and all of its articles [*Bestimmungen*] are based on free personality alone, on self-determination, which is the very contrary of determination by nature" (*Werke* 10: 311).

In the *Philosophy of Right* the following has a central place: "The *universality* of this will which is free for itself is formal universality, i.e. the will's self-conscious (but otherwise contentless) and *simple* reference to itself in its individuality; to this extent, the subject is a *person*" (*Werke* 7: 93). In terms of §5 this formal, abstract will counts as the determinateness of the beginning: my

---

[3] "Spirit as free, self-conscious being is the self-same I, which in its absolute negative relation is first of all exclusively the I of a free being or *Person*" (*Werke* 4: 59).

[4] "The 'pure relation to myself' of personality is therefore the purely cogitative and position-taking (thus voluntary) relation of a self-conscious and embodied individual to itself" (Siep 1992: 101). Cf. Quante 2005: 73–94.

will is respected and legitimated independently of its particularity and independent of all further determination, it is therefore 'justified'. The particularity, the determinateness of the will, is initially disregarded, which is why one can speak of *abstract* right (*Werke* 7: 96). It will be shown, however, that in the last instance nothing at all can be abstracted from particularity (P): the relation individual-particular (I – P) must finally be taken into account, which then marks the boundary of abstract right.

In personality we find the absolute justification of the free will, my universality is this absolute justification, my will counts as universal, without other props or grounds. Law and all its articles rest solely on the free personality, on the concept of the person, which Hegel describes expressly as the fundament of self-determination (*Werke* 10: 311).

2 Personality and Inter-Personality – Recognition of the Person and Legal Capacity

The way out of the simple 'I want' in the talk of the I, the I which wills itself as I, is via what Hegel calls *legal capacity (Rechtsfähigkeit)*. It entails 'being a person', it is the summons to be a subject, to be someone who knows their universality (exactly the justification mentioned above). Insofar as they know themselves as person, every subject ascribes themselves this legal capacity, recognises themselves thus. With this central term of recognition comes a further indispensable element: the idea of the development of self-consciousness towards *universal* self-consciousness – mutually respecting *absolute independence* now has the status of *an absolute justification for every individual person*. Here we have the general as universal, simply what is generally valid, the *absolute equality* of individuals standing in the relation of recognition, who are equal precisely insofar as they are taken exclusively to be *persons*. Relations such as servitude, slavery or despotism fail *a priori* to count as forms of freedom: neither the master nor servant count as free; they 'are in the same relationship' of unfreedom. Here we abstract from non-equivalent, non-symmetrical forms of recognition, though; these have the condition of their possibility in the absolute or universal character of personality.

In the reciprocal being-recognised of persons as persons we have an intrinsic moment of Hegel's concept of freedom. Against the interpretation of Hegel's departure-point as 'individualism' or 'liberalism', against the thesis of "repressed inter-subjectivity" (M. Theunissen) or Hösle's view that Hegel "thought of the person in a way wholly detached from inter-subjectivity" (Hösle 1988: 491), it can be countered that a moment of recognition is implied in Hegel's very starting point. "That the fundamental equality of all legal subjects in Hegel's philosophy of right is indisputable is due to the fact that in the universality of self-knowing knowledge a relation of mutual recognition is already implicit" (Siep 1982: 258). On this Hegel remarks in his *Encyclopaedia*: "I, the *infinite* self-relation, am as a person the repulsion of me from myself, and have the existence of my personality in the *being of other persons*, in my relation to them and in my recognition by them, which is mutual" (*Werke* 10: 307).

The second part of the precept of abstract right thus encompasses inter-subjectivity in the form of *inter-personality* as an under-determined form of inter-subjectivity. It can be formulated as follows: *respect every other individual I as a person, as a subject with legal capacity*. Hegel says, "As person you have existence, being for others, you are free for yourself, you are, you should exist as free, as person for yourself, and *everyone* should be thus" (Hegel 1973, Bd. 4: 174). On the ground of this inter-personality Hegel then builds the various forms of *intersubjectivity* which are further developed in the *Philosophy of Right*, those which can be identified in moral contexts (in the family, in civil society, in corporative-associations which become a 'second family' or 'miniature states') and finally also in the State itself. Fundamentally therefore we can identify three main stages in of inter-subjectivity in the *Philosophy of Right*: a) *inter-personality*, b) *moral intersubjectivity*, and c) *ethical intersubjectivity*. Hegel's philosophy of subjectivity proves itself from the outset to be a theory of inter-subjectivity.

3   Wrong and the Theory of 'Second Coercion'

Contract lies at the basis of *formal-abstract* recognition, the mutual recognition of contracting partners as persons and proprietors, whose particular characteristics remain unimportant. *Inter-personality* proves to be the first form of inter-subjectivity, as *formal-abstract inter-subjectivity*. The second stage of inter-subjectivity, moral inter-subjectivity, places §112 centre stage, in the setting of the moral sphere. Here, on the level of abstract right, my will exists objectively through the externalisation of property; the externalisation is thus objectification, a form of the universal.

This identity consists solely in the similarity of formal willing and the mutual respecting of personality. Contract is posited purely through the person as contracting partner, thus it is not about an in- and for-itself general will but about a still deficient form of universality. This unity or identity of different wills constitutes inter-personality, which combines two moments: I am and remain a proprietor and my existence remains likewise as property, my objectivity counts as " 'free self-consciousness of another" (*Werke* 7: 156).

Hegel's critique addresses all modern contract theories, which built their theorems on the indeterminateness of the contract. Though the *contractual* represents a moment of relatedness, nevertheless ethical associations such as the family and the state cannot be attributed to mere contractual agreement and consensus. Such reductions to the contractual involve invalid extrapolations of regulations of property and of abstract law as such into other, more complex spheres of right and communality. The *contractual-consensual* – which a) proceeds from arbitrary free choice, where b) the identical will is merely common and thereby a still deficient form of universality, and where c) the objects of contracts are *individual external things* (*Werke* 7: 157) – represent a first form of inter-subjectivity, *contractual inter-personality*, which however proves insufficient on its own to ground a conception of the rational sociality of free subjects.

Contract displays the difference between universal and particular wills and with it right as the commonality of particular wills and their accidental or arbitrary agreement; a difference that leads consequently to an opposition of universal and particular wills, to particular right as an illusion (*Schein*) (*Werke* 7: 173). In this sense Hegel introduces 'wrong' (*Un-Recht*) as the third stage of abstract right; according to the *Science of Logic*, the truth of appearance consists in its invalidity or nothingness (*Nichtigkeit*). Abstract right, pushed to its conclusion, can pass over into wrong in the form of infringement. The will, in the form of its outer existence (the body and external property) can be infringed, afflicted, injured or suffer violence, and through such violence can suffer *coercion* (*Werke* 7: 178). Kant had already noted that abstract right has as its object "only that which in actions is *external*" (Kant, 1968 Bd. 6: 232). Hegel adds, the will which is in-and-for-itself free cannot be coerced: the "free will in its concept will not be damaged" (Hegel 1983b: 52). Though an individual may be physically subjugated, they are not necessarily thereby coerced; coercion involves an act of *self-will*: "True, as a living thing a human being may be *overpowered* [*bezwungen*], i.e. their body or any other external part brought under the power of others; but the free will cannot be *coerced* [*gezwungen*], except in so far as it fails to withdraw from the external object in which it is held fast, or from its idea of that object. Only the will that *allows itself to be coerced* can be coerced into anything" (*Werke* 7: 178–9). Hegel adds, "Since it is only insofar as the will has an existence in something determinate that it is Idea or actually free, and since the existence in which it has embodied itself is the being of freedom, it follows that force or coercion is in its concept immediately self-destructive because it is an expression of a will which annuls the expression or determinate existence of a will" (*Werke* 7: 179).

This first coercion must always remain wrong (*unrechtlich*), the abstractly taken coercion destroys itself in its own concept, it is no free act (*Werke* 7: 179–180). Here Hegel follows Kant's considerations on law, where law is bound up with the authority to coerce, and Kant's idea of *second* coercion.[5] If a wrong, illegitimate coercion "is a hindrance or resistance that occurs to freedom" then an opposing coercion can be viewed as "hindering a hindrance to freedom", thus generating the authority to coerce the first coercion. "Right and the authority to coerce therefore mean one and the same thing" (Kant 1968 Bd. 6: 232). Against the coercion of heteronomy a second coercion appears justified. Thus Kant speaks of the law "of a reciprocal coercion necessarily in accord with the freedom of everyone under the principle of universal freedom" (ibid.).

Hegel immediately adds that violence against a natural being in which a will resides also counts as coercion. Insofar as the affected will is only a particular will against the universal (thereby not a free will or will in-itself), we must speak of 'coercion in itself' or of *first* coercion. Against such a particular will, against the merely natural or the arbitrary, against heteronomy, a counter-coercion can be exerted, which according to Hegel appears to be merely a *first* coercion but is nevertheless a *second* coercion – that coercion embodied in, say, teaching or raising taxes: "the merely natural will is a violence directed against the intrinsic Idea of freedom, which must be protected from this uncivilized [*ungebildeten*] will and enforced against it" (*Werke* 7: 179–80). This enforcement is a *second* coercion, which follows the first as its sublation (*Aufhebung*). Coercion is legal "only as the sublation of a first, immediate coercion" (*Werke* 10: 311). It is therefore a question of law or right (*Recht*) against injustice or wrong (*Unrecht*). This situation points ahead to the State, where arbitrary free choice and the merely natural represent a first coercion against common interests and concerns, and where the rational (in the form of the unity of I - P - U) must be invoked (for example, in the form of the levying of duties and taxes or demands for services from the State) against it. *Coercion is thus justified only in the form of second coercion*, as the authority to act against the *heteronomic*.

---

5 "The person has, e.g. a right to property. The freedom of the will thereby receives an external existence. If this is attacked, so is my will attacked. That is violence, coercion. Herein lies immediately the authority of second coercion" (Hegel 1973 Bd. 3: 296–7).

Hegel then makes explicit that abstract right as *coercive right* can only be considered legitimate as a coercion against coercion, as a coercion against wrong (*Un-Recht*) and thus as the *re-establishing* of right (*Recht*).[6] This negation of the negation, this "obstructing an obstacle to freedom" (Kant 1968 Bd. 6: 231) in turn makes right into something valid and compelling – a real power.

Punishment – the expression of second coercion – must indeed be seen as *belonging to the deed of the criminal*. Punishment reverses the first (the wrong, the infringing deed) and thereby *completes the deed* – punishment for a crime is "not an external but rather an essential result of the action, posited by the action itself [. ...], flowing from the nature of the act, a manifestation of the same" (Hegel 1999: 15–16). Punishment is "merely the manifestation of [the criminal's] own will" (*Werke* 8: 277). Herein lies the core idea of an *action-theoretical legitimation of state punishment*. A crime counts (and this forms the basis of the idea of punishment) as "an essentially invalid or void [*nichtige*] act, a violation of free will as will" (Hegel 1983b: 52).

The practical-logical core-thesis thus runs: *crime contradicts the concept of free will and the concept of free action*. In a legal context, wrong represents an unauthorized action – legal guilt – and thus demands a reversal in law, by means of punishment. The infringement of law as "positive external existence" (§97) is intrinsically *void* (*nichtig*) and this infringement is itself destroyed (*vernichtet*) in punishment (negation of the negation).

The real evil is the infringement of right, of the universal. The criminal has, "according to the concept, *done something against himself*, which must be brought to reality" (*Werke* 4: 60, my emphasis). In punishment the infringement of law as law is sublated: "one must focus on justice and reason, that is, freedom must preserves its existence; sensual drives etc. should not be venerated" (*Werke* 7: 188).

It can be maintained that a coercion against wrong has legitimacy solely in the sense of self-defence, certainly not as coercion and violence against substantial personal rights, such as assaults on integrity or property, upon religious views or artistic creation. The strict right of coercion cannot infringe the moral realm, neither can it distinguish here, e.g., between murder and manslaughter,

---

6 Punishment cannot be understood as mere coercion. It is rather "the re-establishing of freedom, and the criminal remains free or is made free as well as the punishment being rationally or freely enacted" (*Werke* 2: 480). The heading mentioned in the *Encyclopedia* – "Right against Wrong" (*Das Recht gegen das Unrecht*) captures the matter well. When Hegel's discussion of these topics is clarified then what Schnädelbach calls "the considerable problems of understanding" the *Rechtsphilosophie* (2000: 298) fall away. (The idea of 'second coercion' is conspicuously absent from Schnädelbach's presentation).

between *deed* and *action*. These require the transition to the sphere of morality, which is here clearly anticipated.

For guilt to be established it must be possible explicitly to ascribe wrongdoing to the free deed of the criminal: injury through *free* deeds. Free omissions belong explicitly to this class of free deeds too.[7] Of course infringements of the law have effects upon a victim, but the law itself remains incapable of injury, the 'positive' infringement is only that of the particular will of the perpetrator. Punishment manifests the necessary annulment of illegitimacy (*Vernichtung der Nichtigkeit*), the sublation of the crime.

In this brilliant and topical theory of punishment, so clearly grounded in a theory of action (cf. Mohr 2005; Pawlik 2004), the procedure of the understanding (*Verstand*) proves insufficient; the theory essentially approaches the concept (*Begriff*). Punishment can be designated 'just' insofar as it constitutes *the perpetrator's will in itself* – one can even say it is their right (!) as an accountable subject. In injuring the universal, injuring right as such, the perpetrator has just as much injured themselves. Punishment is "a right of the criminal himself, is posited in his very action" (*Werke* 7: 190). Punishment can be added to the criminal act because it is already posited in the criminal act, must be conceived as an internal moment of the wrongdoing. Punishment can be viewed as restoring equilibrium, something in which the perpetrator himself has an objective interest (though of course not every law-breaker readily admits as much!).

The Erinyes, Greek Goddesses of Revenge, Hegel notes, symbolize "man's own deed and the consciousness which ails him, torments him, insofar as he knows his deed as evil" (*Werke* 17: 127). These Goddesses are "the just and precisely therefore the well-intentioned" – the Eumenides, likewise, are "the criminal's own deed, which claims him" (Hegel 1999: 4) and in so doing halt the eternal cycle of violence and revenge.

Hegel is implicitly referring us to a 'third' judgment, and his pointing to the *Science of Logic* in §95 and especially to §§497–500 of the *Encyclopedia* requires that we once more bring the underlying logic into view. In relation to law and judgment, we are dealing with the further-determined structure of judgment.[8]

---

7 In the *Allgemeines Landrecht* (ALR) we find the passage: "Morality of the Crime" (§16). "Whoever is incapable of acting freely, with him no crime and therefore no punishment takes place" (ALR Th. II, Tit. XX.; Th. II, Tit. XX, §§7 und 8).
8 This logical anchoring is analysed in both Mohr 2005: 98ff. and Hösle 1987; see also Siep 1982: 269.

4 The Logically Grounded Structure in Judgment

Unintentional Wrong	Deception	Crime
negative judgment	infinite-positive judgment	infinite-negative judgment
"the flower is not red"	"this flower is this flower"	"the flower is not a table"
illusion (*Schein*) in itself universality recognized	law (*Recht*) as illusion universality as illusion	law as void (*Nichtiges*) negation of universality

4.1 The Simple-Negative Judgment

The simple-negative judgment forms the transition to the infinite judgment (cf. *Werke* 6: 317–324). Unintentional wrong corresponds to this transitional form, which will be demonstrated with the example of civil litigation – a mere special right finds its negation, while law as such is affirmed. In the judgment 'this flower is not red' only the particular colour, not colour as such is negated. In relation to a contract it might run: 'this contract is not legal, it doesn't conform to the law', whereby this type of contract doesn't infringe upon the legality of contracts *per se* but "only the title to the right is in dispute; the universal sphere of right is therefore recognized and maintained in that negative judgment" (*Werke* 6: 325). Hegel reveals that such judgments by no means contain truth, although they may be correct within a limited sphere of imagination and thinking. Truth consists in the agreement of the object with itself, i.e. with its concept. It may be true that I take a theft to be an action, but the theft is, according to Hegel, "an act which does not correspond to the concept of human activity" (*Werke* 8: 323).

4.2 The Infinite Judgment

4.2.1 The Infinite Judgment as Identical – Deception

In deception, by contrast, the deceiver knows of his wrong, but gives the appearance of right, by striking an agreement which lacks the universality of law. The formal relationship is maintained, the other will is respected, personality recognized, but the body of the law regarding the disposal of a thing is infringed, injured [*verletzt*]. It has its validity within the contract (a voluntary agreement to exchange a thing), but the aspect of universality-in-itself is missing (*Werke* 7: 177). This wrong of deception is based on the infinite judgment as identical (*Werke* 8: 324, & *Werke* 10: 309).

4.2.2 The Infinite-Negative Judgment – Crime

Unlike the deceiver, the thief doesn't give himself the appearance (*Schein*) of right, he respects neither the will of others nor the universal, respects neither the subjective nor the objective side of legality. In crime, by contrast, we have an infinite-negative judgment in the full sense "a judgment in which even the form of judgment is set aside [...] It is supposed to be a *judgment*, and consequently to contain a relation of subject and predicate; yet *at the same time* such a relation is supposed *not* to be in it" (*Werke* 6: 324). Judgments in the form 'Spirit is not yellow' or 'The rose is not an elephant' are certainly true, but nonsensical nevertheless.

This applies also to the judgment 'Crime is an action', because action (understood in its full, emphatic sense) and crime are mutually exclusive. To do evil is not a sufficient predicate of free action. By negating the universality of deeds, the universal side of the predicate of personhood, crime infringes the *free personality* of others *per se*.[9] It destroys too the particular, the subsumption of a thing under my will, as well the universal, legal capacity itself. It also infringes property, or the right to use things as a right to bodily integrity, the right to life. In the case of 'violent injury to life and limb' my personality also loses its recognition. Therein we see the transition from private law (contract as a means of composition) to criminal law.

It is necessary to distinguish whether the existing will in its entire scope (legal capacity as the infinite in the predicate of personhood) is infringed (death, slavery, religious coercion – an interesting list) or only a part thereof (theft). In theft (as distinguished from robbery), the criminal infringes subjective infinity, insofar as he uses personal violence against me (*Werke* 7: 184). Hegel refers in this context to the judgment-structure: "crime may be viewed as an objective instance of the negatively infinite judgment. The person committing a crime ... does not, as in a suit about civil rights, merely negate the particular right of a person to some definite thing, but the right of that person in general" – he has "violated law as such, that is, law in general" (*Werke* 8: 325).[10] The criminal deprives me of something, negates my particular right (the right of the other) and thereby simultaneously violates right as such.[11] He injures, me (the other),

---

[9] Hegel 1968 – Bd. 13: 227.

[10] The "negatively infinite judgment in which the genus [*Gattung*] and not merely the particular determination – here the apparent recognition – is negated [is] the *violently malevolent* will, which commits a *crime*" (*Werke* 10: 310).

[11] "Whoever unlawfully damages someone by a free act, who commits a crime, makes himself not only responsible to the victim but also to the State whose protection he enjoys" (*Allgemeines Landrecht*, Th. II, Tit. XX, §7).

himself and the universal (*Werke* 4: 60). Crime is, however, "*the infinite judgment*, which negates not merely the *particular* right, but the universal sphere as well, negates *right as right*" (*Werke* 6: 325).[12] Anticipating the stages of morality and ethical life (violently-evil will, evil action), Hegel attaches the epithet of nonsensicality to such actions: the infinite judgment "does indeed possess *correctness*, since it is an actual deed, but it is nonsensical because it is related thoroughly negatively to ethical life which constitutes its universal sphere" (*Werke* 6: 325).[13] It becomes clear how necessary is the step beyond the sphere of abstract right to those of morality and ethical life.

"The positive moment of the infinite judgment [lies in the] reflection of individuality into itself, whereby it is posited for the first time as a determinate determinateness", just as the subject "as individual is posited" (*Werke* 6: 325). The individual, like the universal, is no longer posited as merely immediate, but as *reflected into itself*. The judgment of existence has been sublated in the judgment of reflection.

The remaining steps fall outside the remit of this chapter, but the discussion here has sufficed to show that Hegel's recognition-based philosophical theory of 'interpersonality' and 'wrong' brought something radically new to the history of philosophy, and that these concepts are still highly relevant today. Their intellectual power and fascination *derive from their logical grounding – this is an essential reason for their topicality*.

12 In the negative-infinite judgment subject and predicate fall wholly apart.
13 A bad act has an existence which isn't adequate to its concept. If an act is judged to be bad, still its unreason has an aspect which is in accordance with reason, similar to a badly-built house (*Werke* 4: 55).

CHAPTER 7

Care and Forethought: The Idea of Sustainability in Hegel's Practical Philosophy

In the philosophical treatment of the theme of sustainability, Hegel has – wholly unjustifiably – played almost no role.* This blind spot in the research deserves detailed investigation. Hegel's reflections on sustainability are to be found in his practical philosophy, in his key work, *The Philosophy of Right*, specifically in the chapter on formal right which contains Hegel's theory of the person. My focus here is upon two central concepts – care (*Sorge*) and forethought (*Vorsorge*) – concepts which go to the heart of Hegel's subject matter. These play a crucial role in Hegel's theory of personality, an innovative theory that testifies to the enduring modernity of his philosophy of the practical. Indeed the cornerstone of the entire structure of Hegel's philosophy of freedom is to be found here. In the *Philosophy of Right* a new concept of the person and of abstract right opens up the possibility of a sustainable understanding of rational right and a comprehension of contemporary developments. The palette of problems Hegel deals with encompasses the concept of the person, personality and inter-personality, fundamental rights, property, the formation of the natural as self-formation and formation of external nature, appropriation, intellectual property, contract and wrong.

The early sections of the *Philosophy of Right* unfold the core idea of the human will. At this first stage of its unfolding the human will appears as individual will in itself. "The absolutely free will, at the stage when its concept is abstract, has the determinate character of immediacy … the inherently *individual* will of a subject" (*Werke* 7: 92). "Spirit (*Geist*), in the immediacy of the freedom which exists for itself, is an *individual*, but one that knows its individuality as an absolutely free will" (*Werke* 10: 306). The will of the subject is "still abstract and empty, has its particularity and fulfilment not yet on its own part" (*Werke* 7: 92). In this merely formal, self-conscious and otherwise content-less simple relation to itself, in this exclusive individuality, the subject is a *person* (*Werke* 7: 92–5).[1] Personality entails "that as *this* person: I am completely determined on every side … yet

---

* This chapter is based on the previous publication of the same name in "Readings in the Anthropocene", edited by Sabine Wilke and Japhet Johnstone, Bloomsbury 2019.

1 Cf. *Werke* 4: 59: "Spirit as a free self-conscious being is the self-equal 'I' which in its absolutely negative relation is at first an exclusive 'I', an individual free being or *Person*".

nonetheless I am simply and solely self-relation, and therefore in finitude I know myself as something infinite, universal and free" (*Werke* 7: 93). Hegel's treatment of the idea of sustainability is to be found in his account of how *persons* come to have *property* in things – the appropriation and formation of the natural.

1 Property

Property contains the following basic structure, grounded in the changing relation between person and thing: A) appropriation of the thing (*Werke* 7: 119–128); B) use of the thing (*Werke* 7: 128–140); and C) alienation of the thing (*Werke* 7: 140–150). The individuality which knows itself as absolutely free will – the person – has its distinctiveness and fulfilment not yet in itself (the knowledge of freedom is still abstract and empty), and consequently these exist at first in an *external thing*, "the external material for the embodiment of the will" (*Werke* 10: 303, 306). Property represents the "external sphere of law and freedom … the subsumption of something ownerless (*herrenlosen*) under my power and my will" (*Werke* 4: 59). This pertains to a) the relation to one's own body, as well as b) the relation between the will and an external, found objectivity – the *external things of nature*.

The person, who must create something external, an external sphere for the realization of their freedom (and thereby become a *particular*), has the absolute and unconditional right of appropriation over all immediately diverse things (*Werke* 7: 106). This sphere of freedom can only be "immediate and separable" from the will (*Werke* 7: 102), the external in general, a thing, defined as unfree, impersonal and ownerless. This thing counts as *natural* insofar as it is the conceptual determination of nature to be the "external in itself" (*Werke* 7: 103). A thing is therefore "the Idea existing outside itself", something natural. In contrast to "the subjectivity of intelligence and volition", the thing is "without will or right" (*Werke* 10: 306). The external becomes mine (external empowerment, ownership – I am the owner). My will is housed or dwells in these things and thus they belong to my will, a belonging bound up with the exclusion of others' power over them – possession is the site of voluntary empowerment.[2] Two aspects of appropriation are worth noting here. On the one hand, Hegel discusses things only in their immediacy and the person in their first immediacy – the human as natural being and their behaviour in the

---

2 Cf. Kant 1968: 270: "An external object that – in terms of its substance – belongs to someone is his property (*dominium*), in which all rights in this thing … inhere and which the owner (*dominus*) can, accordingly, dispose of as he pleases".

outside world. We are not yet concerned with developed things, things mediated by the will (*Werke* 7: 103). On the other hand he points out the manifold forms of the natural and the external world (*Werke* 7: 103–4) and already anticipates what is distinctive about actual appropriation – "an other (*ein Anderes*) is whatever I can take into my possession – namely *only individual not general* things, not the *elemental*" (*Werke* 7: 106).

Here in his analysis of appropriation Hegel already anticipates a differentiation latent in the natural; crucially, he follows it with proposals for the *exclusion* of particular items from the sort of appropriation typically undertaken today – of air, water, animals, ecological systems.[3] In acts of appropriation and of making-one's-own, in (private, individual) ownership, the free will becomes for the first time *real* will and each of these subjects become *persons* – the *life of the person is property*. Property means that in owning something I am myself "objective" ("*gegenständlich*"), I am "*by myself*" ("*bei mir selbst*") in this thing; in property the person is incorporated with itself (*Werke* 10: 306). In this personal self-relationship, freedom obtains its first existence (*Werke* 7: 107) and the reality of freedom manifests itself as the actual will of the person in its relation to itself, in its property. "Because I give my will existence through property, property must have the determination that this thing is mine" (*Werke* 7: 110). What count as objects of appropriation or disposal? Firstly, the physical existence of the subject and, secondly, specific "things" in the external world.[4] The person, as individual, has a natural existence, partly in itself, partly in relation to the outside world and is hence both immediate and mediated (*Werke* 7: 104).

2   Property and the 'Formation' of the Natural

Both the appropriation of living being as well as of living external things include the following moments: A) the actual (positive) appropriation, i.e., the

---

[3] The German law on genetics (Bundesverfassungsgericht 2010) adheres in this sense to the elemental: genetic technology "intervenes in the elementary structure of life. The results of such intervention may only with difficulty – if at all – be reversed" (11, 135). In other words we must forego, in the common interest, dangerous interventions in the elemental, in ecological systems.

[4] ALR (*Allgemeines Landrecht für die Preußischen Staaten*) Theil I, Titel 2, §1: "Things in general mean, in a legal sense, that which can be the object of a right (*Recht*) or an obligation". Property is the authority over the substance of a thing with the mandate to exclude others by one's own power (Theil I, Titel 8, §1). On Hegel's close knowledge of the ALR see Rosenzweig 2010: 432ff. Joachim Ritter (2005: 57) sees in the ALR one of the "first legal codes to be grounded in rational law". Hegel was also familiar with the work of E.F. Klein, one of the co-authors of the ALR. He can also appeal to the *Code Civil*.

will has its existence in something positive, something visible to others – "mine" as "universal permanent predicate" (*Werke* 7: 102); B) the use and exploitation of the thing from which follows the negation of each thing as mine; and C) the possibility of disposing of, or alienating, the thing. The logical structure of the positive, negative and infinite judgment thereby comes into play (*Werke* 8: 323–53; *Werke* 6: 311ff). Here only the main line of thought can be considered: appropriation has the following moments, a) of immediate physical seizure, b) of formation (*Formierung*) and c) denomination. And one must bear in mind the precise scope of the concept (*Begriff*) in the Hegelian sense, otherwise too much will be expected of philosophy. From the simple appropriation of objects and what is physically seized, certain problems arise in formal law which no longer concern the concept itself. For instance, the resolution of specific property issues – such as if you were to find Hegel's autograph in your rose garden, or a Roman coin in your Piedmontese vineyard, or flotsam and jetsam on your property on the New Zealand coast – belong to prudence and to positive laws. As Kant notes, "nothing further on this topic can be deduced from the concept alone" (Kant 1968: 82).

2.1 Self-formation – the Appropriation of the Body as the Natural, Immediate Existence of the Person

The thesis that the first object of property must be the body is linked to the idea that the making-one's-own of particular bodies[5] is a fundamental element of personality.[6] According to Fichte, a rational being cannot posit itself as "an individual that has efficacy without ascribing to itself, and thereby determining, a material body" (Fichte 1991: 56). To understand the person as a natural and immediate existence, to understand spatio-temporal individuation, we must first understand Hegel's recourse to *Naturphilosophie* and the Doctrine of Subjective Spirit. The person as a natural being belongs to the realm of living beings, closer to what is animal, and thus has individuation in itself; the person is born (without its will) as just such an individual. In addition, the paradigm of spirit entails a necessary becoming-objective-to-oneself. The elucidations of Subjective Spirit already deliver evidence for the constitution of the spatio-temporal individual – faculties such as the sign-making imagination, the use of speech or language, drives or inclinations. It can be shown that Hegel in no way records this spatio-temporal individuation as fact but rather quite rigorously deduces it.

---

5 On the Hegelian understanding of body and soul, see Wolff 1992.
6 In an illuminating essay, Angelica Nuzzo documents Hegel's view of the body as constitutive condition of free personality. See Nuzzo 2001.

Insofar as the I is taken as person, this must be ascribed to an individual, particular body in its unity of the corporeal and the intellectual, to their *living* will, and it remains within the individual's discretion to appropriate their body merely in part or not at all – self-mutilation and suicide. "No one may force the other to neglect something simply for the reason that the agent would harm himself" (ALR Erster Teil, Dritter Titel, §27). The person can thus be considered as private proprietor of their particular, natural existence. Moreover, this particular living being *demands* the taking-into-possession: the expression 'My life and my body are my own' is an immediate corollary of an act of free will (see Nuzzo 2001: 119). Intellectual capacities are, according to Hegel, the free intellect's own, something internal; they can, however, *via the mediation* of intellect, be posited as something external – a sermon, a speech, a book, an artwork – and thereby become a thing; the person is here the 'author' (*Urheber*), on which copyright law (*Urheberrecht*) is based. For other persons, by contrast, I am essentially free in the form of my body,[7] which I immediately have; it is immediately mine. The inviolability of the person signifies the inviolability of my particular, natural existence, the prohibition of every abuse or even killing of the person as a living thing, or the absolute prohibition of injury,[8] mutilation or torture – a basic principle of modern constitutions. Personality therefore goes together – fundamentally and inseparably – with the right to bodiliness, the individual's right to a living existence. In so far as taking possession of one's own body involves the forming of the natural, the person must also pay attention to the leitmotifs of *care* and *forethought*: keeping the body healthy entails conduct in consideration of the preservation of life and a successful combination of the sensible forming of nature and letting-be.[9] The right to life thus forms the basis for all other rights.

Simple appropriation as simple physical seizure – which is similar to the random picking up of an apple fallen from my tree – and subsequent formation (*Formierung*) of the thing entails primarily the externalizing of what is internal, what is alive and mine and externally mine. With regard to the living being of the person himself, this includes the education (*Ausbildung*) of his self-consciousness, which understands itself as free (*Werke* 7: 122), though this schooling is initially compulsory. Hegel explains this with the example of *lordship*: this belongs in the past, in the time *before* historical progress has brought about general freedom. However, since free beings, those capable of

---

7 Likewise through my own things. For others my will has "its definite, recognisable existence in the thing" (*Werke* 10: 307).
8 Exceptions, of course, are medical emergencies which require surgery.
9 Sensible care of the body and body culture instead of bodybuilding and overwork.

freely-chosen actions, can always neglect what is rationally bidden, that which should be a thing of the past can always break forth again. Negativity, subjectivity, the I and freedom are the same principles which allow evil, vice and pain. Subjugation and oppression may always reappear. Precisely here in the evidence that man can kill himself arises the possibility of the self-destruction of humanity as a whole.

2.2 The Formation of the External World – Property in External Things

Highly relevant to the process of formation is the idea of *appropriate appropriation*, because here a differentiation between natural things emerges clearly. This distinction is based on the position of things in the natural realm, in the infinite variety of the qualitative nature of objects and the diversity of subjective aims (*Werke* 7: 121). It has implications for some contentious present-day issues, particularly environmental matters. What does Hegel's talk of the rational formation (*Formierung*) of the outer world and the conservation of natural living conditions actually entail?

3 The Appropriation of Elemental Things

First, Hegel's discussion implies that so-called *elemental things*, such as air and water – what David Hume called "the most valuable of all external goods" (Hume 1960: 495) – are not to be particularized as private property (*Werke* 7: 108). To these elemental things whole ecological systems must be added too, since they represent the basis for life. From Hegel's perspective these elemental things are to be excluded from appropriation; only *individual things* may be taken into ownership. This idea of a ban on private appropriation of elemental goods deserves particular attention and has considerable consequences. In the 21st Century the availability of *water* and *air*, along with our wider dealings with ecosystems – under the heading "elemental and organic things" Hegel mentions air, water and soil (*Werke* 7: 131) – have become problems which concern mankind's existence as such.[10] Linked to this is the issue of whether the privatization of forests and uncontrolled deforestation may be permitted – these carry fundamental significance for our collective existence because of their role in climate change. The same applies to our dealings with the Earth's water resources – oceans, rivers, the Arctic and Antarctic – and the

---

10 This is highly topical, cf. the International Conference on Water 2009 – *mare liberum* – the freedom of the sea.

protection of the planet's atmosphere. Today the orgy of deforestation that is taking place from Brazil to Europe to Siberia in the cause of maximizing profits threatens humanity's survival. Natural wealth is being destroyed at an enormous rate: each day 20,000 hectares of arable land is destroyed, 50,000 hectares of woodland is cut down and 100 biological species die out, as the consumption of natural resources rises ever higher.[11]

In all these cases what is central is the indisputable relevance to ecological equilibria of the appropriation of *elemental things*, an appropriation which, from Hegel's point of view, represents a fundamental injustice, since these goods form the common preconditions of continued human existence.

4 'Forethought Which Looks to, and Secures, the Future'

Hegel left behind no developed concept of sustainability, but he did sketch substantial outlines of this key issue of 21st century life. His findings on the formation of surrounding nature, the environ-ment (*Um-Welt*), carry extraordinary weight – dealing as they do with an existential problem which in Hegel's time – despite the considerable damage already inflicted[12] – was not yet fully manifest. Certainly, as we have seen, he formulated at the level of abstract right initial thoughts on *care* and *forethought*, and thus the ecological question and the challenge of sustainability. Already in his time at Jena, Hegel had posed the problem, specifically via a sharp critique of the *theoretical abuse* of nature in Kant's and Fichte's transcendental philosophies, philosophies which show the legacy of Cartesian dualism and its attitude of domination towards the natural world. The understanding of nature in Fichte's doctrine of natural right culminates, so Hegel argues in the *Differenzschrift*, in the subjugation and enslavement of nature, our relation to the objective-natural reduced to mere "having" (*Werke* 2: 13, 80ff). Fichte's conception of a realm of freedom goes along with a subduing of nature, complementing the enormous arrogance of the I, which floats above the universe, displaying a hollow loftiness and delusions of grandeur (*Werke* 2: 416ff).

In the modern understanding, an image of humans as amphibians, as living in two contradictory worlds, dominates. On the one side, humans feel themselves oppressed and dominated by nature; on the other they conceive

---

11 *Earth Overshoot Day* is the day in the calendar on which humans' consumption of resources exceeds the annual capacity of the Earth to regenerate those resources. In 1990 it was October 11th, in 2019 it was July 29th.
12 Deforestation in ancient Greece, effects of industrialization.

of a realm of reason and freedom in which they prescribe to themselves universal laws. For Hegel, the limited understanding (*Verstand*) "strips the world of its enlivened and flowering reality and dissolves it into abstractions, and spirit (*Geist*) maintains its present right and dignity only by abusing nature and denying it rights" (*Werke* 13: 81-2). Such a contradiction must be solved by philosophy; the truth consists in *reconciling* spirit and nature, not by ignoring the contradiction but by showing how both one-sided moments "are in reconciliation". An important concern of Hegel's idealistic monism is a consistent solution to the problem of how humans can be at home in the surroundings of their world, how they can be "at one" (*bei sich selbst*) with themselves and consequently free in the natural as well as the cultural en-vironment (*Um-Welt*). Both the natural and the cultural components of this challenge of care and forethought are taken up in the *Philosophy of Right*. To this end it is essential to employ the hitherto overlooked talk of the *formation of the organic* and the corresponding distinction within the sphere of the natural, between the organic as highest form of the external world and the working-upon of the Earth with all its moments, the cultivation of plants and the domestication and husbandry of animals. This corresponds to the thought found in Naturphilosophie of the step-by-step overcoming of the Idea's externality-to-itself.

From this results a necessarily distinct way of dealing with the organic, with plants and animals and with the environment as ecological system at large. Through what Hegel calls 'formation' (*Formierung*), the thing changes into what is a person's own. This owned thing is not ours to destroy, however; it must be *maintained*, must be *durable* or *sustainable*; in Hegel's words, what is mine "ceases to be restricted to my presence here and now and to the direct presence of my awareness and will" (*Werke* 7: 121). The here-and-now of the thing is sublated, allowing its future appropriation. The reason for maintaining and sustaining the natural world, as Hegel makes explicit in his theory of recognition, lies in the communality of the individual's life-needs and the concern for their current and future satisfaction – care (*Sorge*) and forethought (*Vorsorge*). This means replacing the crude consumption and destruction of the natural object with its 'caring' formation and conservation (*Werke* 7: 122). This *form of the universal* is a "permanent means and a provision which takes care for and secures the future", says Hegel (*Werke* 10: 224) – it requires the "forethought (*Vorsorge*) of future use" (*Werke* 7: 122).[13] Bearing in mind the

---

13   In its judgement on genetic technology (Bundesverfassungsgericht 2010: 1 BvF 2/05, II, 135, 142), the German Federal Constitutional Court speaks of the constitutionally mandated "responsibility to protect the natural basis of life for future generations" in accordance with "the greatest possible forethought".

relevance of *measure* in the satisfaction of needs, we can say that there must be *measured* dealings – Hegel uses the example of animal husbandry (*Hegen*) – with the natural resources of life. 'Measured' means here in keeping with the object – the entire ecological fabric, it means acting in a way which respects the peculiarity of a system that is indispensable to the existence of the person – a *husbandry* therefore in the widest sense. It is in this sense that the German Basic Law (Article 14) states: "Property entails obligations. Its use shall also serve the public good".[14]

Hegel notes that on occasion the "specific characteristics pertaining to private property may have to be subordinated to a higher sphere of right, e.g. to a society or the state" (*Werke* 7: 108). This is particularly true of "elemental things". In the case of objects essential for sustaining the ecological balance – these could even be relatively simple things such as woodland or meadows, etc. – the private ownership of these objects could then legitimately be revoked, in part or in full, in the interests of society and the common good. Under the heading of the formation of the organic Hegel also mentions – somewhat cryptically – indirect uses of elemental matter such as the exploitation of wind by windmills, along with "contrivances for utilizing raw materials or the forces of nature and processes for making one material produce effects on another" (*Werke* 7: 122). This raises the issue of more complex patterns of formation, which would likewise require a usage that is rational and in keeping with nature. I act rationally, in a measured way, I act with '*husbandry*', in so far as I forego something which would severely damage the natural ecological balance. My action constitutes a *foregoing*, a holding-back or a suspension before any momentous intervention, out of respect for the natural balance. Husbandry (*Hegen*) or caring (*Schonen*) are at root about a type of "behaviour with consideration for how objects may be preserved" (*Werke* 7: 122) – an early attempt at a principle of *sustainability*, the conservation of life, the truthful, rational dealing with our environment. For Hegel, sustainable use is grounded in a knowledge of current and future situations and takes into account the *current and future rights* of free subjects.

5   Natural Sustainability – the Forest as Paradigm

That the term 'sustainability' originated in the field of forestry – it was first formulated by the forestry scientist Hans Carl von Carlowitz (his decisive definition

---

14   German Basic Law (Grundgesetz), Article 14. The principle of sustainability is also explicitly mentioned in Article 20a.

runs: "continuous, enduring and sustainable use")[15] – is in no way accidental, but arises from the necessity for long-term care of the forest as one of the most valuable goods of the Earth. The forester knows the significance of the forest for climate, soil, and water, knows too the lengthy life-cycles of trees (which will often outlive him or her), understands ecological systems and their vulnerabilities, has knowledge of the eco-logic. The forester is a 'husband' by vocation. Dealings with the forest cannot be conducted according to mere private appropriation and profit-maximizing but must also be oriented towards common interests – the forest as *public good* – and must therefore involve conservation and forethought. The relation to the forest, "forestry consciousness" (*forstliche Bewußtsein*), whose highest concern is the long-term maintenance of the forest as functioning ecological whole, is a model of sustainability. It shows, in terms of the history of ideas, how an intuitive concern for the future crystallises into a concept, a concept which combines gravitas and elasticity, in keeping with the traditional meaning of the terms *conservare* and *sustenare*.[16]

In his study *Sylvicultura Oeconomica* (1713), von Carlowitz, former student at the University of Jena, gives the term *conservare* conceptual shape and modern form: his work is a plea for the "conservation and expansion of the woods". It is crucial, says von Carlowitz, that "there is a continually enduring and sustainable usage, because it is an indispensable thing without which the land may not remain in its being" (cited in Grober 2010: 116). Von Carlowitz's is a masterpiece on conservation that would likely have impressed Hegel. Diverse thoughts merge in his concept of conservation: we can use no more wood than the forest can withstand; we must ensure a balance between growth and removal of trees; the forest must be allowed a right to recovery if it is to sustain itself. *Sylvicultura Oeconomica* sets out its own rational silviculture: the woodlands are "to be *rationally* arranged" (von Carlowitz, cited in Grober 2010: 116)[17] and their usage tied to maintaining their balance. In §56 of the *Philosophy of Right*, Hegel outlined *in nuce* the same idea. The formation of the natural rests

---

15   Hans Carl von Carlowitz (1645–1714) was probably the first to explicitly formulate this notion of "continuous, enduring and sustainable use". See his *Sylvicultura oeconomica, oder Hauswirthliche Nachricht und Naturgemäße Anweisung zur Wilden Baum-Zucht etc.* 1713. For this information I am grateful to Dr. Georg Sperber (Ebrach) who, for decades, has dedicated himself to the principle of sustainability, in particular to the maintenance of our most important life-foundations, the forests of the Earth.

16   On this, see the excellent study by Ulrich Grober (Grober 2010).

17   In 1760 the Duchy of Saxe-Weimar began to reform its forestry in line with the principle of sustainability, Duchess Anna Amalia decreeing that the forests "will receive a new and sustainable forest management established on the correct principles of forestry science" (cited in Grober 2010: 122).

on two pillars: firstly, my will becomes objective, external, and enduring in the thing formed and the determinations of time and space are overcome; secondly, the thing is objectively left alone or permanently sustained, whereby the parameters of space and time are also conserved and we orientate ourselves to permanence. The making-one's-own of the natural should be brought into a rational unity with the *leaving alone* of the natural, the *letting-it-be-so*. This second element upholds Hegel's vital qualification: "forethought for future use" (*Werke* 7: 122). It gives clear support to an appropriate, careful use of the natural, against the extinction of plants and animals (which as living things have an intrinsic value) and makes the case for conservation, in which the principles of respect for alterity and posterity combine.

I suggest that the principles of sustainability (set forth by von Carlowitz) and care and forethought (set forth by Hegel) should be carried over into the economy at large. The present age demands a new *Cultura Oeconomica*, an economy oriented towards *natural as well as social sustainability*, in contrast to the now-bankrupt market fundamentalism with its mania for deregulation and world-plunder. The simple pursuit of profit undermines sustainability and thereby endangers the forest – along with the entire global ecological fabric; with every utilization of the forest its healthy conservation must take precedence, for the sake of humankind's deepest interests.[18] And what applies to the forest can be extrapolated to the entire economic sphere: a new *Cultura Oeconomica* as ecological economy can teach us to treat nature with such care and husbandry that we vouchsafe its enduring usage.

In the present, however, we are confronted – frighteningly – with a very different programme. Not only is the tropical rainforest in Brazil being brutally cut down, the beech woods in Germany and forests in many other regions are being decimated. A perverse frenzy for timber reigns, a drastic violation of our common interest. Despite assurances from some politicians, the forests – the decisive basis for securing the lives of human, animal and plant – are becoming more and more the objects of economic exploitation and profiteering. The moment of natural, ecological sustainability must be considered in connection with what von Carlowitz calls the "promotion of the general wellbeing of the country". Hegel's notion of the formation of the natural and its principles of *care and forethought* serve exactly this end, for instance in the treatment of bourgeois society, in the form of notions of *social care and forethought*, or in the State in the form of an idea of a social State which may guarantee – as far as is possible – social sustainability.[19] In this way, sustainability – both natural

---

18   On this see the work of Josef Köstler (esp. Köstler 1967).
19   Space forbids going further into this issue here, but see Vieweg 2012a.

and social – can be raised to a basic principle of the constitution of a free, modern society.

The so-called 'triangle of sustainability' – economy, ecology and social justice – which was formulated during the 'Earth Summit' in Rio de Janeiro in 1992 points in this direction. With regard to the air as one of our most important external assets, knowledge of increasing – and increasingly dangerous – levels of carbon dioxide in the atmosphere must lead to actions which take into consideration the needs and life quality of future generations. Water, an essential good, requires a similar approach, otherwise this scarce resource will be further depleted and may even become a cause of wars in the coming decades. Those things which humanity needs for life cannot, according to Hegel, "be mere dead means, but rather through them man must feel alive with all of his senses and self and through close connection with them give them their own human soul and individuality" (*Werke* 15: 341). The temple of the world in which we live must be preserved from being turned into logs and stones, the forest grove reduced to a collection of timber. This pertains especially to the preservation of natural diversity, a diversity which, due to various influences (climate change, negative effects of industrialization such as monoculture, overexploitation, pollution, etc.) is increasingly under threat.

Humanity's 'emergency exit', as one leading climate scientist has put it, "stands barely a hair's breadth open.... If we do indeed generate five or six degrees of global warming in this century, then an advanced civilization – as we know it – will no longer be possible on this planet" (Schellnhuber 2009). The external goods which are decisive for the rational preservation of life, such as water, air, forests, ecological systems, are common resources for the common good and belong – this would be a thoroughly plausible conclusion to draw from the Hegelian approach – under strict public supervision and control and must largely be withheld from profit-making interests. The demand for sustainability is a fundamental criterion for belonging to the sphere of modern societies. Societies which fail to act in a sustainable way and so allow, tolerate or even promote these predatory excesses, must consequently be denied the status 'modern'.

CHAPTER 8

Hegel's Philosophical Theory of Action

The following remarks can be considered a contribution to the current 'Hegelian Turn', understood in terms of Robert Pippin's claim for *Idealism as Modernism*.* I should like to demonstrate the far-reaching significance of German Idealism by indicating the contemporary relevance of Hegel's theory of action, and for this purpose I shall focus on two specific examples: a) Hegel's philosophical conception of punishment as one of the foundations of contemporary legal penal theories, and b) the modern character of the precise distinction between 'deed' and 'act' and its significance for contemporary theories of action.[1]

Although it hardly seems disputed today that Hegel's practical philosophy is essentially a *philosophical theory of action* (in this connection Robert Pippin speaks of a "rational agency theory of freedom" (Pippin 2008), and Michael Quante of a "critical theory of action" (Quante 2011), there exist only a few extensive and illuminating discussions of this question. In the *Philosophy of Right*, Hegel's principal contribution to 'the practical domain', the philosopher unfolds the concept of action on three levels, in each case developed in relation to the acting subject. This sequence of levels encompasses a) the *formal-juridical behaviour of the agent qua 'person'*, b) the *action of the moral subject*, and c) the *action of the ethical subject*.[2]

Hegel's *Philosophy of Right*, it can be noted, develops the concept of action not only be reference to philosophy and law but also by reference to an interpretation of specific works of art, particularly ancient Greek drama, an approach which helps to define this concept more sharply in the context of practical philosophy and contributes to a more precise analysis of the components, types, and forms of action and of conflictual behaviour as well. In this the *Philosophy of Right* complements the *Aesthetics* (specifically the third chapter on 'Artistic Beauty and the Ideal') which contains a special section titled 'Action' (*Die Handlung*) in which he expressly draws attention to the internal relationship between action, language, and poetic speech. There he writes: "Action

---

* This chapter is based on the previous publication "Hegel's Theory of Action", in "The Impact of Idealism. Volume III", edited by Nicholas Boyle, Liz Disley, Christoph Jamme and Ian Cooper, Cambridge University Press 2012.
1 I have developed some of the fundamental concepts involved here in Vieweg 2012c
2 For further discussion see Vieweg 2012a.

is the clearest revelation of the individual, of his temperament as well as his aims; what a man is at bottom, and in his inmost being comes into actuality only by his action, and action, because of its spiritual origin, wins its greatest clarity and definiteness in spiritual expression also, i.e. in speech alone" (*Werke* 13: 385). Hegel's entire philosophy of art, and especially his account of literature, undertakes to show the validity of this principle by reference to a variety of poetic works, and thereby contributes to a more precise understanding of the concept of action and of literature in general. This mutual enrichment and illumination of practical philosophy and aesthetics will be illustrated in what follows by reference to specific aspects of the concept of action and to some selected works of art.

After a few preliminary observations, I shall explicate my basic thesis by reference to two issues in the theory of action: a) crime and punishment and b) the distinction between purpose (*Vorsatz*) and intention (*Absicht*), and to two works of dramatic art that are directly relevant to these issues. As our starting point we shall take the discussion of 'The Ideal' in Hegel's *Aesthetics*, and specifically the aforementioned section on 'Action', since these passages present his reflections on the relationship between the 'practical' or socio-political world and the world of art, between the realms of objective and absolute spirit. These ideas are well known to those familiar with Hegel and will merely be sketched here, albeit from the specific perspective of the concept of action. The specific and determinate character of the Ideal in Hegel shows how the Idea goes out of itself to assume actual determinacy, how it emerges into the realm of externality and finitude (*Werke* 7: 230). This process of determination, insofar as it advances through particularity to difference within itself and to the resolution of the latter, is described as 'action' in the context of art. Insofar as the Idea determines itself in this way it divests itself of abstraction, of mere unity and universality, and connects up directly with the realm of images and sense perception (*Werke* 13: 231). Hegel writes:

True independence consists solely in the unity and interpenetration of individuality and universality. The universal wins concrete reality only through the individual, just as the individual and particular subject finds only in the universal the impregnable basis and genuine content of his actual being' (*Werke* 13: 237).

It is thus necessary for us to conceive of the logical unity of the universal, the particular, and the individual. The principle of particularity implies the representation of the universal by means of fantasy and imagination, of intuitive and pictorial presentation, and this produces a manifold range and variety of further determination. Images and representations always appear in multiple form, while the Concept only presents itself as something individual.

The work of art thus synthesises universality and particularity, unites the spirit that is embodied in activity with an enduring tranquil form that has the unshakeable certainty of freedom. As examples of such effectively accomplished symbiosis Hegel specifically mentions Hercules, the Greek gods, the figure of Don Quixote. In the particular actions of determinate characters, directly involved and bound up as they are with the conditions of external reality, these agents are able to preserve their freedom, can remain self-possessed in the realm of otherness and externality. The self-relation of the agents is thus concretely presented in vivid and imaginative form. Modern romantic poetry and literature in particular concentrates on relating the fictional life-stories of irreplaceable and particular subjects, the paradigm here being Theodor Gottlieb von Hippel's novel *Lebensläufe in aufsteigender Linie*, with its striking and unforgettable opening line: 'I'. According to Hegel, it is 'characters' that furnish the real central focus of artistic presentation. Or to formulate the claim the other way round: agents we can specify by name, such as Oedipus, Orestes, Wilhelm Meister, Josef Knecht, or William of Baskerville, do not appear as such in the theory of action in the context of practical philosophy, and cannot be thematised expressly in that context.

The protagonists of poetry and literature preserve the universality of freedom within themselves, even if their action manifests itself as a particular, determinate, and externally directed form of action. This in relation to the decisive logical transition from §5 to §6 in the *Philosophy of Right* – the necessary logical transition from universality to particularity[3] – Hegel emphasises that freedom must reveal itself immanently as a whole and at the same time as the possibility of particularising itself, as the potentiality for anything (*Werke* 13: 232–233). And this yields a provisional definition of action in the poetic and literary context, namely as the internally differentiated and dynamic determinacy of the Ideal. The particular is here wrested from the realm of mere contingency, and concrete particularity is thereby vividly presented in its universality. As Hegel puts it: "spirit's particularization, turned out from within into external existence is immediately bound up with the principle of *development*, and therefore, in this relation to externality, with the difference and struggle of oppositions" (*Werke* 13: 233). The appeal and power of the work of art springs from this development, shaped as it is by tension and internal conflict, and from the resulting self-reintegration of spirit.

---

3 For more detailed discussion of this point, see Vieweg 2012a.

1   Crime and Punishment – the Eumenides and Hegel's Grounding of
     Punishment in the Theory of Action

Hegel's theory of wrong and of the nature of punishment has been accorded an extraordinary degree of attention in the field of contemporary legal theory, and it is regarded as one of the most significant contributions to the modern theory of punishment. Hegel treats 'wrong' – the *negation of right* – as the third level of abstract right. The latter, driven to an extreme, is capable of reverting to its opposite (*summum ius summum iniuria*) as the infringement of right. In the form of its outer existence (as body and external property), the will can be affected, violated, and injured, that is to say, can suffer *violence*, and through this violence can thus be subjected to *coercion* (*Werke* 7: 178). Abstract right "generally has as its object only what is external in actions" (Kant, 1968 Bd. 6: 232). In his theory of punishment, Hegel follows Kant's reflections on the concept of right (which is intrinsically connected with the possibility of legitimate coercion) and his idea of a second coercion.[4] A wrong or illegitimate case of coercion is, Kant says, "a hindrance or resistance to freedom", and the coercion that is opposed to this can be regarded as "a hindering of a hindrance to freedom" (Kant 1968 Bd. 6: 231), which yields the permissibility of coercion with respect to the first or original coercion. As Kant puts it, "Right and the authorization to use coercion therefore mean one and the same thing" (Kant 1968 Bd. 6: 231–232). Against the coercion of heteronomy a *second* act of coercion appears to be justified. Kant speaks of "the law of a reciprocal coercion necessarily in accord with the freedom of everyone under the principle of universal freedom" (Kant 1968 Bd. 6: 232). Hegel takes up this thought directly: violence against a natural form of existence that embodies a will must be regarded as an act of coercion. Insofar as the relevant will is only a particular will in opposition to the universal will (and thus no free will at all, or merely will 'in itself'), we must speak of 'coercion in itself', or of *first* coercion.

Against such a particular will, against the merely natural or arbitrary will, against mere heteronomy, it is permissible to exercise a *counter-coercion*, which according to Hegel only appears as a *first* coercion but is actually a *second* coercion, as in the context of education or the raising of taxes. We are dealing therefore with a *second* coercion that follows upon the *first* as the *sublation* of the latter (*Werke* 7: 179). Coercion is permissible "only as the sublation of an

---

4 "The person has, for example, a right to have property. In this way the freedom of the will acquires an external form of existence. If this latter is attacked, my will is thereby attacked. That is violence, or coercion. In the latter the permissibility of second coercion is immediately contained" (Hegel 1973, Vol 3: 296–7).

initial immediate coercion" (*Werke* 10: 311). *Coercion is therefore justified solely as second coercion*, as the authorisation of *autonomous* action over against *heteronomous* action. It is only *second coercion*, as sublated first or illegitimate coercion, that can be treated as rightful (the sublating of coercion through coercion), as coercion directed *against* the denial of right and thus as the *reestablishment* of right. Through this negation of the negation (this "hindering of a hindrance to freedom"), right becomes something binding, something capable of being enforced, a real power.

Punishment as an *expression of second coercion* must be ascribed to the deed of the agent, and reverses the first aspect, that of the original transgression that violates right. *And it is only then that the agent's action is completed.* The punishment that answers a crime is "is no external consequence, but rather an essential one that is posited by the action itself" (Hegel 1999: 15–16). This analysis provides the central concept for a legitimation of legal punishment that is grounded in the theory of action. Punishment must be regarded as "in and for itself a null form of action, an infringement of right as right, of the free will as free will" (Hegel 1968 Bd. 26.1: 52).

The strict right to coercion cannot be exercised with regard to the moral dimension, so that *here*, for example, we cannot draw a distinction between theft and robbery, murder and killing, between *deed and action*. The necessary transition to the sphere of morality is thus already announced and unmistakeably anticipated at this point. It must be possible to ascribe the action in violation of right explicitly to the agent as a fee act: as damage or injury produced by *free action*. Free acts of omission also belong explicitly to this class of free acts.[5] The infringement of right certainly brings about damage or injury to the victim, but 'right' itself remains inviolable and untouched, and the 'positive' injury only involves the particular will of the agent. What punishment makes manifest is the necessary nullification of a nullity, the sublation of the crime, a form of retribution as the infringement of an infringement (*Werke* 7: 190–196). This brilliant and thoroughly contemporary theory of punishment, explicitly grounded in a theory of action (cf. Mohr 2005), indicates the limitations of an approach based solely on 'the Understanding', when what is required is precisely the logic of 'the Concept'. Punishment can be described as just or rightful inasmuch as it presents itself as the *will in itself of the agent himself*, even as the agent's claim and right (!) to be regarded as a subject responsible for his acts. In violating the universal character of right the agent has thereby also violated

---

5 Compare the passage regarding the 'morality of crimes' in the *Allgemeines Landrecht* (ALR), §16: "For one who is incapable of acting freely, no crime is committed and thus no punishment is incurred" (ALR Th. II, Tit. XX.; Th. II. Tit. XX, §§7 and 8).

himself. Thus punishment also presents "a right posited in the criminal himself, ... in his action" (*Werke* 7: 190). The punishment must therefore be added and attached to the criminal act, is indeed already posited in the agent's act, and must be conceived as a moment internal to the wrongful action. The punishment is regarded as a reversal and equalisation in which the agent himself has an objective interest, even if this would certainly not be admitted or accepted by everyone who violates the law. Punishment may thus be regarded as the manifestation of the crime itself, as the *'other half' of the agent's action*, as the reversal of the criminal act now turned against himself. The central thesis, from the logico-practical point of view, is this: *crime contradicts the concept of the free will and the concept of free action.*

The avenging goddesses of antiquity, the Erinyes, give symbolic expression to this very thought. In the context of his various reflections on the nature of deed and action, whether in the *Philosophy of Right*, in the *Aesthetics*, or in the *Lectures on the Philosophy of Religion*, Hegel refers repeatedly to this point, appealing in fact to a specific example from the realm of artistic imagination. In these particular passages, as well as in Hegel's autograph note and the Addition to §101 of the *Philosophy of Right*, the three mythological 'conditions' of the avenging Furies are interpreted in terms of the three levels of right, wrong, and punishment. Thus a) we first witness the sleep of the Eumenides, then b) they are awoken by the transgressor and his heinous deed, and c) we see the avenging punishment,[6] through which the goddesses are appeased. In the condition of right or justice the Furies slumber, but "crime awakens them, and hence it is one's own deed that asserts itself" (*Werke* 7: 195). The idea of avenging punishment as a reversal of wrong is emphasised in other lecture transcripts too: the Eumenides "are the very deed of the transgressor, a deed which makes itself felt in the transgressor himself" (Hegel 1983a: 87).

The Eumenides embody "the very deed of man himself, the consciousness that afflicts and tortures him, insofar as he knows this deed as an evil in him". They are "the Just Ones and precisely therefore the Kindly Ones" who "will the right, and whoever has violated the latter bears the Eumenides in himself" (*Werke* 17: 127). These Furies are represented as at once *external* and *inner* powers. The external pursuit of the victim is equally "the inner Fury which penetrates the transgressor's breast. Sophocles uses this too in the sense of the man's own inner being", as in *Oedipus at Colonus*, for example (*Werke* 13, 295).

---

6 What Hegel calls "the right of the hero" (Hegel 2005: 97) is a merely immediate exercise of right, still an expression of the merely particular will, a form of vengeance rather than a due process of law in the modern sense.

When vengeance and punishment are at issue, Hegel of course also thinks of Aeschylus' *Oresteia*. The Furies, the terrifying avenging goddesses from Tartarus who pursue Orestes for the killing of his mother Clytemnestra, are only assuaged by the goddess Athene and the council on the Areopagus. For here a "human court, at the head of which stands Athene herself as the concrete spirit of the people, is to resolve the conflict" (*Werke* 14, 68). Here Apollo and the Euminides are both honoured in equal measure, which avoids the need for sacrifice on both sides (*Werke* 15, 532).[7]

In his poem 'The Cranes of Ibycus', Schiller created a modern poetic form in which the cranes represent the 'power of the Eumenides' who have been called forth by the act of murder and provoke the criminal to an unintended confession. The perpetrators themselves have roused the punishing goddesses of vengeance and the ensuing punishment is therefore the effective result of their own deeds. Thus Schiller's ballad also presents the idea of a fully accomplished action, from the original crime to the effect of the punishing goddesses, to the act of punishment, to 'the burning ray of vengeance' that completes the action.

1.1 *The Necessary Self-Transcendence of the Structure of Wrong*
Insofar as *avenging* punishment simply reproduces the preceding structure of wrong, we find ourselves confronted by what Hegel calls the 'bad infinite.' The successful overcoming of this deficient form of judgement expressed in the idea of vengeance can only be accomplished through a *third* kind of judgement, through the resolution of a *third* form of authority, that of punitive justice, the judgement of *right in itself*, in the sense of a neutral or disinterested judgement on a particular case (*Werke* 10: 309). In the context of Hegel's logical

---

7 Apollo admits to Orestes, "It was I who moved you to slay the body of your mother", and enjoins him to enter the city of Pallas, where he will find judges who are just. Once the votes have been cast equally in favour of condemnation and of release, it is only the white ballot-stone of Athene which decides in favour of Orestes (and Apollo). "The direful maidens pursue Orestes on account of his mother's murder which Apollo, the new god, ordered him to commit so that Agamemnon, her slain husband and King, might not remain unavenged". Here Hegel clearly distinguishes between the Erinyes and the Eumenides, or Kindly Ones (*Werke* 14: 58). The right of the husband and lord is also emphatically defended, or "the clear, conscious and self-conscious ethical life" (*Werke* 14: 59). "It is only the connection between the political and the divine that can accomplish the freeing of Orestes and establish reconciliation in place of retribution. In that the Erinyes are transformed into the Eumenides, the Kindly Ones, tragedy gives way to harmony … The realm of injury and blind rage gives rise to helpfulness and benevolence, the Erinyes become the Eumenides … Fundamentally speaking, this reconciliation is a victory for reason. For the process of persuasion, the weapon of reason, has brought about the reconciliation in which Athene takes pride … Reason now takes the place of Fate and its chain of predestined events" (Sokel 1963: 13–16).

theory this requires a move to the *judgement of reflection* and the long path that leads to the judgement of the concept (*Werke* 8: 325–6). It is only when we reach the judgement of reflection (the judgement of the Understanding) that we can truly speak of a power of judgement, or only when an action is expressly assessed as good or bad. In the *Philosophy of Right* this further development of the argument is indicated in part by reference to the necessary process of reflection-into-self and in part by reference to the 'disinterested' resolution of a dispute. The indeterminacy here points ahead to a will that is capable of judging, a will that acts both as an individual and as a representative of the universal, namely a *judger* in the sense of a court and a '*judge*'.

Here, as well as in his claim that the Understanding is not sufficient to grasp the full significance of punishing justice and must therefore give way to the *Concept*, Hegel indicates that the sphere of 'abstract right' immanently points beyond itself to the spheres of 'morality' and 'ethical life' that are still to be conceptualised if, for example, we wish adequately to determine the role of the *judge* who acts authentically on behalf of right. Punishment can only properly transpire within the context of the State. The 'judge' cannot simply rely upon negative-infinite judgements, but must, amongst other things, 'present' the spirit of the Constitution (an essential moment of ethical life) in his decisions, although this means we have attained a logically higher kind of 'judging' and transcended judgement itself. For the authoritative role of the judge can only completely be determined on the level of *ethical life*. And here the sphere of ethical life already reveals itself as the authentic ground of practical philosophy.

As a whole, we can say that Hegel presents the relevant "criteria even for a contemporary theory of punishment" (Mohr 2005: 122ff). Hegel's philosophical theory of punishment (indeed his entire 'idealism of freedom') represents a highly original contribution to the field and a conception that retains its relevance to this day. It draws its intellectual power and appeal precisely from *the logical foundation* that underpins it, and indeed *this is the fundamental reason for its continuing contemporary significance*. And in view of this explicitly philosophical grounding of punishment it is also well worth pursuing these Hegelian paths of thought even further.

1.2 *The Transition from Abstract Right to Morality*

On the final level of formal right, with the exercise of rightful punishment, the will is thrown back upon itself (in what Hegel calls 'reflection into itself'). The *singular individual in its 'simple' universality* thereby accomplishes a return to the *particular* will through the determination of punishment as the *right of the agent himself*. The previously encountered form of self-relation must thus be extended: on account of the limitations which have been revealed the self-referential structure can no longer remain simply 'external', but must pass on to internal reflection, to particularity. The negativity of abstract right which has now been diagnosed – and which found its turning point in crime, in the denial of right as such – has led to its own negation. The will has increasingly revealed itself not only as free intrinsically or *in itself*, but as explicitly free *for itself*, and the determinate particular will therefore now becomes *its own object*. In the movement through abstract-formal right it has become increasingly evident that the assumed immediacy of willing is mediated through the *subjectively particular will*, and thus that immediacy itself must be thought in terms of mediation. What became quite clear was the necessity of advancing beyond the formal-abstract level (both from the perspective of logical theory and that of practical philosophy itself). We can thus no longer ignore or abstract, as we had to at the beginning (*Werke* 7: 96), from this particularity of the will. The will itself is thrown back upon itself in its specific individual selfhood. The thought of particularity emerges necessarily from the examination of the logical structure of singularity and universality. Universality, as identity, has divided itself into difference, into non-identity, into opposition. The *judgement of existence* inevitably sublates itself and passes over into the *judgement of reflection*: "The individual, posited in the judgement as individual (as reflected into itself), has a predicate, in comparison with which the subject, as self-relating, still remains something *other*" (*Werke* 8: 325–6). The singular or individual thus immediately comes into focus as something particular, as subjective will that is reflected into itself. Since the determinacy of the will is thus posited *inwardly*, the will exists at the same time as a *particular* will, and thus arise further particularizations of it and the relations of these to one another" (*Werke* 10: 312).

The universal here can no longer be identified with abstract universality, for we are now dealing with a universal which comprehends itself as one through the connection of different moments (*Werke* 5: 67). As Hegel writes: "In *existence* the subject ceases to be immediately qualitative, but is here in *relation* and *interconnection with something other*" (*Werke* 8: 326). The judgement 'this action is bad' relates not only to the particular subject (without reference to other subjects), but also to the intersubjective context itself.

To recapitulate, then, we can say that personality here becomes its own object and is reflected into itself. The object of the second sphere (that of morality) can be understood as a strict result of the dynamic unfolding of the first sphere (abstract right) and not as something that is simply added on in an external fashion. At the same time, the being-for-self that has been attained here presents the *inner subjectivity of freedom*, and also the moment of contingency, which has been posited through the particular and contingent will. This subjective-contingent will, however, possesses standing and validity only in its unity with the universal will, insofar as the subjective will "is within itself the existence of the rational will" (*Werke* 10: 311), is reflected into itself, and represents the infinite contingency of willing in itself (*Werke* 7: 199). That the *subjective-particular* will intrinsically relates in this way to a *universal* will is what Hegel designates as *morality*.

From abstract determinacy, from the immediacy or being-in-itself of the will – which manifests itself in relation to 'things' and focuses upon action as negative, upon prohibition – Hegel's argument moves onwards to subjective-particular determinacy, to *action that is concretely required or demanded*, to the inner self-determinacy of subjectivity. Thought moves from juridical action to moral action, from the *abstract-formal recognition of the singular person* to the *reflective recognition of the particular person as a moral subject*, from abstract formal right to morality. And morality, as the *sphere of particularity*, acquires an extraordinary significance for determining the essential character of modernity (*Werke* 7: 233).

2 Orestes and Oedipus – Heroic Self-Consciousness and Modernity

Most forms of contemporary analytical philosophy show no real awareness of Hegel's theory of action. But the emphasis upon the internal connection between motivation and deed, between the inner constitution of the subject and its realisation in action, upon *the conceptual tie between genuine action and intention*, is not a discovery or unique achievement of 20th century analytical philosophy, of thinkers such as Donald Davidson for example.[8] In fact, this thought is fundamental to Hegel's account of action, an account in which he distinguishes terminologically between deed and action (between *Tat* and *Handlung*). Only when attention is given to the notions of purpose and intention (*Vorsatz* and *Absicht*), in contrast to the deeds analysed in the context of formal right, can we properly speak of 'actions'. An inner conscious motivation belongs to action in the complete sense, and the motivating grounds are constitutive for the free will. We thereby arrive at a higher level of right and freedom. Action in the full sense is *an outer expression of the inner determinacy of the will*, so that the free will recognises, and allows to be ascribed to

---

8 It has been expressly claimed that Hegel adopts "a position which is recognisably akin to that of Davidson himself in recent times" (Knowles 2002: 174).

itself, only that which it has *itself knowingly willed* (Werke 10: 312–3). In *acting*, in the expression of the inner spirit, we have the actual realization, *the exposition of our inner intentions and purposes*. What belongs to the deed (*Tat*) is the whole range of determinations which stand in an immediate connection with "a change that has been produced in external existence" (Werke 4: 206–7). What belongs to action (*Handlung*), on the other hand, is only that which "lies in decision, or was present to the consciousness in question, that which the will therefore ascribes to itself as its own" (Werke 4: 206–7). Through action the subject (the human being) enters actively into the concrete world of actuality (Werke 15, 485). The *further determination of the concept of action* and the judgement passed upon particular forms and courses of action now constitute the real object of attention and concern. For free activity cannot be reduced to a question of whether it is 'formally right' or permitted, but it must also be capable of being evaluated, of being described as morally valuable or 'good'.

Insofar as activity or 'actuosity' is a constituent of the will, this philosophical theory of free willing involves an 'ongoing preparation' for the full concept of action, and indeed on *three principal levels* which together present the essential dimensions of free action. This sequence of levels encompasses a) the *formal-legal activity of the agent as 'person'*, b) the *acting of the moral subject*, and c) the *acting of the ethical subject*.

Essential determinations of action already come into view on the first two of these levels, albeit from a limited perspective in each case, namely that of abstract right and morality respectively. And to that extent we still are unable to provide a fully adequate determination of the concept of action. It is only on the third level, that of *ethical* action, that we can properly fulfil this demand. But it is under the rubric of morality that the *concept of acting* is expressly introduced. This is the first place where we can deal with the phenomenon of action itself.

Here is where *action* appears for the first time. Something that is connected with right can also be action, yet it does not possess the formal nature of the latter in itself … It is the activity of moral subjective willing that belongs to action … without purpose (*Vorsatz*) there is no *action*, but only *deed*, in which judgement does not yet enter (Hegel 1999: 11). But the concept of action is by no means exhausted in this regard, and truly becomes an object in the highest sense only in the chapter on ethical life. On the level of morality we are moving in the realm of particularity, on the terrain of the merely subjective-formal dimension of action, the achievements and limitations of which are clearly exhibited by Hegel. These reflections are concerned with the moral standpoint, which represents the 'reflective judgement of freedom' and thus the work of 'the Understanding'. This is a logically necessary intermediate stage, but one on which the concept of action cannot be explicated fully. Just as the phenomenon of punishment broke open and exceeded the framework of abstract right, so the emergence of morality also breaks open and exceeds its own framework on account of its inner contradiction. Both juridical action and moral action will reveal themselves, taken on their own, as two one-sided ways of determining action, deficient in virtue of their isolation, and finally as *two moments involved in ethical action*. In this sense, Hegel's practical philosophy is essentially concerned *from the first* with ethical action, with the genuine determination of the free will, and with nothing else. It is essentially a *philosophical theory of ethical action*.

This insight into the conceptual connection between authentic deed and intention requires further concretisation, particularly with regard to an understanding of the conceptual dimension that is specifically in play here and with regard to those who engage in action (the agents). In the first place, we must ascribe personhood to the agents in question. Insofar as the motivating grounds are in question, we are talking about moral persons, about *moral subjects*. This requires consideration of all the consequences that sprang from abstract right and the role of personality. To put this in an even pithier and sharper fashion: not every deed is an action, and not every kind of directed movement can properly be described as an action. The spider that runs across Harry Frankfurt's table, the remarkably skilful manner in which my cat Francis succeeds in catching flies, or the way that a small child manages to run backwards or snatches and hides an object do not count as moral actions, since action in the strict sense always signifies the acting and interacting of free and intelligent beings, of moral persons, which involves but is not reducible to deeds which lack the other required component, namely intention. Even the activity of appropriating or taking possession of something is not described by Hegel as an action, and nor does a deed that infringes right count for him as a positive action. Thus the moral action of the subject unites the external perspective of the person and the internal perspective of activity, or *genuine action and intention*. The *person* advances to the *moral subject*, *personality* to *moral subjectivity*, and the *formal deed* is developed into *moral action*, into the *right of the subjective will*, and this results in a higher form of self-determination, or *moral freedom*.[9]

---

9 The freedom of the moral will, moral right, consists in the fact that "something is recognised as good by me" (Hegel 2005: 102). What is central here is the inner character of willing, which determines itself as particularity.

2.1 Hegel's Doctrine of Judgements as the Logical Ground of Morality

For Hegel, all things are a judgement, that is to say, they are singulars which are a universality or inner nature within themselves, or a universal that is singularized; the finitude of things consists in the fact that they are a judgement, that their existence and their universal nature are different and separable (*Werke* 8: 318–9). Once he has determined the basic form of the judgement in the context of his doctrine of logical judgement, Hegel proceeds to assesses Kant's attempt to provide a logical division of judgements on the schema of a table of categories. In spite of the inadequacy of this schema, it does reflect the insight that it is the universal forms of the Idea itself through which the various kinds of judgements are determined. In accordance with Hegel's *Logic* it is necessary to distinguish three principal kinds of judgement, which correspond to the levels of being, essence, and the concept (*Werke* 8: 322). The middle term here is internally doubled, in accordance with the nature of essence as the sphere of difference. "The various kinds of judgement do not simply subsist alongside one another with the same value, but must rather be regarded as a series of levels, and the distinction between them rests on the logical significance of the predicate" (*Werke* 8: 322). On this basis Hegel unfolds a developing series of practical judgements, that is, of judgements which relate specifically to actions.

In §114 of the *Philosophy of Right* Hegel defines the fundamental structure of moral right, or the 'movement of the judgement' as he describes it elsewhere (*Werke* 6, 309). This passes through three stages of imputation:[10] a) the *abstract formal right of action as action that can be ascribed to me*, as purposeful action, characterised by knowledge of the immediate circumstances (the transitory of this first level is revealed here, precisely as the abstract-formal right of imputability which the final level of abstract right logically anticipated): the criminal act as an infinite judgement; b1) the *intention* of the act and its value for me, and b2) *welfare* as the content of action, as my particular will supported by reflective knowledge; c) the *Good* as the inner content in its universality and objectivity with its opposition in *subjective universality*, the knowing of the concept, the judgement of the concept, and thus finally the "determinate and fulfilled unity of the subject and the predicate as their concept" (*Werke* 6: 309), the transition to the logical form of the syllogism,[11] the conceptually necessary transition from morality to ethical life.

---

10   Quante describes Hegel's concept of imputation as "cognitivist ascriptivism" (2011: 226); and talks in illuminating ways of "Hegel's map of our ascriptive practices" (ibid.: 224).
11   The *Science of Logic* refers to the "syllogism of action" and the "syllogism of the Good" as ways of bringing together and uniting the moments of the concept of action, of subjectivity and objectivity (*Werke* 6: 545–6).

2.2 The Right of Knowing – Acting in Knowledge

In the opening sections of his theory of moral action, as part of the scientific exposition of practical philosophy, Hegel formulates a fundamental right and thereby also a duty, namely the *right to knowledge*. The focus lies on the inner knowing self-determination of the will, on the subjective grounds that determine action, on my insight, my inner motivations, my knowing and my purposes, on the 'ethically right' – all of this is an essential determining moment of moral right. In the case of morality we are concerned with "the subjective aspect, i.e. knowledge of the circumstances, conviction of the good, and the inner intention, constitute for us a chief element in the action" (*Werke* 13: 247). Such knowing in the form of our rational maxims must be inherent in moral action: *insight belongs to intention* and is the 'soul' of action. The ethically good depends on what is ethically 'right', and this is identified, as Kant argues, *independently of the consequences of the act*. Hegel is attempting, as Kant did before, to articulate an ethics based on the autonomy of reason (cf. Wood 2005).

Acknowledgement and justification is explicitly accorded here to the motivating grounds of my action, to my free inner process of self-determination. It is only through the *self-ascription of responsibility* that one can speak of *my* action at all. It is possible to clarify Hegel's position in more detail by reference to §105 of the *Philosophy of Right*, and his own hand-written notes on this section of the text. Once the standpoint of the will as that which is 'infinite' in itself, as identity for itself over against immediacy and what is merely in itself, has been clearly determined (and the first level, abstract right, has thus become the object of the second level), it is possible to draw a precise distinction between a) subject, b) object, and c) the determination of the concept, and thus capture the thought of the *right of knowing*. The subject now *knows* itself as free, *knows* the freedom within itself – consequently I *know* myself as being for myself. The object remains the will itself, and thereby its being within itself, or the right of subjective willing as a knowing. The modern understanding of freedom draws attention to the motivating *ground* of our activities rather than simply the *consequences* of action, it focuses on "how the matter stood inwardly within me" (*Werke* 7: 204), on my inner judgement, my inner consent, knowing as *my* knowing, on the ethically right. We are essentially concerned with the willing something that I *know* – something that already stands before me, before the actual expression of action, in this sense as something 'theoretical'.[12] This corresponds to the basic idea of deontological ethics, the relation

---

[12] Hegel understands the urge or impulse (*Trieb*) in general as "internal self-movement, self-movement proper" (*Werke* 6: 76).

of ethical evaluation to obligation in the sense of ethically right action, as this finds expression in commands, prohibitions, or duties (Quante 1993: 130ff).

The judgement of 'good' or 'evil' refers exclusively to the actions of subjects, rather than to things. Here, again, we should consider the initial characterisation of willing as the pure thinking of itself in §5 of the *Philosophy of Right*. It is insight, knowing, thinking, the 'theoretical' dimension as such, that will provide the basis for the inner determinacy of the subject. We are concerned with action that *knows* what it is, and it is this dimension of *knowing* that first brings the real and distinctive privilege of the free being into view. We are talking about the only law that the will of every rational being gives itself (Kant), or about the will that knows itself as absolutely valid (Hegel). From the moral standpoint all the acts or circumstances of potential injury or infringement in terms of formal right may be ignored, because morality itself cannot fall victim to theft, assault, violence, or murder. For 'thoughts are free' (*die Gedanken sind frei*), in the words of an old German song.[13]

In the first instance the moral standpoint can lay claim to unlimited right and unconditional validity. It unfolds as a process on the basis of three levels of knowing, passing from merely abstract purpose through concrete intention to the right of the subjective will to know the Good, and to the knowing that is con-science (*Ge-wissen*). Expressed in logical terms, it passes from particularity to universality. In this way we rise to a full conceptual comprehension of action, in a logically supported procedure aimed at producing knowledge without the intrusion of *any illegitimate claims, unfounded prejudices, unjustified assertions, or mere assurances*. In law, a person charged has a right to *know* what he has done. Here we are not yet concerned with the consequences of action, but with the inner spirit of the action in terms of *increasing levels of imputation or imputability*.[14] "The spiritual (*geistig*) aspect of action must possess an absolute value" (*Werke* 7: 236). The agent is thus at once recognised, respected, and honoured as a *thinking* and *willing* subject.

2.3 The Right to Knowing and Heroic Self-Consciousness in Works of Art

Morality is treated as the first realm of particularity, and §117 of the *Philosophy of Right* specifically conceptualises this thematic in a pregnant manner: the issue is the ascription of responsibility and the imputation of acts, the 'right to

---

13 The second verse runs: "I think what I want, and what delights me, / though silently and as is suitable. / My wish and desire, no one can deny me / and so it will always be: Thoughts are free!" The *Altes Landrecht* (Part III, §2) provides the relevant juridical formulation: "Only external free acts can be circumscribed by laws".

14 On the concept of 'imputability' see Kant's *Critique of Pure Reason* (1968 Bd. 3: B 476).

knowing'. In this section of the text too Hegel illustrates the theoretical problem of action with examples drawn from poetry and mythology: the deed committed by Oedipus was strictly speaking a slaying rather than a murder, and cannot be regarded as parricide since the deed in question lay neither in his knowing nor his willing (*Werke* 7: 217). His deed is done 'unknowingly', with no awareness that the victim is his father. Both §118 of the *Philosophy of Right* and the section on 'Action' in the lectures on *Aesthetics* discuss the achievements and the one-sided aspects both of the heroic self-consciousness and also of modern conceptions of ethics. The heroic consciousness insists in an immediate way that the entirety of the deed be imputed to the doer, and takes responsibility for the action as a whole. But according to Hegel the doer here has not yet advanced out of their substantial simplicity "either to reflection on the distinction between deed and action or that between external events and their intention" (*Werke* 7: 219).

Hegel's specific discussion of action in the *Aesthetics* includes a perceptive treatment of the problem of imputation which combines practical-philosophical reflections with a developed poetological-aesthetic perspective. This is well illustrated by the following extremely insightful passage which undertakes to identify the difference between the ancient and modern worlds. These lines effectively encapsulate the core components of the concept of action as it is unfolded in the *Philosophy of Right*:

> But just as, in the Heroic Age, the subject remains directly connected with his entire willing, acting, and achieving, so he also takes undivided responsibility for whatever consequences arise from his actions. On the other hand, when *we* act or judge actions, we insist that we can only impute an action to an individual if he has known and recognized the nature of his action and the circumstances in which it has been done ... a man nowadays does not accept responsibility for the whole range of what he has done; he repudiates that part of his act which, through ignorance or misconstruction of the circumstances, has turned out differently from what he had willed, and he enters to his own account only what he knew, and, on the strength of this knowledge, what he did on purpose and intentionally. But the heroic character does not make this distinction; instead he is answerable for the entirety of his act with his whole personality (*Werke* 13: 246–7).

It is on the basis of virtue, as the immediate and not yet mediated unity of substantiality and particularity, and out of this independence of spontaneous will and character, that ancient heroes "take the whole of the action upon themselves". Oedipus has unknowingly struck down his father, and the *action that can be ascribed to him* was the killing of an aged man, not the murder of *his father*. Yet he acknowledges this atrocity in its entirety as his own, even though this lay neither in his knowing nor in his wiling. The *heroic* character repudiates any division of guilt and knows nothing of *this opposition between subjective intentions and the objective deed and its consequences*. The subject wishes that "what has been done, has been entirely done by him alone and that what has happened is completely his own responsibility" (*Werke* 13: 247, my emphasis).[15] The action of these heroes correspond to the positive-infinite judgement, which does not yet distinguish the external circumstances of the act from the interior independently specifiable dimension of the agent, and where the external aspect is identified undistinguishably with the inner, Here my deed is identical with my action.

Thus the agent is the law to himself, in a kind of pre-juridical condition, which is prior to the political state. This means that in the heroic age, in a social structure without publicly established power or authority, the heroic agents cannot be recognised as explicitly *moral* heroes since the distinction between deed and action has not yet been drawn. Expressed in modern terms, the concept of action has not yet been sufficiently specified or differentiated (cf. Vieweg 2012a). The protagonists of the Homeric poems act out of their own exclusive sense of virtue, and in the modern sense must be regarded as *outlaws*. The hero stands up unambiguously and unreservedly for whatever consequences spring from his own deed, and in this sense appears as a natural consequentialist. Modern thought, on the other hand, typically distinguishes, where action and our judgement upon action is concerned, between premeditation, purpose, and intention, and the consequences and circumstances of the deed. In order to be able to impute a given action to the individual we demand that the individual "has known and recognized the nature of his action and the circumstances under which it has been done" (*Werke* 13: 246). Modern subjects insist upon the right of knowing, for what is at issue here – as Hegel points out with regard to the *Oedipus Rex* and *Oedipus at Colonus* – is the right of awakened consciousness, the justification of what an individual has accomplished through their self-conscious willing in contrast to what they have done unconsciously and without will in accordance with the decision of the gods. The right of our deeper contemporary consciousness lies in the fact that deeds such as those of Oedipus, since "they lie neither in our own knowing nor

---

15 In his hand-written notes to §118 of the *Philosophy of Right* Hegel refers to Orestes as a poetic representative of heroic self-consciousness who takes full and unreserved responsibility for his deeds (*Werke* 7: 220–221).

our own willing, cannot be recognized as the deeds of one's own self" (*Werke* 15: 545).

This modern position can be described as a *moral* one insofar as purpose and intention in the moral context, the subjective aspect of our knowledge regarding the circumstances and our conviction of the Good, constitute a principal component of action. And Hegel interprets this as an example of progress: the agent takes responsibility only for their own action, which implies for example that the thought of *collective guilt or responsibility* (long before Karl Jaspers) is repudiated in principle, as well as the idea of punishing the *family* of the offending individual. For the agent is now capable of drawing a sharp distinction between the subjective act and the act of the family or community. In an impressive passage, Hegel protests against the notion of somehow simply inheriting merit or blame. The idea that a person is simply what his forefathers were, what they suffered or perpetrated, implies an irrational submission to a blind destiny. "Just as, with us [moderns], the deeds of ancestors do not ennoble their sons and posterity, so the crimes and punishments of our forebears do not dishonour their descendants and still less can they besmirch their subjective character" (*Werke* 13: 247). The confiscation of family property, for example, is regarded by Hegel as a form of punishment that "violates the principle of deeper subjective freedom", the principle of modernity itself (*Werke* 13: 248). But Hegel also draws attention to the more plastic character of ancient life as a whole, where the heroic individuals can appear and stand out in a more ideal manner precisely because the substantial character of ethical life is immediately expressed here in individual terms, and the individual is thereby already 'substantial' in himself. This is one aspect of the classical form of art, characterised as it is by an intrinsic congruence between the Idea and its sensuous configuration, which has irrevocably been lost in the conditions of modernity. Yet modern art can now transpose its own ideal forms of art into the age of art and myth in order to mitigate the more prosaic character of modern life, which manifests itself in the development from the way crime and transgression is represented in tragedy right up to the genre of the criminal story. And this change also involves the possibility of a certain reinvention of forms: the modern 'romantic' artist "must remain entitled to create always anew from what is already there, from history, saga, myths ... indeed even from materials and situations previously elaborated artistically" (*Werke* 13: 281). The material of drama emerges from conflicts involving the crucial powers of social and cultural life which have been challenged or violated – firstly by unwitting and unintentional acts (Ajax), secondly by an intentional and conscious transgression (Agamemnon against Iphigenia, Clytemnestra against Agamemnon, Orestes against Clytemnestra), and thirdly through indirect forms of violation.

The story of Orestes, finally, illustrates the distinction between purpose and intention, between imputation in the *first* and *second* sense, which is essential to the question of responsibility. For now the inner aspect of imputability is separated from the deed at large, and the action divides into the moments of universality and particularity (*Werke* 7: 227). Orestes a) kills his mother, and b) avenges his father. On the one hand, the right of the husband and ruler is thereby defended, the demand of the clear, conscious and self-conscious ethical life, but in these pre-modern conditions it is the law of particular virtue rather than right as such that prevails. The ensuing chain of vengeance must be broken, for it is based upon the logically deficient pattern of infinite repetition. This transition to the political realm prefigures the thought of a modern political structure where the state alone possesses the monopoly of force and is the only legitimate source of punishment. Hegel also illustrates and confirms this difference between the ancient and the modern world by considering the contrasting treatment of the legendary story of Iphigenia by the ancient authors and by Goethe, and by the different way in which the Eumenides are interpreted as external or as inner powers. This moral dimension is well conveyed in Hegel's remarks on the Eumenides that were quoted earlier: "it is man's own deed and consciousness that afflicts and torments him insofar as he knows this deed as something evil in him" (*Werke* 17: 127). And with specific reference to Oedipus at Colonus Hegel glimpses a kind of inner reconciliation that "on account of its subjective character comes very close to the modern" (*Werke* 15: 551). The heroes presented by Euripides, on the other hand, according to Hegel, "no longer possess the same intrinsically plastic and ethical character" (*Werke* 12: 318) and in them (as in those of Aristophanes) it is the principle of the corruption of ancient life which clearly comes to the fore.

CHAPTER 9

Beyond Wall Street: Hegel as Founder of the Concept of a Welfare State

In an article in the New York Times with the title 'Hegel on Wall Street' the New York philosopher J.M. Bernstein diagnoses the reasons for the failure of neoliberal market-fundamentalist Wall-Street capitalism and recommends turning to the ideas of Hegel: "the primary topic of [Hegel's] practical philosophy was analysing the exact point where modern individualism and the essential institutions of modern life meet.... If Hegel is right, there may be deeper and more basic reasons for strong market regulation than we have imagined" (Bernstein 2010). In the years since Hegel was writing, the gap between rich and poor has widened so far that the very foundations of democracy are threatened. 1% of the population now presides over one fifth of total wealth. Over one billion people today suffer from chronic hunger or malnutrition, as a result of which one dies every five seconds. One sixth of the world's population – the so-called 'bottom billion' – is condemned to live in extreme poverty, while at the same time there are 1,826 billionaires with an aggregate wealth of $6.5 trillion (Dolan 2016).

That Hegel's philosophy is highly relevant to social, economic and political problems is something already suggested over 100 years ago, in an article in Harper's *New Monthly Magazine.* There it states that "Hegel is the most conspicuous of the liberals, a main figure of the liberal movement in Europe – the true philosopher of progress", "the philosopher par excellence of the only true political liberty". What American readers glimpsed over a century ago is *the profundity of Hegel's practical philosophy.* And a key part of Hegel's practical philosophy is his theory of civil society and the idea of a rational regulation of the market. This, I argue, is the foundation of Hegel's theory of a social state.[1] Hegel's concept of civil society, of the rational regulation of the market and the idea of a social State will be my themes here.

At the outset we may note that the pattern of thinking one finds among the Wall Street market fundamentalists actually shows remarkable similarities to that of their professed opponents, namely supporters of the People's Republics – both display an *untenable economism* and *a tendency towards state*

---

1 For further discussion see Vieweg 2012a.

socialism. Today these two conceptions form an unholy alliance and lead to a dead-end. Both reject one of the main achievements of the 20th Century, namely the social State based on a market economy, a rationally designed, regulated capitalism. In so doing, these two diametrically opposed economic worldviews endanger the very project of modern freedom. One of the most significant economists of the 20th Century, John Maynard Keynes, got to the heart of this issue with the title of his book *The End of Laissez Faire* and its key finding: "the decadent international but individualistic capitalism ... is not a success. It is not intelligent. It is not beautiful. It is not just. It is not virtuous. And it doesn't deliver the goods" (Keynes cited in Roubini & Mihm 2010: 23).

The copyright on the notion of a modern society of freedom and a rational, social State belongs to Hegel. To demonstrate this requires a short, if by no means straightforward, tour round the infamous 'lumber room' of philosophy. The following discussion can be understood as a contribution to the so-called 'Hegelian turn' in philosophy, because Hegel proves himself to be the thinker who until now has provided the most convincing foundation for freedom in modernity. Since Hegel, I suggest, no other thinker has stepped forward who is even in the same league.

1 Civil Society as Modern Community of Market, Education and Solidarity

The theoretical foundation and at the same time bone of contention of Hegel's political thought is to be found in his concept of ethical life (*Sittlichkeit*), in particular in his theory of civil society.[2] In his *Philosophy of Right*, Hegel was "the first to conceptualise the separation of state and society" (Koselleck 1989: 388). His overcoming of the traditional equation of civil society with State provides a significant contribution to a "proper theorization of modern political and social conditions" (Horstmann 2005: 203–4), it gives us the foundation for a modern theory of society and State.

With civil society, ethical life enters the sphere of particularity. An immediately ethical association in the form of the family is dissolved, the immediate unity experiences its first sublation (*Aufhebung*) – into a unity of reflection, a unity of understanding. The concrete individual person thereby wins the possibility of their particular self-determination, they exist "in independent freedom and are particular for themselves" (*Werke* 10: 321). At the same time,

---

[2] A theory that draws on the political economy of Ferguson (1966) and Smith (1981).

the concrete individual initially loses their ethical-communal determinations and enters the realm of contingency. At first, the concrete person is necessarily conscious of, and takes as their purpose, not the unity of the ethical but their own particularity. The immanent negativity of the ethical finds expression in its 'diremption', its division into extremes. Civil society is *"ethical life split into its extremes and lost"* (*Werke* 7: 340). In this atomistic system the ethical substance mutates into a general relationship of independent extremes and particular interests.

Hegel sets out the idea of a *modern* world, an idea of freedom built on the notion of a *modern* state, an idea that underpins modern forms of life. In the notion of civil society we find a foundation stone for this theoretical construction. Two basic elements characterise civil society: a) *the principle of particularity*, the concrete person who has particular ends and who comprises particular needs, natural desires and impulses, and b) *the principle of universality*, the necessary relationship between particular persons. Each particular person may assert themselves only via mediation with this universality. What distinguishes civil society from the State is that the former is shaped by the market principle, a system of all-round dependence, a community of need and understanding, while the latter is governed by structures which sublate (*aufheben*) this market principle, by simultaneously respecting and overcoming the impulses and accidents of particular individuals.

The market system, Hegel tells us, cannot sufficiently regulate or control itself, it tends towards market fundamentalism; left to its own logic it will damage or even destroy itself. As in what Hegel calls 'the understanding' (*Verstand*), so it is in a state based on the understanding, the structures are "essentially unstable and shaky and the building they support must [without rational regulation] collapse with a crash" (*Werke* 8: 109). The Hegelian State does not do away with the market. It respects the capitalist market order and grants it a role within prescribed limits. The State, however, must protect the market from its own immanent self-destructive power. Its task is to regulate this sphere, to provide it with a framework and to supervise it. The Hegelian State has the duty to restore the ethical life that has been 'lost in its extremes' and thus to bring *the understanding* to *reason*. The State may not let itself by determined by market principles.

Civil society contains three moments:
1. The Economic "System of Needs". Satisfaction of the individual's needs through his or her work and through the mediation of the work and satisfaction of the needs of all others. Sphere of inequality.
2. Constitution of Law (administration of justice). Realization of the universality of freedom and protection of rights. Legal equality of persons.

3. Oversight and Regulation – social care and provision. Provision for residual contingencies in each system and the fulfilment of particular interests as a common good, basis of a social State, universal provision for the welfare of individuals and for the subsistence of rights, foundation for creating justice.

2   All-round Dependence in the 'Community of Need and Understanding'

Individual persons are conscious of their own particularity and their being-for-themselves and take these as their own purpose. This is the principle of independent particularity, the "principle of the self-subsistent inherently infinite personality of the individual" (*Werke* 7: 342). Here we find a defining feature of modernity: the *right to particularity on the part of subjects*, the *right to subjective freedom*. Only in the modern world, according to Hegel, do we find this form of life – civil society – intervening between family and State. The formation of civil society belongs exclusively to modern times. The particularity of the actor, their interests and goals, form an inescapable aspect of their freedom. This constitutive principle of civil society, namely the particularity of the individual and his or her *relative and insufficient* association with the community, represents an *essential constituent of a free community* and the *core principle of modernity*. The rejection of this principle, in whatever form of political or economic organization, implies the destruction of freedom. Thus Hegel cannot be read as a critic of such a civil society since it is for him the *sine qua non* of a free society, nor can he be read as a critic of modernity. On the contrary, Hegel provides the decisive foundations for a philosophy of modernity, a philosophy of freedom.

However, another necessary constituent of modernity is the moment of particularity with its enormous potential for danger. Hegel's approach provides a theoretical analysis of the threat civil society poses to itself and how this threat can be rationally overcome in the State. Civil society as a system of dirempted ethical life must therefore preoccupy us here. The concrete person as a sum of interests and needs has only himself or herself for his or her purpose, but he or she exists in mutual relations to other particulars, in a community of concrete persons, and in this way particulars are supposed to be equal. They are not, however. On one side we find the selfish goal of meeting one's own needs, while on the other we find that our rights, welfare and subsistence are bound up with the rights, welfare and subsistence of all. The private person aims to satisfy their own merely particularistic needs and inclinations, but needs the other private person. They depend on each other, they have need of each other, they stand in a relation of *external* necessity to one another, they exist in a situation of need as accidental necessity.

When Hegel talks of a State based on 'understanding' (*Verstand*) he is referring to its logical status, to its *formal universality*, its *understanding-universality*, to a unity that establishes understanding. The 'understanding' is here a deficient form in which universality appears. Particularity has the right to give itself universal existence, to develop itself in an all-rounded way, to realize itself. All human possibilities can be developed, including all the accidents and inequalities of birth or fortune. On the other side we have an inescapable context in the form of a community of mutual dependence.

The unlimited satisfaction of desires, impulses and subjective pleasures is, Hegel tells us, an infinite process, a bad infinity, one which encapsulates the logical problem of the understanding itself: desire, impulse, opinion and need are all *boundless*. Civil society cannot, on its own, define any rational measure or limit; it suffers chronically from *boundlessness*. A striking indication of this is to be seen in the permanent instability and crisis-ridden nature of the industrial market economy, which is accompanied by a ubiquitous myth of stability and self-healing. The actual cause of boundlessness is the very human *particularity* which is a defining principle a modernity. Satisfying the needs of the particular person within a system of all-sided dependence and arbitrariness is itself *accidental*; it presents itself to the individual as the work of a mysterious, hidden power, as fate, as a lottery with happy or disastrous results. In this necessary feature of civil society the *arbitrariness* of its satisfaction of human needs comes dramatically to light: our needs may successfully be satisfied or they may not; the particular can be identical with the universal, or it may diverge from it. Putative freedom may turn into fatalism, into faith in an external necessity and civil society come to resemble an aggregate of necessities.

Individual parts of this giant machinery and indeed the entire machine itself may break down and so hinder or prevent the realisation of needs. The continual possibility of economic crises is for Hegel an essential feature of the capitalist economy (cf. Stiglitz 2010). Civil society thus involves the setting-free of particularity, it appears as a "battlefield of the private interests of each against all" (*Werke* 7: 458), as a "theatre of debauchery and misery" (*Werke* 7: 341).

Concrete persons can raise themselves only to *formal freedom* and to a *formal universality of knowledge and willing*, they can educate themselves only in the sense of reflection and understanding. Education nevertheless gains an infinite value: in its absolute determination it is the only way to freedom. The education or formation (*Bildung*) of the concrete person thus presents a fundamental milestone on the road to freedom – *only the educated and thus self-determining free citizen* (*Bürger*) can guarantee the survival of a free community. Modern civil society must therefore be not only market – and welfare-based but also a society grounded in *education*.

3   Political Economy and the Regulated Market

For Adam Smith the functioning of the market was guaranteed by a mysterious power, *the invisible hand*, a process by which the egoistic and often conflicting interests of individual economic actors converge in a stable and self-regulating economic system. Out of the chaos of countless individual decisions arises order (Roubini & Mihm 2010: 61). Ignoring Smith's own caveats, market fundamentalists make this idea into a doctrine of self-balancing, self-repairing markets, "the conviction that free markets themselves generate economic wealth and growth" or "that markets regulate themselves and that the self-interested behavior of market participants guarantee markets' proper functioning" (Stiglitz 2010: 11).

Hegel respects the market as the basis of modern economies, but he finds in it no self-regulating structure. On the contrary, the market involves a sphere of the arbitrary and accidental, a context which requires rational organization (by the State) and which cannot function properly on its own (cf. Stiglitz 2010: 10ff). He points to the crisis-prone character of market mechanisms and explains their causes. As Roubini puts it, in the same spirit as Hegel, "capitalism is anything but a frictionless, purring, self-regulating framework. On the contrary it is an extremely unstable system" (Roubini & Mihm 2010: 66). Contrary to the ideology of markets' stability and rationality of markets and contrary to the evangelism of deregulation, privatization and liberalization, the market structure proves to be highly fragile, precarious, risk-laden and crisis-prone.

Hegel's proposed solution and the set of conceptual tools he employs to this end prove (and he is confirmed in his solutions by present-day day economic theory) a major contribution to our understanding of world economic conditions. The keywords here are: regulation instead of deregulation, oversight instead of arbitrariness and chaos, legal frameworks instead of 'voluntary' self-regulation, natural and social sustainability instead of market fundamentalism, rational international organisation of markets instead of exploitation of the Earth and the impoverishment of billions. These are the general outlines of a concept of a regulated market constitution, a *rational and socially-organized capitalism*. The ideology of deregulation, with its disastrous results, needs to be abandoned. A modern market *only functions at all* with the aid of elaborate regulative institutions. With Hegel one can say that the idea of the market needs to be *protected* from the market fundamentalists, whose gospel leads directly to the collapse of market structures themselves.

4 Regulation and Social Organization

The *relative* unity of the principles of particularity and universality is achieved in various institutions of *order* and *regulation*. Relevant here too are forms of 'public welfare' and organizations based on diverse professions, interests and locations. Society is under obligation not only to respect the formal rights of particular subjects but also to *help realize those subjects' right to welfare*. Civil society as an assembly of free persons has to be not only a market economy but a *community based on solidarity*, not only an economy based on individual performance but also a *community based on welfare*, an alliance of the *solitary* and the *solidary*. Only in this synthesis can it prosper, i.e. only thus can it constitute a community of free beings, and guarantee their freedom. A meaningfully functioning civil society implies the solidary-social. Here we already find the foundations of Hegel's theory of a social State, which stands in direct opposition to the views of market fundamentalists, for whom talk of social justice is a heresy and for whom giving the State a welfare function would destroy the market.

Central to Hegel's theory are the ideas of *oversight*, of *regulation* and of *social help*. These, it should be emphasized, are functional conditions of modern societies, they are constitutively entwined, essential categorial elements of Hegel's theory of modernity. Until now, however, Hegel's significant contribution to this field has been either forgotten or neglected. But precisely here we find one of the major achievements of his practical philosophy: the conceptualizing of a *regulated and socially-organized modern community*, the foundation for a constitutional and social State based on a market system. Hegel insists on the unity of rights and well-being and pushes the idea that we address not merely formal rights but that rights must have a content – this content is the common good of all members of civil society. The subsistence and well-being of every individual emerged at the level of the System of Needs only as a *possibility*, whose realization was dependent upon natural particularities and accidental conditions (*Werke* 7: 382). But the accidents which derail the goal of well-being must be overcome, the particular well-being must be treated as *a right for all* and be realized.

5 Oversight and External Regulation

A first dimension of oversight comprises *legal oversight and intervention* in the form of a guarantee of *security* along with a certain *control and management of collective public action*, for instance commercial or market activity. It involves "general institutions [...], which must have a public power" (Hegel 2005: 217) and these must have a public power precisely because the entire set of market relations and mediations cannot be viewed and controlled by individuals alone. These public interventions, which must be relevant and reasonable, relate firstly to the testing and approval of products for technical or health usage; they are undertaken by health authorities, building planning offices, bodies responsible for technical safety, food safety, consumer protection, etc. Secondly, intervention aimed at the rules of the market – involving oversight of all areas of buying and selling such as the industrial market, banking and exchange. In both cases, the intervention is about stipulating sensible procedures and preventing cases of serious violation or injustice. The health care system and the design of infrastructure also come under this heading.

The tasks performed by such public bodies, which we often take for granted, show that internal oversight on the part of the market is insufficient and that legitimation and regulation by the state, oversight by a higher public authority, is indispensable. Matters essential to the survival and flourishing of a community, such as health, environmental protection and infrastructure, must be preserved from the influence of the market principle, an idea that contrasts starkly with the current mania for privatization. The right to a share of the common wealth must be guaranteed to *all* individuals, each concrete person has the right to join in civil society, and every exclusion from civil society and the common wealth should be considered a crime.

6 Social Care and Forethought – Foundations of Hegel's Conception of a Social State

In thinking about our relationship with *nature* Hegel developed the ideas of 'care' (*Sorge*) and 'forethought' (*Vorsorge*), in the sense of *natural sustainability*;[3] now we move on to the terrain of *social forethought,* of *social sustainability*. A brief example can be given here, namely three forms of social

---

3 See Vieweg, 'Care and Forethought: The Idea of Sustainability in Hegel's Practical Philosophy', in this volume.

help and the interaction between them: *subjective help* as a first form arises out of individually felt moral duties, benevolence, beneficence, charity, individual solidarity as the moral duty to assist in times of need. A second form of social help is *charitable* or *non-governmental help* where individuals come together in a type of mutual aid and solidarity, a sphere of civic charitable engagement. The word 'charitable' (*gemeinnützig*) is used here very much in Hegel's sense – it is about universal usage, one *harnesses* the *universal*, and thereby serves the *general good* or the *common wealth*. This form of help does not fall under the aegis of the market principles, but neither is it a form of State aid. Nevertheless, while extremely important and not to be underestimated, such subjective forms of help remain random and accidental; there is no guarantee of them lasting and so sufficient guarantees for the well-being of those affected are lacking. Help remains here a contingent principle, and may fail.

For this reason, individuals in need also have a right to *universal, public help*, from which arises a whole set of aid and welfare institutions, and which go beyond the capabilities of civil society (for example social welfare organizations, child and youth welfare organizations, bodies which care for the elderly and disabled – these are all forms of public-governmental solidarity). Today one also finds particular combinations of subjective and public help, sustained by engagement from their participants and by charities, themselves supported by public, governmental institutions. What is decisive for the governance and resourcing of social help is, for Hegel, the instrument of *taxation*, particularly the model of a progressive income tax, whereby a portion of one's income, relative to one's wealth, goes into the collective pot, allowing *collective* obligations to be fairly met. All the above-mentioned types of social help form the cornerstone of a social State, the most decisive condition for a functioning market order in a modern society – "the well-designed welfare state", as Stiglitz puts it, supports "an innovative society" (Stiglitz 2010: 256). It is the *sine qua non* of freedom in the modern age.

The State, the political, then manifests itself as the 'true ground' of civil society, as the presupposition of its subsistence. This notion stands diametrically opposed to the thesis of Marx concerning civil society as the basis upon which the superstructure of the State rests. It is also in stark contrast to the economistic credo of the market fundamentalist Chicago Boys. It stands opposed to both the omnipotent fantasies of Wall Street and the bureaucratic capitalism of the great People's Republic, that is, against concepts which threaten the foundational principle of modernity – individual freedom. Nor can Hegel be denounced as someone who would limit individual freedom, let alone viewed as a precursor of totalitarianism. The idea of the State as a community of free citizens, of free citizenship, stands at the centre of Hegel's practical philosophy, at the centre of his thinking of freedom.

But without the unfolding of the particular concrete person – with all their contradictions, especially the contradiction between their *potential for innovation* and that for *destruction*, and the conflict between *progress* and *insecurity* – the idea of a free community cannot be adequately established or grounded. The proponents of market radicalism celebrate the market as the holy grail of freedom, but clearly the market is a nexus of the arbitrary and accidental, a 'swarm of caprice', most spectacularly embodied in the stock market on Wall Street. Arbitrariness and randomness are (inadvertently or deliberately) confused with freedom and one remains stuck at the level of the Understanding (*Verstand*), of a deficient universal. Meanwhile, against the backdrop of the vast series of 'capital offences' recently committed in the financial system, the neoliberals with their promise of self-regulating markets have some explaining to do.

At least since the time of Hegel one could see that the market, while forming an essential pillar of a free community, cannot alone – precisely due to its determinacy – generate rational structures, and so must be rationally organized, that it requires appropriate regulatory frameworks. The market-radical mantra that "regulation kills innovation" has now lost its attraction (Stiglitz 2010: 40). The market is to be neither demonized nor glorified; though it is an important *enabling condition* of freedom, one can in no way describe the market itself as 'free'. Both the deregulated capitalism of Wall Street and the bureaucratic-socialist People's Republic (or an explosive mixture of the two) endanger and undermine the principle of the freedom of all particular individuals that has shaped modernity. The current shipwreck of deregulated capitalism does not mean the foundering of our journey towards a free society. Nevertheless the deficiencies and unsustainability of both models – *socialist collective ownership and market fundamentalism* – exhibit two contradictory claims to a share of the wealth of nations.

To take up Hegel's project is, at core, to aim at a new conception of an environmentally and socially sustainable and just society, and a corresponding world order. It is to further Hegel's philosophy of freedom. Now is the time for such a fundamental transformation in thinking, now is the time for the *Hegelian turn* in philosophy.

CHAPTER 10

The State and Its Logical Foundations

It was the great Italian architects who defined the term *chiave de volta* or 'keystone', a concept that fits perfectly Hegel's theory of the political state.* In architecture, the keystone is placed at the apex of an arch: it finalises the edifice by crowning it, it bears its load. Hegel's concept of the state as the objective form of justice forms the apex of the "gothic cathedral" (*Werke* 12: 67) of his practical philosophy – a philosophy of freedom.[1] Without this concept of the state, the whole structure of Hegel's temple of freedom could not stand. It is the foundation and reason of everything, the foundation of a world of freedom. In the elevated form of the state we have the beginning and the end of Hegel's philosophy of objective spirit that is his theory of free will and action. This theoretical construction is akin to the breath-taking *Palazzo della Ragione* in Padua that in its interior and exterior architecture unites free beings' various modes of living: law, market, art, religion and intellectual culture.

In the *Philosophy of Right*, Hegel speaks of the "the architectonic" of the state's rationality, which he says is characterized by "determinate distinctions between the circles of public life and their rights and by the strict proportion in which every pillar, arch, and buttress is held together" (*Werke* 7: 19). According to Eduard Gans, the merit of the *Philosophy of Right* is to be found "in this wonderful architectonic with which each page and room is treated, in the assiduity that is bestowed upon each corner of the edifice, and all in this regular and yet varying style that can be observed from top to foundation" (Gans 1981: 3).

Hegel's *Philosophy of Right* can thus be condensed into the words that appear in its subtitle: its philosophy of freedom and of right is a *science of the state*. The highest determination of the thinking of practical freedom in the realm of politics is to be found at the standpoint of the "highest concrete universality" (*Werke* 7: 474).

Hegel took on the Herculean task of finding a new *legitimisation of the political*, of justifying the state as the supreme form of free willing by means of *comprehending thought*. This means that his conception seeks to describe the state as idea, and as idea moreover in the form of the *highest level of ethical*

---
* This chapter is based on the previous publication "The State as a system of three Syllogisms", in "Hegel's Political Philosophy", edited by Thom Brooks and Sebastian Stein, Oxford University Press 2017.
1 For more detailed discussion see Vieweg 2012a.

actuality, the state as the highest form of objective spirit. Hegel's state is thus defined as the "actuality of the ethical Idea" (*Werke* 7: 398) that has completely developed its form.

This fundamental theorem must be explicated as precisely and systematically as possible for it to become clear that the "construction of the state" is the "realisation of the edifice of freedom" (Hegel 1973, Bd. 3: 716), i.e. the *objective manifestation of justice*. The aim of Hegel's science of the state – to comprehend and depict the state as something inherently rational – thus requires that we pay close attention to a demand that Hegel articulates in the *Philosophy of Right*'s preface: "the whole, like the formation of its parts, rests on the logical spirit [*dem logischen Geiste*]. It is in these terms above all that I should like my book to be understood and judged" (*Werke* 7: 12–13).

Hegel is here pointing his readers to the *logic of the constitution*, i.e. to the state's logical foundation. He is telling us, in other words, to read his work of political philosophy alongside the 'speculative mode of cognition' developed in detail in the *Science of Logic*. According to H.F. Fulda, this kind of interpretation, one that pays close attention to logical foundations, is something that has nevertheless "to this day still barely been realised" (Fulda 2003: 197). The thoughts I present in what follows aim to remedy this deficit. They further the project initiated in two seminal articles by Dieter Henrich and Michael Wolff.

Henrich writes: "It lends weight to Hegel's theory that he attempted to construct his philosophy of freedom with recourse to a logical theory" (Henrich 1976, p. 230). Robert Pippin likewise insists on the necessity of taking the *Logic* into account: "no adequate treatment of Hegel's practical philosophy can ignore [logical] claims" (Pippin 2008: 8). Jean-François Kervégan also emphasizes that Hegel's *Philosophy of Right* is not to be read simply as a political philosophy but rather as one element within his larger system, the *Encyclopedia of Philosophical Sciences*, which in turn has a logic at its heart (Kervégan 2009: 7). Unless the fundamental coordinates of the *Science of Logic* are brought to light, substantial contents of the *Philosophy of Right* will remain hidden.

Yet even today, most commentators on the *Philosophy of Right* ignore its logical foundation. We live in an ostensibly post-metaphysical age and pick-and-mix approaches to Hegel drawn from sociology and political theory are in fashion. While some admit that a number of Hegel's thoughts are worth engaging with, his notion of logical justification is ignored or denigrated, many considering it out-dated and burdensome. My approach breaks with this fad: I pursue a strategy of uncovering the *Philosophy of Right*'s systematic intentions, its logical foundations and thus the innermost core of Hegel's thought.

1   The State as a Whole Consisting of Three Syllogisms

It is not only the state in the sense of civil or common law and the political state (the constitution) that can be considered a whole consisting of three syllogisms, but also (indeed first and foremost) the overall structure of the idea of the state as defined in the *Philosophy of Right* §259. The application of the syllogistic triad thus takes place within the interpretation of a single totality, a whole, with its internal logical mediation deriving from speculative reason, according to which "only the idea that, through the power of the concept, has become an actual totality, forms a self-referential, closed whole of syn-logisms" (Henrich 1982: 445).

The syllogistic triad

U	–	P	–	I
P	–	I	–	U
I	–	U	–	P

These three configurations of universal, particular and individual must be explained in some detail. Firstly, the sequence of the middle (P-I-U) remains identical, secondly, the last figure ends with P, and thirdly, Hegel shows that the positioning of the terms in figure 1 is logically identical to that in figure 2. The first syllogism implies that the individual (initially understood as qualitative determination) is posited by the universal. This individual, i.e. spirit as the active individual, moves towards the middle, into the mediating position. Finally, the truth of the first syllogism is posited by the second (*Werke* 6: 365–6). The second sequence is also defined by the idea that "since the particular and the universal are extremes and represent immediate, indifferent determinations vis-à-vis each other, so their relationship itself is indifferent; either one or the other can be taken as the major or minor premise" (*Werke* 6: 368). The conclusion is universality, which must therefore move to the centre of the third syllogism. The sequence I – U – P represents the truth of the formal syllogism so that according to Hegel, the syllogism becomes legitimate but the conclusion becomes necessarily negative: "Consequently, it is also indifferent which of the two determinations of this proposition is taken as predicate or subject, and whether the determination is taken in the syllogism as the extreme of singularity or the extreme of particularity" (*Werke* 6: 370).

Despite this formalism "the conjunction ... must likewise have its ground in a mediation that lies outside this syllogism" (*Werke* 6: 371). Hegel's syllogistic reasoning has a "very fundamental meaning" which "rests on the necessity that, as a determination of the Concept, *each moment* becomes itself the *whole* and the *mediating ground*" (*Werke* 8: 338–9). Everything rational forms such a threefold syllogism, in which the terms ultimately become interchangeable.

One can observe the path through the levels of the idea in Hegel's description of the 'syllogism of the idea' in the *Encyclopedia*'s final section – including that argumentation's culmination in the 'absolute syllogism'. The transition from subjectivity – especially from syllogising as its last step – into objectivity has its roots in the nature of the syllogism itself, which gives itself external reality through particularity. From then on, the logical form of the syllogism continues its path on a higher level and cannot be called an "empty framework" (*Werke* 8: 345). We are dealing with a *rational* syllogism insofar as here "the subject unites with itself through mediation. Thus it first becomes a subject, that is, the subject is itself the syllogism of reason" (*Werke* 8: 333).

2   The State as a Triad of Syllogisms

Qualitative Syllogism: I   –   P   –   U
 state as individual   relation of particular states   world history
 inner law of the state   outer law of the state   law of the world
Syllogism of reflexion: U   –   I   –   P
Syllogism of necessity: P   –   U   –   I

It is the state's duty to re-connect (con-clude) what has been divided and torn apart into its extremes in the context of civil society. This constitutes the state's meaning as a form of integration and connection in the sense of a constitution of freedom. The last syllogism effects the sublation of the structure of the syllogism and the constitution of a system of syllogisms that is a whole and in which the determined, fixed positions of the extremes and of the middle are dissolved and each determined moment itself represents the whole.

1. The individual state is connected with the universal via its particularity (as a national state). Individual states are attached to the universal through their external particularity and their particular interests and needs.
2. The activity of the individual state (I) serves as the mediating factor that gives actuality to the relationship of the states (P) and the world-context (U) by 'translating' their ethical essence into the extreme of actuality. Individual states constitute inter-nationality through their relations: the external sovereignty of the state and international law.
3. The universal is the substantial middle, in which individual states and their particular welfare find their mediation and subsistence. World history is the "absolute centre" (*Werke* 6: 425) which connects the poles of

individual states (I – constitution) with their external circumstances (P – international law).

This first explication of the three syllogisms is informed by Hegel's claims about the individual state as a system of three syllogistic mediations: "It is only through the nature of this con-cluding, or through this triad of syllogisms with the same terms, that a whole is truly understood in its organisation" (*Werke* 8: 356; *Werke* 6: 425).

3 The Inner Law of the State or Domestic Right – the Second System of Three Syllogisms

The triad of three syllogisms also informs the explication of the inner law of the state, i.e. the constitution. We here encounter a *second* system of three syllogisms that Hegel – as quoted above – alludes to in his *Logic* and in the *Encyclopedia*:

The state is a system of three syllogisms just like the solar system. (1) the *singular* (the person) con-cludes himself through his *particularity* (the physical and spiritual needs, which when further developed on their own give rise to civil society) with the *universal* (society, right, law, government). 2. The will or the activity of individuals is the mediating [term] that gives satisfaction to their needs in the context of society, right, etc., and provides fulfilment and actualisation to society, right, etc. (3) But it is the universal (state, government, right) that is the substantial middle term within which individuals and their satisfaction have and preserve their full reality, mediation, and subsistence. Precisely because the mediation con-cludes each of these determinations with the other extreme, each of them con-cludes itself with itself in this way or produces itself; and this production is its self-preservation (*Werke* 8: 356).

The following triad can be identified as the basic code of the state's internal right. Hegel does not develop this train of thought in the *Philosophy of Right* but it still represents the foundation of his idea of the state's inner rational structure, i.e. the constitution.

3.1 *The Qualitative Syllogism I-P-U*

A subject as individual "is con-cluded with a *universal determinacy* through a quality" (*Werke* 8: 335). The concrete person connects by means of its qualities, its particularity, i.e. its physical and spiritual requirements and interests (which civil society defines in more concrete form) with the universal (U) – right, law, government, so that individuals are connected to the universal of the constitution via their needs and their external existence. In other words, the subject connects by means of its properties and interests – abstract particularity – with the universal determinacy. However, P is subsumed under U (civil society is subsumed under the constitution) and I is subsumed under P (the concrete persons are subsumed under civil society). This creates only a dualistic relationship and no real mediation. Its logical deficiency lies in the 'imperfect middle': the *medius terminus* remains a concept-free quality. U, P and I face each other as abstract entities but in truth all three moments of the concept are more concretely determined than that. At the same time, U and P are connected and U becomes the mediating term of the extremes (P-U-I). However, this U only represents the abstract-universal and so this results in the total indifference of the moments, an external identity of the understanding.

There are two important lessons to be learned from this development. Firstly, individuality cannot be thought of as an isolated being, as a monad. Instead, it must be thought as a universality, the individual is an *individual citizen*. Second, the logical order of the syllogism's elements takes the shape of a circle of mutually presupposing mediations (*Werke* 8: 340). Its inherent lack motivates the further determinations of the qualitative syllogism. And since the individual is determined as an abstract universal, it assumes the middle position and becomes the mediating term. This constitutes the transition to the syllogism of reflexion where the middle is defined as all the concrete, individual subjects.

3.2 The Syllogism of Reflexion U-I-P

Now, all individual citizens as individuals (I) represent the middle, they *enact* the universal. When they bring the universal into external existence, they translate their ethical essence (U) into the extreme of reality and thus constitute the actual constitution of state order. So the will and the activity of individuals function as the mediating term, which brings satisfaction and reality to the citizens' needs and interests and which bestows actuality upon the constitution and universal right. Now, individuals reconcile within themselves the extreme of the independently knowing and willing individuality and the extreme of the substantially knowing and willing universality. They are actual as private and as substantial persons and achieve their particularity and universality in both spheres (P and U). The citizens' essential selfhood is partly found in the universal institutions of the state, which is the being-in-itself of their particular interests, and partly these institutions allow them to engage in an activity that aims at a universal purpose. This reflexive syllogism is deficient because the syllogism of all-ness (*Allheit*) ('all individual citizens') is first revealed to be a syllogism of induction and then a syllogism of analogy. In the meaning of the determined genus (i.e. universality) that is now disclosed, particularity becomes the mediating determination and universality becomes the middle term in accordance with the syllogism's third form.

3.3 P-U-I the Syllogism of Necessity

The universal (the 'universal part of the constitution') constitutes the middle term in which individuals (I) find their satisfaction and interests (P) have their reality and continued existence. The laws of the state and its institutions are the absolute centre in which the pole represented by individuals (I) is united ('con-cluded') with their external, particular existence (P). The laws articulate "the determinations of the content of objective freedom" (*Werke* 10: 331). Concrete freedom consists in the fact that personal individuality (I) and its particular interests (P) find their complete development and recognition within the state, the universal of the constitution (*Werke* 7: 406–7).

Insofar as the acting subject has the status of *'citizen'*, the agent achieves the *highest form of recognition* within an individual community, namely in the form of the unity of the dimensions of subjectivity. These are: personality, moral subjectivity, membership in a family and in civil society and these determinations find their acknowledgement and guarantee in the status of citizenship. My rights as person, as moral subject etc. are inherent in my rights as citizen. The right of the citizen as a whole unites all the rights (and duties) that were determined so far and it is more than the sum of its parts. As a citizen, I have grasped my individuality also as a universality (for example by respecting rational laws as something universal) and thereby prove my true freedom. §263 of the *Philosophy of Right* explicitly refers to the syllogism of necessity: spirit appears as objective universality (U) to the moments of the state (individuality and particularity) that have their immediate and reflected reality in the spheres of the family and civil society. Here spirit is the power of the rational within necessity, in form of the laws and the institutions.

At first, the syllogism of necessity takes the form of the categorical syllogism: the state as universal, the genus of *citoyens*, makes a case for a just system of education and against environmental destruction. The particular appears in the meaning of a determined kind or genus. The genus 'citizen', i.e. 'citizenship' is a 'positive unity', it is the oneness (das *Eine*) of the state, which finds its expression in the *one* constitution. This positive singularity requires mediation by individual citizens, i.e. by the individual representatives of the genus 'state' so that the logical form of the hypothetical syllogism is defined by the schema U-I-P. This constitutes the necessary relationship but there is still no steadfast necessity in the sense of an inevitable destiny as there is no necessary demand for the genus' unity. It is only a hypothetical demand because it is grounded in the contingency that comes with the structure of individual citizens' arbitrariness. At the same time, however, it includes the demand for a completion or affirmation of the hypothesis.

According to this syllogism's form, the mediation lies in the activity of individual citizens: they ought to constitute the free community – but can also fail to do so. The necessary, i.e. the universal, thus steps into the *middle position*: schema I-U-P. This mediating universal must be thought of as the totality of its particularisations and as an excluding oneness. Here, it is one and the same universal that is differentiated into all these forms, it is the disjunctive syllogism: citizens as universal, individual and particular. This logical structure exposes the moments of the concept in their *speculative unity*, each of these three moments represents the whole and contains the respective others within itself. Only a citizen logically-speculatively thought of in this way can serve as the foundation of a political state that is truly free. So at the end of the system of the syllogistic trinity we now have the *universal and rational will*. The achievement of the disjunctive syllogism provides us with a criterion for evaluating individual states and their constitutions. It follows logically that *every moment of the concept's determination (I, P, U) is itself the whole* and the *mediating ground* – citizens, civil society and the political state as *community* of citizens. Every syllogistic moment has the function of the middle and is "itself the totality of the moments and thus proven to be the entire syllogism" (*Werke* 8: 344). Everything rational must be grasped as threefold syllogism, as system of a threefold syllogising. This also means that the formalism of syllogising itself is overcome.

§260 of the *Philosophy of Right* articulates precisely this 'being con-cluded together' (*Zusammengeschlossenheit*) as a core feature of the formation of modernity: "The principle of modern states has prodigious strength and depth because it allows the principle of subjectivity to progress to its culmination in the self-sufficient extreme of personal particularity, and yet at the same time brings it back to the substantial unity and so maintains this unity in the principle of subjectivity itself" (*Werke* 7: 407). The rights of the universal, particular and individual must be thought of as a unity of mediation. "Precisely because the mediation con-cludes each of these determinations with the other extreme, each of them con-cludes itself with itself in this way or produces itself; and this production is its self-preservation" (*Werke* 8: 356). The freedom of the person and the freedom of the concrete person, i.e. the formal participant in civil society, are united in the freedom of the *citoyen*, i.e. the individual citizen, the state member. Personhood must be acknowledged and formal right must be actualised; the particular well-being of the individuals must be nurtured, the public good secured, the family protected and civil society must be rationally regulated and designed.

4 A New Conception of the Separation and Interdependence of State Powers

The basic structure of the separation or differentiation of the state into its substantial bodies – *Hegel's conception of the division of powers*[2] – can only be hinted at here. After Hegel had been championing the traditional model for a long time, the *Philosophy of Right* offers a new conception of the 'trinity' of the powers, a theory of power-interdependence that represents a paradigm shift in the history of political philosophy:
 (a) the power to determine and establish the universal – the legislative power;
 (b) the subsumption of individual cases and the spheres of particularity under the universal – the executive power;
 (c) subjectivity, as the will with the power of ultimate decision
   Werke 7: 435

PR §275, §287, §298
I   the power of the crown
P   the power of government
U   the legislative power

The first schema contains the moments of the concept of the constitution and pays special attention to how force is being used. The ultimate decision marks the endpoint and is the beginning of the actual realisation of the common will. The inversion of this sequence (I-P-U) that begins in §275 is grounded in the notion set out in §273 that the monarchical, ultimate power is ascribed the function of 'apex' (*Spitze*) and 'beginning of the whole'. A further reason for the inversion can be found in the fact that Hegel does not focus on the functioning, activity and application of the legislative process from §275 onwards but hones in on a possible *fundamental order of the powers* that includes the dominating role of the monarch – this is supposed to be absolute 'self-determination' that contains the three moments within: the *universality* of the constitution and the laws (U), the counsel as relationship of the *particular* to the universal (P) and the moment of ultimate decision-making (I) (§275).

However, it must be noted that the schema above – and comparison with Hegel's *Logic* proves this – fail to sufficiently develop the *fully developed concept*

---

[2] These reflections are based on the very lucid piece 'Hegels Theorie der Gewaltenteilung' by Ludwig Siep (1992: 240–269).

and the transition into the idea. Hegel's perplexing proposition consists in two forms, U-P-I and I-P-U, and in both, the particular takes the middle position. The form of the syllogism of the trinity, i.e. the *whole of three syllogisms* does not apply here. But it is only this logical form that enables a sufficient determination of the concept of the state as something entirely rational, i.e. as a complete universal. The following passage underlines the crucial importance of the logical structure for the philosophical understanding of what the state is. The origin of the different spheres or powers of the state's organisation as something intrinsically rational lies in the *self-determination of the concept*. "How the concept and then, more concretely, how the Idea, determine themselves inwardly and so posit their moments – universality, particularity, and individuality – in abstraction from one another, is discoverable from logic, though not of course from the logic commonly in vogue" (*Werke* 10: 338). This last caveat retains its topicality today.

Unless one unearths the *Philosophy of Right*'s specifically Hegelian logical foundations, i.e. their status as *new* logic, the architecture of political rationality remains a merely pragmatic or sociologically oriented description without legitimacy, an edifice in need of completion. Hegel comments succinctly on this issue: "What disorganizes the unity of the logical-rational, equally disorganizes actuality" (*Werke* 10: 338). Political reality as a whole comprising different functions, i.e. as a system of powers, must be grasped as a system of three syllogisms *of the same terms*. According to Michael Wolff, Hegel wanted to "place the three syllogistic forms of mediation also at the heart of the political constitution" (Wolff 1985: 166–167). And for Ludwig Siep, there is no doubt that Hegel "thought of his doctrine of the division of powers as such a system of three syllogisms" (Siep 1992: 263f).[3]

5   The Constitution as a System of Three Syllogisms – a Reformulation of the *Philosophy of Right*

Surprisingly, it is exactly this key thought – the trinity of syllogisms – that in the chapter on the state is neither explicated in detail nor is strictly consistent with the requirements of the *Logic*! The above-mentioned schema can be found in the *Philosophy of Right* §273 und §275ff where the essential moments of the state are defined. There are also several important hints as to the

---

3 According to Siep, Hegel was able to "use the resources of the speculative doctrine of the syllogism to describe the three constitutional powers as the three 'ways in which the state's will is enacted', each representing a syllogism" (1992: 263).

structure of the syllogisms and the specific relevance of reciprocal implication and mediation. But the reader is somewhat taken aback upon realising that the brilliant logician Hegel does not properly demonstrate the connectedness (the 'con-clusion') of the three syllogisms here and fails to explicate the moment of the systematic whole, i.e. of the three syllogisms' unity, in sufficient detail.

Michael Wolff has already demonstrated that taking the monarch as the ultimate political power involves a deficient syllogism of reflexion (U-I-P) and that on the contrary the legislative power must have this function. However, this would contradict the very primacy of the monarchical power that Hegel's text insists on. How are we to make sense of this? The cardinal problem can be found in the fact that Hegel only relies on the logic of the *not yet developed, not realised* concept instead of relying on the *triad of syllogisms* that would be necessary here. Although the determinations of the concept ought to appear as 'moments of the idea', one finds no convincing explication of the logical theorem: the syllogism-triad. This amounts to a profound gap in the logical sequence of the *Philosophy of Right*. It is difficult to find reasons for this and in my attempts at an explanation, I must venture into the risky realm of conjecture: one reason may be the times in which Hegel wrote: the available historical-constitutional models as well as the debates surrounding constitutional theory may have inspired him to find in constitutional monarchy a guarantee of stability and order and motivated him to clearly delineate this notion of monarchy from other versions and varieties of constitution. Hegel's monarch appears as the apex (*Spitze*) in the notion of the will. The principle that there is a first – and final decision-maker – a head of state – is certainly respected by all modern states, although it also means that natural i.e. arbitrary factors play a role. Hegel is not to be argued with on this point – he profoundly altered the doctrine of the division of powers and provided a justification for the *ultimate decision-maker*, i.e. the head of the state, as one of the three state powers.

However, the *Philosophy of Right* also suggests that constitutional monarchy is the political form adequate to the modern world. Hegel's insistence on logical foundations particularly in *this* context could be read as an indication that he has identified a problem at the logical level but that political reality does not live up to the standards of logic. It is possible that political caution guided his thinking here, and that he trod warily to avoid a comprehensive discussion of the real issue. According to Dieter Henrich, "Hegel's reconstruction of the state as a system of syllogisms develops the logic of the ethical state in a form that articulates its intrinsic systematicity; but there are reasons why this form does not become explicit to the same degree in the *Philosophy of*

Right" (Henrich 1982: 443f).[4] It is well-known that there were several attempts to denounce Hegel to the Prussian king because of his concept of the monarch. Most likely, Hegel's was no accident or categorial mistake but a cultivation of the art of what Goethe called 'impish disguise'. The philosopher saw the dangers that might arise from publishing a logically grounded political alternative.

The absence of the expected syn-logistics appears to be the only logical faux pas of the *Philosophy of Right*. Hegel has – so my rather daring interpretation – fooled the Prussian censors with considerable finesse and chutzpa and placed his faith in his subsequent interpreters to realise a *reconstruction and correction of political reality in accordance with the requirements of his Logic*. The crucial elements for the understanding of the three spheres of the state were conceptualised by Hegel, leaving the logical systematicity – especially the syllogism-triad – still to be finished.

This seems to be the only way to explain his insufficient realisation of the principle of the whole as a system of syllogisms. My interpretation here follows the intentions of Henrich and Wolff, who maintain that the "form of the concept of Hegel's theory of ethical life and of the ethical state is not easily deduced from the development of the published *Philosophy of Right*. Hegel himself has explained with some clarity in passages that were more suitable for the task of conceptually determining formal relationships the logic in which this conceptual form has to be constructed" (Henrich 1982: 450).

The following description connects the two already mentioned principles of interpretation: a) adoption of the discussed syllogistic forms, including the relations of the three powers and b) systematic construction of the three spheres of the political in accordance with the requirements of the triad of syllogisms. Particularly the latter *deviates from Hegel's own explicit claims* but is faithful to the *logical spirit* and seems entirely appropriate given the intentions of the author of the *Philosophy of Right*. In what follows, this passage of the *Philosophy of Right* will be reformulated with the help of Hegel's *Logic*.

As stated above, what matters is the 'spirit' of Hegel's conception, the issue at hand is a *theory of the organic state that relies on the insights of the triad of the syllogism of Hegel's Logic*. The most crucial change concerns the explanatory sequence of the state powers: According to syllogistic logic, the qualitative syllogism (I-U-P) has to stand at the beginning. The executive power constitutes the middle of the scheme, the syllogism of reflexion. The third form is the syllogism of necessity – the legislative power, which is the only one capable of

---

4 Klaus Hartmann identifies the "mistake" in the will of the political state in the *Philosophy of Right* – Hegel is said to have forgot his "categorial insight" (Hartmann 1982: 311). I argue that it is no accident on Hegel's part.

truly tying the three conceptual moments together and bringing them into the unity of the *universal rational will*. According to the *logical* reading, this reveals the foundation of the state's structure: the constitution and the constitutional laws, the constitution itself and the legislative power. The ground (and reason) for the state's legitimacy can only lie here. Insofar as the legislative power in its function as terminus major (U) takes the middle position in the figure of the third syllogism (P-U-I), it renders it "the true syllogism of state-life, in which all powers originate in the people as such" (Michelet 1970: 185).[5] As Hegel's student Michelet put it: by the standards of the *Logic*, the schema should take the following form.

6 The State as a System of Three Syllogisms – against the Letter of the *Philosophy of Right*

Syllogism of Dasein (Qualitative Syllogism)

I	P	U
power of ultimate decision	power of government	legislative power
head of state	executive	legislative
monarchy (autocracy)	aristocracy	democracy
'one'	'some'	'all'[6]

Syllogism of Reflexion

| U | I | P |

Syllogism of Necessity

| P | U | I |

The middle terms of the syllogistic triads – *ascending* from the third syllogism and thus from the U – contain the structure of willing and of purposeful action: U – the universal will, the *cognition and determination* of the purpose of the state (*staatlicher Verband*); I – the *examination* of the purpose regarding its conformity to constitutional and legal standards and of the *ultimate decision*

---

5   Michelet adds: "The true heart of the rational constitution consists in the fact that the demands of ethical life also find expression in form of a written document" (Michelet 1970: 185).
6   In his essay 'On Perpetual Peace', Kant speaks of the different kinds of government of the body politic (*forma imperii*): a) One – autocracy b) Some united amongst themselves – aristocracy or c) All together – democracy (Kant AA VIII: 352).

regarding the realisation of the purpose, und P – the relation to the particular, the *application and execution* of the purpose. The question of the nature of the purpose can be precisely answered: The people as *populus* is the "sole purpose of the state". Furthermore, the structure that is determined by the schema within the three syllogisms can be deciphered: *Every single syllogism represents the whole of syllogisms*. In the first syllogism, this means that figure 1 I-P-U dominates, in the second, figure 2 U-I-P, the syllogism of induction, and in the third syllogism figure 3 P-U-I, the disjunctive syllogism. According to Georg Sans, the three figures of the syllogism originate in "the complete permutation of the terms individual, particular and universal. All of these, one after another, pass through the positions of the two extremes and of the middle. This is exactly what Hegel describes as 'syllogism of three syllogisms': a systematic whole of three concepts, each of which is capable of mediating the two others with each other. And because each term is able to justify the relationship of the other two, there arises a 'circle of mutually presupposing mediations' (§189)" (Sans 2011: 167–181).

syllogism of Dasein	syllogism of Reflexion	syllogism of Necessity
<u>I – P – U</u>	I – P – U	I – P – U
U – I – P	<u>U – I – P</u>	U – I – P
P – U – I	P – U – I	<u>P – U – I</u>

On the one hand, this schema registers a change in the syllogism's moments (*terminorum*) but on the other hand, it also captures the foundation of the entire syn-logistics: the universality that stands in the middle of the disjunctive syllogism (U). This is the *universality of being a citizen* and its representation in the legislative, i.e. the law-making assembly.

7 The Universal, Law-Making Power – the Syllogism of Necessity (P-U-I)

From the perspective of Hegel's logic of the syllogism, the legislative power supplies the cornerstone of the state's entire structure. This power has the special function of *cognising* and *determining* the specific purposes of the state. It is part of the constitution, which is prior to it. This power in its function as particular power is also revealed to be a *universal* power that serves as the foundation of the division of powers. In the election of their parliamentary representatives, the citizens ('the people') reveal their function as justifier and founder of state power. It is here that the system of political powers finds its ground, i.e. the *universal rational will*, which manifests itself as constitution and as legislative assembly. Both represent the *civic will* (*bürgerschaftlichen Willen*), i.e. the *universal will of the citoyen*, which mediates individuality with particularity, i.e. with the other constitutional bodies. The assembly of the polities (*Politen*) has the task of developing the constitution, which is also further specified in the process of defining the specific laws and the constantly changing governmental affairs (*Werke* 7: 465). The crucial problem that Hegel has to face is clarifying the relationship between the will of all and the universal will, i.e. the issue of the grounds for the *legitimacy of the modern state*. This is connected to the question of who wields this power, i.e. the specific form of participation of the *citoyen* in the process of determining the ends of the state – how *citizens participate* in the affairs of the state that is connected with the highly contemporary question of *how participatory politics are formed* and from which the justification of state power can arise. "The principle of any sovereignty resides essentially in the Nation", as the *Déclaration des Droits de l'Homme et du Citoyen*, Art. 3 puts it.[7] The parliament must be – as the French constitution of 1793 determines – at the centre of the state's structure, the people embody the sovereign in this 'republican' sense.

Every *citoyen* must be enabled to participate equally in the creation of the universal – be it by way of membership of political parties and societies, or by way of direct (plebiscitary) democracy or indirect, representative institutions. These days, alongside the classical forms of political action, new, non-classical forms (e.g. popular grassroots movements, citizens' initiatives, roundtables, participatory budgets etc.) become ever more important. However, these do not represent an alternative to parliamentary action but are a complementary element with regards to the concrete participation of the citizens in political life. In this context, Hegel's thought presents itself as a challenge and an inspiration, asking us to keep thinking – we must not simply assume that today's form of democracy is by definition the best of all these forms. The criteria by which we evaluate these different ways of political activity must be the successful participation in the *res publica*, the most adequate form of representation, and in general the realization of freedom in the sense of the achievement of the disjunctive syllogism – the guarantee of the freedom of every individual particulars in one modern political community.

According to Hegel's syn-logistics, the syllogisms of necessity – the categorical, the hypothetical and the decisive final syllogism, i.e. the disjunctive

---

7 According to Hegel, the main site of governmental power in the democratic constitution of 1793 France is the parliament; the legislating power has been victorious (*Werke* 11: 117–118).

syllogism, which at the same time represents the sublation of the syllogistic form – supply the required logical connection. In the middle position of the necessary syllogism, we find universality: it is the political will as universal, rational will, i.e. actuality in the form of universal, political representation of the citizens' will. This is the actual presence of the will that is free in and for itself as universal will. This universal (U) connects the universal, rational will in its immediate individual political representation – the individual subject of the head of state (I) – with the universal rational will in the form of its particular political actualisation – the governing power (P). Unlike the previous syllogisms, universality here does not have 'some immediate content', its content is not arbitrary, but it has the reflexion of the extremes (P and I) within itself, while the latter have their inner identity in the middle which in turn is determined in its content by the formal determinations of the extremes – all moments are expressions of the universal and rational will of the citizens.

	universality (U) as middle term	
a) categorical syllogism I – P – U	U as P	executive power
b) hypothetical syllogism U – I – P	U as I	power of ultimate decision
c) disjunctive syllogism P – U – I	U as U	legislating power

8 The Categorical Syllogism

In the categorical syllogism, which is defined by the schema of the first figure of the formal syllogism (I-P-U), we have universality as particularity, in the meaning of the determined kind or genus. The government as particular expression of the universal will of the citizens, i.e. as mediating determination, as universal, rational, political will in its necessary particularity, i.e. in its particular representation as executive power, is responsible for *particularising the universal and its realisation*. The creation, realisation and application of the laws must *incorporate the universal in the laws' determinacy*. However, the other independent powers are also part of government, are also ultimate decider and legislator "because their independence is exactly that substantial universality, the species" (*Werke* 6: 394.). Governing can thus be understood as a determination of the whole (cf. Cesa 1982: 205).

9 The Hypothetical Syllogism

In the hypothetical syllogism, universality moves to the centre in the form of individuality. The ruler in the meaning of 'individual' is 'equally mediating as well as mediated'. In contrast to the syllogism of reflexion, no premises are simply presupposed for the syllogism.

The universal political will in the form of an ultimate decision mediates the universal law (legislative power) with the particularisation of law (power of government / executive power). The initial and ultimate decision connects the cognition of the state's purpose and definition of that purpose (U) with the realisation and application of the purpose (P). The adequacy of P in relation to U is tested and there is an ultimate decision about the law. This power remains *mediated* through the necessary information, counsel and expertise of P and by the determination of the actors in U, i.e. the determination of the ultimate decider is realised by the citizens and their representatives, i.e. via the constitutionally legitimated inclusion of the traditional forms of the monarchical principle.

10 The Disjunctive Syllogism

The decisive concretisation of 'realisation' of the middle is realised in the disjunctive syllogism, the centrepiece of the syllogism of necessity. This is about the universality of universality, about the "universality that is filled with the form", the "*developed objective universality*" (*Werke* 6: 398). The middle of the syllogism includes the universal as genus (categorical syllogism) and universality as completely determined (hypothetical syllogism) and thus the objective universality in the totality of its formal determinations. This universality cannot logically be regarded as the all-ness of reflexion but is the totality of its particularisations – it is individual particularity, an excluding individuality.

The universal presents itself here as the 'universal sphere of its particularisations' and as determined individuality, the *medius terminus is U, P as well as I*. This has fundamental consequences for the syllogistic triad of the political organism. The middle of the disjunctive syllogism as totality of the concept itself contains both extremes in their complete determinateness, the *political trinity* in the *universal rational will* and in *the sovereign law-giver* as universal. In all three powers, one and the same universal is posited, the identity of these powers, the universal in the shape of the *rational political will*. The universal manifests itself here in this *doubled* form, as double identity: as *constitution in general* and as *legislative power*. The legislative power's privileged position is grounded in this briefly sketched syllogistic logic, especially in the logic of the disjunctive syllogism. The positioning of universality in the middle of the last figure creates a successful syllogism. *One of the powers necessarily becomes the ground of the whole, i.e. the foundation of the political organisation of the state.* Recognising Hegel's syn-logistics leads to a very surprising result compared to the claims made in the *Philosophy of Right*: Logic entails the *theoretical legitimisation of a republican, democratic constitution* and of the fundamental meaning of the legislative assembly as expression of a representational-democratic structure. The universal, rational will manifests itself in form of the constitution and in form of the legislative power. Of course this insight cannot be found in the text of the *Philosophy of Right* itself – it must be developed by way of a continuation of Hegel's project.

So the *political trinity* has its ground in the 'holy spirit' of the universal rational will of the citizen, the educated *citoyenneté* as lawmaker and sovereign. The notion of the citizen's self-determination offered here, i.e. of the citizenship's self-government, is also logically grounded in the disjunctive syllogism, which is a syllogism *and* the sublation of the logical form of the syllogism at the same time because the difference between the middle and the extremes is dissolved. In this way, the constitution and the legislative assembly can be thought of as a living unity filled with positive tension. Now one can speak of con-cluding (*zusammenschliessen*) the subject not just with others but with *sublated others*. This is the subject's *syllogising with itself,* which, strictly speaking, is no syllogising anymore. It enables the citizen and citizenship in general to be autonomous, i.e. free, *within* the rationally structured, legislative power in which universality, particularity and individuality are united.

Within the legislative power, universality is present as universal will of the citizens – the democratic principle. Individuality is manifest as head of state – in form of the *monarchical* principle of the ultimate decider. And finally, particularity is present as government – the *aristocratic* principle. At the same time, all three moments represent the unity of the three dimensions and appear as sublated. The 'best constitution' must live up to what the concept of the state expresses and so it must articulate the three components' unity – the state as ethical idea. Now, the political element finds its highest determination in the inner constitution, we have assumed the point of view of the *highest concrete universal*. In all moments we find "the actual presence of the spirit that is in and for itself as the universal spirit" (*Werke* 10: 377). It is the actuality of the ethical idea, the idea of freedom as the concept of freedom that has become the political reality of the state as well as political consciousness. The state is the structure that satisfies the needs of the citizens as it is the product of the free activity and unification of the legal subjects and it is its very own form of right and freedom.

Following Dieter Henrich, one could thus imagine the successful achievement of Hegel's goal "to justify the notion of the state with reference to the notion of 'free spirit' in such a way that the freedom of this spirit is contained and active in the developed concept of the state. The description of the state in the form of three syllogisms is conceptually committed to this goal" (Henrich 1982: 450). In this spirit, I have shown that only an explication and application of the syllogism's triad enables an adequate comprehension of Hegel's 'science of the state' as a thinking of freedom.

CHAPTER 11

The Right of Resistance

From a very young age, Hegel had been interested in the topic of tyrannicide, in the right of resistance against despotism.* In the Tübingen fragment *'Unsere Tradition'* ('Our Tradition') we find a reference to Harmodius and Aristogeiton, who are considered to be republicans because they assassinated the tyrant. In Hegel's view, both attained eternal glory because "they slaughtered the tyrant and gave equal rights and laws to their citizens" (Hegel 1968 Bd. 1: 80). It is probably hard to imagine Hegel as a rebel or as a protagonist of the idea of rebellion – he is usually considered to be exactly the opposite, and to this day the dominant cliché sees him as an advocate of restoration or as an apologist for Prussian state paternalism. Since this wholly erroneous view is still widespread, I will present here a few of the main features of Hegel's theory of the 'inversive' right of resistance.

Hegel presents some basic elements or building blocks of such a theory in his *Philosophy of Right*. According to Hegel, the combination of a great misfortune and severe poverty along with the *higher right to preserve one's existence* give rise to the right of resistance: this right is granted to each subject who rebels against the need they suffer. Hegel's reflections on the right of necessity (*Notrecht*) present an essential foundation for reflection on the gulf between wealth and poverty as a basic problem of civil society. The following passage could be formulated today with as much urgency as when it was written: "It would require but limited resources to alleviate the misfortune of many people, yet these resources are the free property of others" (Hegel 1973 Bd. 3: 398). Thus, the principle of the right of necessity is also of considerable relevance for our time, in which every day countless free beings starve or die of preventable diseases due to a lack of medicine and environmental degradation; from Hegel's point of view, these are blatant violations of *rights*.

The following reflections comprise three parts: first, some observations on the foundations of Hegel's legitimising of the right of resistance; second, a presentation of the theory of 'second coercion'; and finally, a sketch of the successive stages of the right of necessity or emergency that I take to be implicit in the *Philosophy of Right*. In this regard I will argue that for each of the

---

* This chapter is based on a previous publication of the same name in "Hegel and Resistance", edited by Rebecca Comay and Bart Zandvoort, Bloomsbury 2017.

three stages of the concept of right and freedom distinguished by Hegel – abstract right, morality and ethical life – there is a corresponding determination of the right of resistance, which secures the subject's rights against possible violations.

1   Considerations on the Right of Necessity

A passage from a student's notes on a course given by Hegel may serve as an introduction, because it *explicitly* addresses the right of rebellion and resistance in relation to the right of necessity. According to Hegel, the widening gap between great wealth and abject poverty (*Werke* 7: 389–90) gives rise to indignation (*Empörung*) and thus "revolt against the order that denies every realization of the will of free people" (Hegel 1983a: 20). Hegel here formulates the idea of a *necessity* to revolt, that is to say: the right of the poor and discriminated to start a revolution in order to restore justice. It is the appalling misery of abject poverty, Hegel says, in which bitterness, anger and outrage arise from a situation of unimaginable distress, that has been dramatically portrayed by "deep thinking and feeling" minds such as Rousseau (Hegel 1973 Bd. 4: 477).

In Hegel's eyes, the right to *recovery or restitution of the foundations* of the legal state does not in any way stem from an *arbitrary* insurrection or an *illegal* usurpation of power, but concerns the legitimate claim of the citizen to a guarantee of his or her rights. Hegel esteems Rousseau here because he was deeply moved by the misery of the people and because he depicted the inner bitterness and justified indignation of the poor in an especially appropriate manner. However, the conclusion that Rousseau drew from this circumstance, namely the rejection of civil society altogether, led to another extreme, one that denied and despised the principle of subjective particularity as a core element of modernity. The French Revolution that Rousseau helped inspire created a situation where it seemed the "only alternative was to completely abandon such a system [of modernity]", to sacrifice it entirely (Hegel 1973 Bd. 4: 477). The French Revolution's *elimination of the principle of particularity* came at a high and totally unacceptable price: it fundamentally undermined freedom. Hegel refers to the kind of fanaticism and fundamentalism that marked the period of Revolutionary Terror as an expression of an "intolerance towards everything particular". Any distinction, any particularity with respect to talents and institutions was contrary to the revolutionaries' "abstract" and "one-sided" understanding of equality (*Werke* 7: 50). It should be emphasised here that Hegel only takes issue with the *abstract* understanding of equality, and not at all with the concept of *equality as such*. What is at stake in rebellion is a *reconstitution* of civil society based on right, rather than the creation of a fundamentally different society. The clear, profound and even insurmountable conceptual divide between Hegel's and Marx's ideas should therefore be clear, despite the futile attempts still made to bring about a rapprochement between Hegel and Marx.

For Hegel, there is *a right of resistance to violations of the principle of modern freedom*. In legitimate forms of resistance, the civil-societal and political dimensions are interconnected. The preceding forms of indignation (*Empörung*) are present in the ultimate, decisive form of politics, that of the resistance of citizens as political protagonists. Resistance against chronic poverty, environmental degradation, educational discrimination or the aspirations of indigenous people to social and political recognition are considered to be examples of *juridically* permissible actions, that is, in the name of self-defence, as resistance against injustice.

Where there is no law, insofar as it has ceased to guarantee the existence of individuals and the wellbeing of society, the individual is left to themselves without any rights. To the extent that the discriminated or excluded person thereby reverts to the status of a slave, they are left with nothing but "the right to break their bonds at all times; [...] this right is imprescriptible" (Hegel 1973 Bd. 4: 239). The right of resistance stems from this condition. In addition to this formal-legal side – the 'slave principle' – the right of resistance also springs from the sphere of morality: firstly, proceeding from the 'Socrates principle' of a demand for legitimation through one's own testing of the legitimacy of the existing order and inner resistance; secondly, on the basis of the right of necessity with respect to wellbeing. The progressively determined right of resistance rests on these pillars. "Within the conditions of society, hardship at once assumes the form of a wrong inflicted on this or that class" (*Werke* 7: 390), from which springs the right of *moral self-defence* within the sphere of civil society and which anticipates the current political context.[1] Insofar as civil society has particularity and thus self-interest as its principle, it suffers from conflicts that are a sign of its imperfection, and is in need of rational control and regulation, of a rational design by the social state that guarantees justice. As Rousseau writes, "One of the most important things for a government to do, therefore, is to prevent extreme inequality in wealth, not by depriving the rich of their possessions, but by denying everyone the means of accumulating

---

1   In contrast, Schnädelbach asserts that Hegel restricted the right of resistance to *inner, psychological* defiance. See Schnädelbach 2000 Bd. 2: 241.

them; and not by building poorhouses but by ensuring that the citizens do not become poor" (Rousseau 1999: 21). This still applies today to impoverishment in terms of subsistence, education or healthcare. On the whole, poverty and social injustice today give rise to a considerable reduction in opportunities and a limitation of the right to full and equal participation in society. The right of resistance, therefore, concerns the claim of social actors to the legal grounding and protection of their rights.

2 The Concept of Second Coercion

Hegel views resistance as the inversion of injustice, in the tradition of John Locke, and in the sense of rebellion as *re-bellare*, as a response to the initiator of the 'war', as a 'turning the tables'. The legitimation of such a right of necessity, *ius resistendi* as *ultima ratio*, builds upon the Kantian idea of a legitimate 'second coercion'.[2] It is useful to draw a comparison with Kant's position in order to highlight the significance of Hegel's innovative argument for the right of resistance. If a wrong, illegitimate coercion "is a hindrance or resistance that occurs to freedom" then an opposing coercion can be viewed as "hindering a hindrance to freedom", thus generating the authority to coerce the first coercion. "Right and the authority to coerce therefore mean one and the same thing" (Kant 1968 Bd. 6: 232). Against the coercion of heteronomy a second coercion appears justified. Thus Kant speaks of the law "of a reciprocal coercion necessarily in accord with the freedom of everyone under the principle of universal freedom" (ibid.).

Although Kant allowed, in the political field, for a procedure to submit grievances and a right of parliament to refuse government orders, he categorically refused the political right of resistance in its most important and significant form, that of rebellion. Consequently, a decisive element of political self-defence is missing: people cannot offer any resistance to the legislative head of a state that would be consistent with right. There exists "no right to *sedition* (*seditio*), still less to *rebellion* (*rebellio*), and least of all is there a right against the head of state as an individual person (the monarch) … on the pretext that he has abused his authority (*tyrannis*)" (Kant 1968 Bd. 6: 319). For Kant the people should indeed bear the unbearable, for the active rebellion against the highest legislation could never be anything but unlawful. According to Kant, for it to be lawful there would have to be a public law that

---

2 See Vieweg, 'Interpersonality and Wrong', in this volume.

allows resistance to authority; this would imply, however, that the highest legislation contains a provision stating that it is not the highest one. Consequently, any resistance of this kind would be high treason and subject to the death penalty (ibid). Only a type of passive ('negative') resistance would be permissible. Even if the unlawful revolution proved successful, the subjects could not refuse to honestly obey any new order that was established by unlawful means![3] Even if the ruler makes decisions completely contrary to the law, "subjects may indeed oppose this injustice by *complaints* (*gravamina*) but not by *resistance*" (ibid.).

Although Kant conceived the subtle idea of second coercion, this same great thinker of autonomy does not refer to it in the decisive passage above, but in the end prefers subservience, subalternity and paternalism. He prefers the principle of a state of politically subjected citizens, who understand themselves to be subordinated, and who do not possess any right to actively abolish injustice by means of wholesale political self-defence. Political or social improvement arises not from the *bottom up* but only from the *top down*. The sovereign of the state "has only rights against his subjects and no duties" (Kant 1968 Bd. 6: 319). Hegel directly criticizes this view and defends one diametrically opposed to it. Nevertheless, his position is still based on the Kantian idea that second coercion is legitimate. He also refers to the principle of the unity of right and duty, which means that in a state of law no one can be above the realm of duties.[4] According to this principle, the duties of the state and the rights of the citizens are to be defined just as are the rights of the state and the duties of the citizens. The critique of the principle *fiat justitia, pereat mundus* indirectly targets Kant's view on resistance.[5] For Hegel, a (precisely diagnosed) state of extreme need that constitutes a state of unlawfulness gives rise to the right *to invert this situation*, that is to say, to the right to restore law, even if this takes the form of resistance to fundamental violation of rights (tyranny) or to individual violations by the state authorities. Here lies the key idea of a modern 'inversive' right of necessity and right of resistance.

---

3   Kenneth R. Westphal provides a detailed analysis of Kant and the right of resistance in Westphal 1998: 171–202.
4   Some accounts of the monarch in the *Philosophy of Right* mistakenly elide Hegel with Kant's approach.
5   The state of emergency holds for Hegel as a "ground of justification", this "principle, which is new and surprising for his contemporaries, is pronounced with maximal severity", and, as it seems "polemically against Kant (not *ius aequivocum*, not fairness, but law)" (Bockelmann 1935: 22).

3   The Stages of the Inversive Right of Resistance

The (largely ignored) facet of Hegel's *Philosophy of Right* discussed above deals with the series of stages of the right of reason from the perspective of the transgression against rights, and in this way implicitly unfolds the essentials of a *series of stages of 'rights of emergency or necessity'*. On every level, this state of emergency must be tested and the respective instrument of opposition must be determined – *la resistance à l'oppression*. Hegel's view, which builds on Locke and Hume's conceptions of the right of resistance,[6] refers both to the right of resistance against the fundamental violation of the principle of right – the keyword being 'tyranny' – and a resistance against violations of right in the constitutional order. The foundation for the legitimacy of a political right of necessity consists in the *right to oppose the first unlawful coercion with a second coercion*. The legitimacy of the second coercion, and this has hitherto been neglected, grounds the *inversive right of resistance*.

At least on a structural level, Hegel follows Locke: resistance against the violation of right by state institutions (declaration of a 'state of war') is a case of '*re-bellare*'[7]; the violation of the law may itself be violated. Hegel also uses (in different terminology) the notion of a 'disturbance of the peace' (see Hegel 1983b: 230), which it is admissible to oppose. It is always warranted or justified to resist the inversion of rights and any large-scale injustice. This can be viewed as a consistent principle in the *Philosophy of Right*.[8] The state authorities and institutions must adequately manifest or embody the *substance of the state* – the 'being a citizen', 'citizenship' – in which *natural law becomes the law of reason*. If this is not the case, or is only insufficiently the case, the citizenry has the irrevocable right to establish or to reconstitute this adequate form of the state. However, the different levels of opposition, of the right of necessity, of the *inversive right of resistance*, are treated unequally in the text, even though all the main elements receive attention. These are: self-defence against all forms of infringement of the basic right of personhood, 'juridical' self-defence, the right of necessity, moral resistance, resistance to a state of

---

6   According to Ludwig Siep, Hegel accepts the corresponding position of Hobbes. See Siep's commentary in Locke 2007: 310.

7   See also Euchner 1996: 119–23 and Siep's commentary in Locke 2007: 372ff.

8   According to Thomas Petersen (1996: 473, 475), 'in the state of the Hegelian *Philosophy of Right*, justified resistance [is] possible'; Hegel recognizes 'a right to resistance in principle'. However, Petersen fails to consider the crucial notion of a second coercion. On the subject of emergency law and state of emergency in Hegel, see also Bockelmann 1935.

emergency in the sense of extreme need and poverty, and political resistance to perverted forms of the state.

3.1 The Right to Personhood

The point of departure is the most basic right, the principle of the *right to personhood* as the *ground of all rights* – the *Droits de l'Homme* states that "personhood is that which is the highest in man", his "highest dignity" (Hegel 2000: 15). All further articles of law that are required due to the abstractness of the right to personhood and all forms of resistance against the violation of this right have their foundation in this status of the free person, in his or her self-determination, in the *unique* and *universal* right of personhood. This implies the obligation to respect *myself* and *all others* as abstract persons. The equality of subjects with regard to their abstract personhood, as an abstract identity, is for Hegel the first principle of freedom. The prohibition against violating this right follows from the principle of freedom itself, and it must be considered as inviolable: 'the dignity of man is inviolable'. The inviolability, the unimpeachable or inalienable character of this basic right of the person encompasses the substantial goods of my freedom of will, my being an end in itself, my intelligence, my morality, and my understanding of the world. Domination or slavery, subjugation or oppression, coercion of conscience or religion are impermissible and unlawful attacks on the right to personhood. "The right to such inalienable things is imprescriptible, since the act whereby I take possession of my personality and substantial essence and make myself a responsible being with moral and religious values and capable of holding rights removes these determinations from the very externality which alone makes them capable of becoming the possessions of someone else" (*Werke* 7: 142).

Every transgression against or violation of this basic right is a first coercion, i.e. an injustice, against which the affected persons can legitimately and proportionally defend themselves. All infringements of this fundamental right allow for a second coercion, resistance is then an infringement only of prior infringements, i.e. the affirmation of the inversion of the first, unlawful coercion. In this way, actions that aim to overthrow or invert the conditions that violate the basic right to personhood are justified and authorized, and the right to resist is established. When my right is infringed in this way, "any temporary or other justification that could be assumed from my previous consent or acquiescence lose its validity" (*Werke* 7: 142). Every slave, every servant exists in a state of 'emergency' (*Not*), of a lack of recognition and respect for his or her person. He "has the right to break his bonds at all times", the slave "has an absolute right to free himself" (Hegel 1973 Bd. 4: 239, 251).

This line of argumentation helps Hegel to clearly define in an abstract-formal way the basic foundational element of the right of resistance, which then needs to be further defined in the relevant higher spheres of action. The right of self-defence against a first coercion never expires, it is inalienable and has absolute validity. "This return on my part into myself, whereby I make myself existent as Idea, as a person with rights and morality, supersedes the previous relationship and the wrong which I and the other person have done to my concept and reason" (*Werke* 7: 142–3). In resisting a first coercion, in fleeing from my 'emergency situation' or personal 'state of exception' I 'revoke the alienation' of personality. As will be argued further on, this clear plea for legitimate resistance in states of emergency relates not only to pre-modern social conditions but necessarily to potential instances of oppression, subjugation and discrimination in modern societies.

3.2 *Self-Defence*

Self-defence (*Notwehr*), as it is understood in formal law, means legitimate *coercion against injustice*. It is preceded by a violation of the law by another person, e.g. by an act of physical violence. The attacked and threatened person can lawfully resist by means of a force that is appropriate to the violence of the attack. In this way, an 'inversion' of right takes place: if the other person illegitimately uses violence, I can violate the state's monopoly on force and thus infringe the ban on violence by defending myself in an appropriate manner. This 'inversion' or 'reversal' applies to all forms of emergency law. A deed always follows from the violation of a certain right that inverts the existing principle of right. *Self-defence* is the inversion of the rejection of violence.

3.3 *The Right of Necessity*

The *right of necessity* (*Notrecht*) is based on the *right to self-preservation*. When one's life is seriously in danger, one is in danger of *losing all rights*, which is in fact a threat to *the existence of freedom*. Accordingly, formal right is annulled by a higher right, the right of necessity. This right proceeds from acute states of emergency such as being in danger of starving. The petty theft of food, for instance, is a right, if it helps the person to avoid starvation. Both the person and the right "must have life" (*Werke* 7: 241). The right of necessity is thus a basic right, a *human right* in the universal sense of a guarantee of *personhood*, a right to physical integrity, nourishment, protection from illness and from the destruction of the means of one's livelihood.[9] In the German constitution, this

---

9 A debtor has a right to keep what he needs for nourishment and clothing and the means to guarantee a continued existence (for instance, the tools of a craftsperson or farmer).

is enshrined as follows: "Every person shall have the right to life and physical integrity".[10] Abstract liberalism, by contrast, is based on the rigorism and fundamentalism of formal right, especially property right, the limits of which are ignored – abstract liberalism considers a starving person stealing bread to be committing a theft and therefore an injustice.[11]

3.4 Moral Resistance

Both the *moral right of resistance* and the *white lie* (*Not-Lüge*), the right to provide false information, are based on the violation of a subject's right by a community or state, and thus on a state of emergency. The latter legitimates a form of *moral self-defence* that expresses itself by rejecting and 'deceiving' the existing order. In this vein, moral self-defence points to the critical dimension of morality. In line with Hegel, we could speak of a right of morality and conscience, of a '*Socrates principle*' on the one hand, and of the *white lie* on the other. Socrates symbolizes moral resistance, since he expresses a principle that undermines the existing order. He demands that the existing order be legitimized by means of one's own subjectivity, through its impartial examination from the standpoint of a singular self or I. With reference to *The Philosophy of Right* §138, we can discern the validity of *moral resistance* also with regard to the state. There it is discussed in terms of a sublation of the Socrates principle: decisions to act in the modern world are based on the 'depths of self-consciousness', on the 'I want' (*Ich will*). The reasons for these actions are not to be found in oracles or mantic authorities, but rather *within* the human being as such. The forms of *the absolute legitimacy of self-consciousness* and of *free thinking* provide us with a "sufficient condition to appoint the subject the guardian of the constitution, and to provide it with a right to resist, especially since Hegel knows very well that the state is in need of such a guardian" (Petersen 1996: 478).

The need for moral justification arises when an individual, a particular citizen, demands that the existing order be justified. If such a justification cannot be provided, the individual begins to doubt the basic principles of the existing

---

This right holds even if it violates the property right of the creditor – *beneficium competentiae*. As soon as the person who steals food out of necessity or the debtor have financial means at their disposal again, property rights come back into force. Thus, the right of necessity does not destroy the formal right to property but rather temporarily suspends it for the duration of a state of exception.

10 See German Basic Law (Grundgesetz), Article 2 (2).
11 An abstract, 'procedural' liberalism constructs an insurmountable opposition between the rights of an individual and the rights of the collective.

state or even to reject them entirely. Accordingly, the individual orients her actions not only on the basis of positive law and the existing order, but also reverses this order on the basis of her inner authority, which is now based on comprehending thought. This is also the basis for world-historical 'reversals', for historical revolutions, which are only valid as such if they present an action after a preceding injustice, i.e. in the sense of a 'second action' of *historical self-defence* – Hegel's paradigm was the French Revolution. Furthermore, the moral subject has the right, in a certain context of injustice, to supply false information, for example in a dictatorship. It is not accurate to describe these acts as lies, but rather as upright actions. One particularly interesting case of a white lie, of inversion and moral resistance may be found in a novel by Jurek Becker, where the character of Jakob resists the Nazi dictatorship by providing false information.[12]

3.5   *Resistance to Poverty*

A state of extreme poverty legitimates a right to resist in the sense of a restoration of right, that is: the right to participate equally in civil society. As mentioned, the burgeoning gulf between great wealth and severe poverty gives rise to the *emergency right of the poor and discriminated to resist and rebel*. However, the aim of this right is to *re-establish the basic constitution of civil society* rather than destroy it. Therefore, at each of the three levels of the development of the concept of right and freedom, this right of resistance must be defined against possible violations of this right. The right of avoiding abject poverty within civil society is based on a) the right to the integrity of the person that is laid down in the category of abstract right, and the justification of self-defence, and b) the principles of moral resistance and the right of necessity. Both *self-defence* and *moral resistance*, as well as the right of necessity and the right to resist poverty, are always a *re-action*, a 'second' action, the reaction to an existing injustice in a state of exception.

It should be recalled that here we are talking about resistance to blatant offences against the law, about the *reclaiming* of rights. With respect to civil society, this in no way concerns the right to found *another* society.[13] If the constitutional principles of civil society are being violated on a massive scale, or do not exist – i.e. the right to equal participation in civil society – there arises the right to the *restoration or reclamation of these founding principles*.

---

12   See Becker 1969. For a detailed discussion of inversion in the context of dictatorship, see Vieweg, 2012a: 183–215.

13   Of course, this does not involve formal-abstract right, nor the claiming of this right, but the right to well-being in civil society, which can only be achieved politically.

For Hegel, there is not in any sense a right to overthrow, a right to abolish these foundations, because these are the very *conditions that make freedom possible*.

3.6 Political Resistance

With regard to the theme of *political resistance,* Hegel also consistently relies on the principle of the *legitimacy of a second coercion,* although this principle is not made explicitly clear – perhaps a result of Hegel's political caution and the camouflaging of his position because of censorship.[14] In any case, the thesis that Hegel does not provide for rights of defence and resistance requires critical examination (Siep 2010: 112). In fact, Hegel deals with the *political state of exception* and the *political right to resistance* only briefly and indirectly in two ways: firstly, in the context of the 'guarantees' of a state constitution based on freedom, which can be ensured through intelligent institutions and free citizens; secondly, with respect to the 'disturbance of the peace' in relation to the discrepancy that may arise between the self-conscious thinking of citizens and the existing institutions, which may fail to live up to the level of consciousness of the citizens (Hegel 1983b: 230). This issue is further discussed with respect to forms of decay in the state, in connection with the debates about tyrannicide,[15] and most likely also in response to the positions of Locke and Hume. But it remains decisive that here the *legitimacy of the inversion of injustice to justice,* the *justification of second coercion,* and the right to political resistance in any form, must be conceived on the foundation of the basic logic of Hegel's thought. In this sense, Hegel's view of freedom is fundamentally directed against repression, arbitrary rule and tyranny.[16] There is no right of resistance that results in the *dissolution* of the modern structure of right as it is conceived in the *Philosophy of Right,* because that would be an insurrection against reason and freedom, and therefore not a *legitimate* resistance but a rebellion oriented in a backwards direction, a form of restoration, which however is always possible.[17]

---

14 Petersen (1996: 475) argues that the right to resistance "remains implicit" in Hegel.
15 "The right to resist originates in the right to resist a tyrant, an illegitimate ruler" (Siep 2010: 112).
16 Hume (1960: 563) emphasizes that "when there is enormous tyranny and oppression it is lawful to take arms even against the supreme power: government is merely something that people invented for mutual advantage and security, so when it stops having that tendency there is no longer any natural or moral obligation to obey it". This right must be ascribed to the citizens of Cambodia under Pol Pot, or to the citizens of Chile under Pinochet, indeed to all citizens living under dictatorships and other inhumane regimes.
17 The dictatorships of the twentieth century represent restorative, pre-modern forms of this kind.

But, as already remarked, there also exists a *right to resistance against the violations of the principle of modern freedom*, of the individual freedom of individuals in all their dimensions, a right to correct the shortcomings of modern society, a *right to indignation at regressions from the modern principle of right*; i.e. the right to revolt against recently established totalitarian systems, against ochlocratic and oligarchic forms, etc. Such a right does not necessarily have to be explicitly expressed; it follows necessarily from Hegel's understanding of right and freedom. In this way Hegel can be read as a resolute anti-restorative thinker. Against all attempts to retreat from the principle of freedom there is a right to resistance and revolt, both in the sphere of civil society and of the state. These protests are to be seen as models of legally permitted action, of *social and political self-defence*. The right to resistance and revolt in order to secure and restore the foundations of civil society and liberty is predominantly a *political right*, because the possibilities within civil society remain limited. Because of this, it is situated in the sphere of the state, but should nevertheless always be considered as a form of right (in the Hegelian sense). As with the right of necessity (e.g. the petty theft of food), one should definitely take into account that deciding whether or not there is an emergency, or a state of exception (say, acute starvation), remains very difficult to determine in the political sphere, and a thorough assessment is always necessary. The main conditions for the legitimacy of resistance and rebellion would be, firstly, the blatant and permanent violation of the laws that protect basic rights ("if a long train of actions show the councils all tending that way", as Locke (2003: 193) puts it); secondly, the assessment of the legitimacy of the indignation of the persons resisting (the 'Socrates principle'); and thirdly, the existence of a situation that poses a general threat to all citizens (Locke 2007: 372). These conditions hold especially also for the murder of a tyrant, which can often have other negative consequences.[18]

In addition, in Hegel's account the state and the governed are protected from the abuse of power by the government and state officials through an 'internal protection' (collegiate structures), a protection from 'the very top' (the final decision maker), and also a protection 'from below' against the subjective arbitrariness of the ruling powers, and therefore through special rights of

---

18   The members of the resistance group of '20 July' discussed this set of problems at length. I am grateful to Dieter Henrich for drawing my attention to them. Hume already pleads for careful assessment of the advantages and disadvantages of the practical application of resistance. Although "the general principle" of the right to resistance is "authorized", "neither laws nor even philosophy can establish any particular rules that would tell us when resistance is lawful" (Hume 1960: 563).

resistance against government institutions (although these rights are mainly focused on collectives such as corporations, associations and communities). The corrective function of the legislative power is largely absent here. The *Philosophy of Right* also discusses vertical structures of authority, in the sense of a form of 'top down' and 'bottom up' organization. Hegel considers the 'actual strength' of states to consist in well-organized professional bodies, communities and cities. Corporate structures are capable of connecting the general interest closely with the particular interest, of protecting the citizens against unlawful infringements and enabling resistance (*Werke* 7: 460).

According to Hume, there is a legitimate political right of resistance in situations of 'exception', in states of emergency: "There will be no crime or injustice in our resisting the more violent effects of supreme power" (Hume 1960: 552). In a state of emergency, for example in case of tyranny or dictatorship, breaking the law of the state can be seen as a right, as a defence against 'the enemies of public well-being.' This resistance cannot be condemned: it is certain, says Hume, "that in all our notions of morals we never entertain such an absurdity as that of passive obedience, but make allowances for resistance in the more flagrant instances of tyranny and oppression". This is because people owe "obedience to government merely on account of the public interest" (Hume 1960: 552–3) and when government ceases to serve the public interest it loses its legitimacy. The citizens not only have the right to free themselves from tyranny, but also to prevent it (Locke 2003: 197). With this, Hegel can concur: someone who is politically oppressed is robbed of her political rights, and she is allowed to rectify this robbery, or better, this injustice, to defend herself and to reclaim her rights in the sense of a second coercion. In as far as she falls back into the state of a disenfranchised subject, i.e. a 'slave' (cf. Locke 2003: 197), she has the right to break free of her bonds and reclaim her rights as a *citizen*. For Hegel, the enslavement and servitude of the human being count as 'the absolute crime', because the personality of the slave or servant is negated in all its manifestations (Hegel 1983b: 51). Resistance is the right of inversion against the unlawful inversion.

The political right of resistance is based on the pillars of the right of necessity of the previous steps; it entails different forms, and culminates in the *right to rebellion*.[19] Throughout his life, Hegel saw the French Revolution as a

---

19   Losurdo maintains that Hegel "decisively rejects the right of resistance" (2000: 113–22. esp. 119). On the other hand, Losurdo agrees with Hegel's reflections on the right of necessity. The thesis formulated by Siep concerning the absence of rights of defence and resistance in Hegel, of insufficient protection for basic rights, appears unjustified because through popular assemblies, citizens "are themselves enabled to watch over the implementation and protection of their freedom" (Lübbe-Wolff 1986: 421–46). With regard to

legitimate form of resistance against the old structure of injustice: "The development of Spirit unaccompanied by a corresponding development of institutions, so that a contradiction arises between the two, is the source not only of discontent but also of revolutions" (Hegel 1983b: 219). In the state of society, deprivation immediately takes the shape of injustice (*Werke* 7: 390), which gives rise to the right to *moral self-defence*; the latter exceeds the sphere of civil society and also concerns the political sphere. Insofar as the substantial foundations of the liberal constitution of the state are attacked or even destroyed, the individual citizens and the people in a society may take up their right to political resistance – always with the goal of restoring a rational constitution. On this point, the preamble to the American Declaration of Independence stipulates: "That whenever any Form of Government becomes destructive of these ends, it is the Right of the People to alter or to abolish it, and to institute new Government". In accordance with the correlation of rights and duties, which Hegel always emphasizes, it is to be further noted that it is not only one's right, but also one's duty to remove an unjust government. Likewise, since 1968, in addition to the highly problematic emergency regulations (*Notstandsverordnungen*), the German constitution includes the juridical codification of the right to rebellion: "Against all those who seek to abolish this order, all Germans have the right of resistance, when no other forms of redress are available".[20]

This duality entails that the political emergency, the state of exception, can be caused both by political institutions as well as by the citizens, in which case each side can legitimately make use of forcible, 'tyrannical' means with regard to the other side. In the former situation this may take the form of, for example, resistance of the citizens to the unreasonable regime by the forceful occupation of government buildings, police stations or secret service centres, politically motivated nationwide strikes, declarations concerning the overthrow of the old government and the proclamation of a new order; in the latter case, state authorities may offer resistance when the "existence of the whole is compromised" (Hegel 1968 Bd. 8: 237), for example in case of the unlawful intimidation of the reasonable order 'from below'. In this sense, a democratically legitimate state power would have had the right to prevent, from above and with forcible means, the takeover by the National

---

resisting poverty, Henrich writes: "There is no other place in Hegel's work where he does not just understand revolution as a historical fact and necessity, but rather derives and explains a right to revolution on the basis of a systematic analysis of an institution that existed also in his own time" (see Hegel 1983a: 20).

20   Grundegesetz, Art. 20 (4).

Socialists – clearly representatives of dictatorship and despotism – with the aim of avoiding tyranny.

For Hegel, knowledge of the truly universal, that is, an assessment of the existing political order *supported by knowledge*, remains crucial. The criteria for such an objective evaluation are the fundamental elements of freedom and the forms in which freedom is realized, i.e. the law of reason and the constitution based on freedom, as they are developed in the *Philosophy of Right*. Without restriction, despotism is denounced as a state of lawlessness, as an *inner state of emergency* of the state, against which political self-defence must be admissible. In such a case, citizens do not merely request special rights, but rather demand their right as the right of the *actual sovereign*. In this sense there exists a right to revolution, against the *inversions of modern statehood*. The demands of those who resist politically are characterized by the slogan 'Wir sind das Volk' ('We are the People'), which expresses the essence of the German revolution of 1989, which was initiated and successfully realized by East German citizens. It was the result of peaceful resistance by citizens under favourable historical circumstances.[21]

The inversive right of resistance thus includes the determination of a state of need or emergency at levels of increasing generality, and of a justified struggle against need and oppression: the various stages of self-defence, that of second coercion and that of the right to resistance. The idea of a second coercion has to be conceived at all levels in the development of the concept of freedom and right, up to the sphere of the state (including in international law and world history). This account clearly shows that the accusations of paternalism, statism, excessive institutionalism, and the essentialization or sacralization of the state levelled against Hegel's theory[22] are exaggerated and do not get at the core of his idea of the state.

---

[21] One of the most important protagonists of this insurrection, Matthias Platzeck, rejects the trivializing talk of 1989 as a 'turn *(Wende)*' and rightly argues for the designation 'peaceful revolution' as one of the most "successful contributions to European history of the twentieth century". For a vivid presentation of the revolutionary process and its analysis, see Platzeck 2009.

[22] Ludwig Siep bases the thesis of a 'sacralized' and 'inflated' concept of the state in Hegel on the limited power of the legislature, the conception of a hereditary monarchy, the absence of a right of resistance and the idea of offensive war. See Siep 2010: 112. This criticism of Hegel appears to be untenable, as soon as one is prepared, following the logic of Hegel's thought, to put certain passages in the *Philosophy of Right* into context, and to reinterpret them on the basis of the logical course of his thought, taking into account that a number of passages in the chapter on the state were written under the influence of the censor.

4 Conclusion: State of Exception and Second Coercion

Of course, political states of emergency are essentially based on the situation in civil society (the 'system of need' and 'the understanding'), a system of mutual dependence, of ethical life "lost in its extremes". The self-inflicted and burgeoning gap between rich and poor threatens the foundations of civil society and signals an excess, it points to its own sublation. Civil society is pushed to go beyond itself, *not towards another order*, but towards its own ground, which is a rational form of society based on conceptual thinking, that is, towards a state of freedom.

Civil society does not have its *own* sufficient means of countering these existential threats. As a result, it is a breeding ground for various forms of despotism and fundamentalism, forms built on an attitude of injustice flowing from a lack of education or half-education that can threaten freedom. The most dangerous of these *unfree* forms is that of tyranny, because here the rights of citizens are in no way sufficiently protected, but rather existentially threatened (*Werke* 4: 248–9). In this context, Hegel's repeated and constant emphasis on *the right to education* becomes especially illuminating: no modern order, no democracy, can thrive without educated citizens – the ignorant is unfree. Developing the universality of thought undoubtedly supplies a vital instrument against inhumanity. In unjust societies, *spiritual and intellectual impoverishment* always reigns supreme; their crimes are based on fundamental violations of the *concept* of right. Philosophy has the responsibility to bring these violations to light; this is *philosophy's right to intellectual self-defence and resistance*. The knowledge and education of citizens are the only sustainable way of guaranteeing resistance against all forms of inhumanity.

From a Hegelian perspective, the codification of a legal state of exception (constitutionally defined emergency powers, emergency legislation) would be the dissolution of the legal order, the aporia of positive emergency law. Following Carl Schmitt, Agamben once again raises the question of how such a suspension of the constitution may still be contained in the legal system, if the defining characteristic of the state of exception is the (total or partial) suspension of the legal order (Agamben 2005). The essence of emergency law is to stand outside the legal system and yet belong to it, Schmitt claims. The dilemma lies in the fact that any state of emergency declared to save the democratic state could – with equal probability – be misused for its destruction, because chartered rights of freedom are suspended and the separation of powers (and thus the rational structure of the state) is partially dissolved. The supposed rescuing of freedom would then be 'reversed', it would be turned into its opposite (into partial dictatorial measures and powers) and would thereby ultimately threaten or even destroy the state as an organism of freedom. The emergency laws in Germany entail the aporia that fundamental rights may be restricted, but constitutional amendments are prohibited. Accordingly, only *resistance by the citizens* (whether it is codified or not) can prevent a coup. The citizens of the state in question then place themselves outside of its positive lawful order, but have recourse to the law of reason. Under a dictatorship carrying out mass murder, terror and war, it is reasonable to form resistance groups, to provide citizens with information, to sabotage the economy, desert from the security forces, or in the last resort, to employ violence in order to assassinate the tyrant.

Only *educated citizens* can be the force to guarantee a free constitution – *education, in an absolute sense, is liberation.* This view of freedom and emancipation understands education as the "immanent aspect of the Absolute" and proves its "*infinite value*" (*Werke* 7: 345). The legitimacy of the state and of political resistance has its source in the *law of reason*. Existing positive law must be measured by the criteria of a theoretical constitution of freedom; ultimately, the *nervus probandi* of a free state can only be *conceptual thought*.

PART 3

Hegel on Art and Religion

∴

CHAPTER 12

Hegel's Conception of the Imagination

Hegel's praise of a concept that is more than 2000 years old and his abiding insistence on the concept, on the *logos* of knowledge, may appear oddly anachronistic in light of current theories of knowledge.* Nevertheless, 200 years after Hegel I am going to recommend precisely such an apparent anachronism and argue for the enduring and decisive value of Hegel's concept of the imagination for current philosophical reflection on knowledge. What might at first look like a dusty attic of intellectual history will soon reveal rich and unfamiliar treasures and provide the cornerstone for a modern philosophy of knowledge and aesthetics. Hegel's theory of the imagination is an Ariadne's Thread leading out of the labyrinth of conflicting opinions in today's philosophy of mind. Here, however, I will only be able to point out a few of the basic outlines of Hegel's thinking.

1 Imagination and Mind

The fact that Hegel situates his conception of the imagination within the Philosophy of Mind in the *Encyclopaedia* gives it a serious advantage. This relocating into the system-architectonic can only be treated cursorily. For textual support to the discussion that follows, a reader should turn to the section titled *Philosophical Psychology* in Hegel's *Encyclopaedia of Philosophical Science*. The key points are as follows:

a) The imagination is held to be a special formation or developmental phase of Geist. The German term *Geist* is a philosophical, metaphysical principle that is only inadequately translated by the English words "spirit" or "mind", words which we must nevertheless use. To grasp what spirit (*Geist*) means, one must understand it as the stages of a self-production. This self-generation means self-determination or autonomy, the self-determination of spirit as self-liberation. The formal essence of spirit consists in freedom and can be grasped as a process of "freeing itself to itself", as realization of the concept of its freedom. In this way, spirit makes itself free from everything that does not correspond to its

---

* This chapter is based on a previous publication of the same name in "Inventions of the Imagination", edited by Richard T. Gray, Nicholas Halmi, Gary Handwerk, Michael Rosenthal and Klaus Vieweg, University of Washington Press 2011.

concept, *free from every form that is not adequate to it*. To be free does not mean to exist alongside an other, but to come to itself.

b) This self-relation as active self-production is conceived as a logically based step-by-step movement on a path of spirit's activity. From the lower, abstract determinations, the higher, concrete determinations are deductively generated according to the necessity of thought. In this way the previous determinations then appear as moments in the higher stages and there attain their partial validity. This logical process of grounding the progress in a return to the foundation avoids, for example, the common but mistaken view of the activity of knowing as mere collection, as mere aggregation of capacities that is to be found, analysed, and then brought into interconnection (cf. Düsing 1991: 298–307). In clear contrast to an empirical-psychological process, Hegel conceives this step-by-step process as the *self-development of spirit*. From the very beginning this movement is present as a thought that attains its justification along the logical path itself. The path and manner of ascent to determined knowledge "is itself rational and involves a determined, necessary transition by the concept from one determination of intelligible activities into another determination" (*Werke* 10: 240). In this way, Hegel can determine the contours of a *logic of knowledge*, of an epistemology in the strict sense, in clear distinction to a merely analytic and synthetic account of mental capacities.

c) The faculty of imagination (*Einbildungskraft*) belongs to the second level of theoretical spirit, a level Hegel gives the term representation (*Vorstellung*). A prominent place in his system belongs to theoretical spirit or intellect. Within the sphere of subjective spirit, there occurs the change from phenomenology, from the standpoint of consciousness, to the standpoint of intellect. In this way, we stand at the formal beginning of philosophizing – science must "presuppose the liberation from the opposition of consciousness" (*Werke* 5: 45). The result of phenomenology was shown to be the one-sidedness of the *paradigm of consciousness* and the dualism of consciousness and object, of mind and world, of subject and object. Their principle identity was demonstrated in the sense that we are not concerned with external relations but rather with an internal relation, with intellect as a *self-relation*, as a *self-determining universal*. Everything about which we want to obtain knowledge, all that we want to know, must therefore be taken as a *self-forming of intellect*; this is a core moment of Hegel's *monistic idealism*. This being-one implies, in Hegel's words, the identity between the nature posited by the mind as its world and the presupposing of the world as independent nature, between the *posited* and the *pre-supposed* world. It has to do with the identity of the determinations as inherent – existing in nature itself and existing as constituted by spirit. Objectivity shows itself to be subjective and subjectivity shows itself to be objective.

The path of knowledge as a logical transition, in stages, of theoretical spirit or intellect, of subjective-intelligible inwardness, of abstract self-determination and its expression in the language of knowledge, passes through the chief stations of *intuition, representation,* and *thought* – whereby imagination occupies the middle, the seam between *aisthēsis* and *noēsis* (see Fulda 1991: 326). We are dealing with the path from mere certainty to true justified knowledge. From the form of the external-singular, of common subjective universality, the content – rational in itself – is raised to the form of true identity of singularity and universality, to determined knowledge. This intellectualizing of knowledge shows the necessity of the translation of the true content from a *still insufficient form inadequate to spirit* into the form of the concept. The stage of representation or the faculty of imagination is presented as an indispensable transition or middle in the self-constitution of finite subjectivity (Düsing 1991: 311–312).

2   From Intuition to Representation

For these initial stages of the self-determination of intellect, the chief characteristics of *intuition* must first be briefly outlined. This is the absolutely necessary presupposition for understanding the faculty of imagination, and it has serious philosophical implications. On the basis of the paradigm of consciousness that has been overcome, intellect doesn't relate to its content as to an object, but rather relates *exclusively* to its own determinations. The intellect's separation of its determinations of the subjective and the objective is shown to be merely apparent.

The initial form of this logical structure is found in intuition, in which a given inner or outer sensation (or affection) emerges as an identity of the subjective and the objective. A singular, particular content belonging to an object appears at the same time as posited by a singular, isolated subjectivity. A content ostensibly merely found or given to the subject in a sensation of something outside, something received via impressions or as the influence of external things, proves to be identical with what is posited subjectively. The *impression of what is objective* reveals itself to be the *expression of what is subjective* – the *finding* turns out to be a *positing*. The 'Myth of the Given' remains a semblance that as such is to be exposed and refuted, which also holds for the opposing 'Myth of Construction'. In Hegel's view, intuition constitutes the immediate, most present form in which subjectivity relates to its determinations as to a supposedly given, encountered content. Intuition is the immediate presence, the "presentation" of the individual I, here and now, it is the identity of receptivity and activity (*Werke* 19: 205). We are not concerned with a panoply of duplicated intuitions but rather with the immediate unity of *being that already exists and being that is created* (*Werke* 3: 231–232). The assertions "What I see is blue" and "There is a blue object" are identical; in intuition the effect of both propositions is posited as one.

The one that sees and the one seen, hearing and sounding, mind and world, are taken as identical. In this is revealed the simple mental structure of intuition, its "logos-authorship" (Welsch 1987: 140–152). Pure intuition (as well as pure representation) is an appearance that proves itself to be such; intuition and the faculty of imagination are contaminated by thought from the very beginning. Intuition is sensual *and* intellectual, natural *and* rational at the same time. Producing and being produced come together in a unity.[1] Hegel's insight here finds resonance in the words of that master of seeing and intuition Paul Cezanne, who in a conversation with Joachim Gasquet suggests that the nature that is seen, nature there outside, and the nature that is sensed, nature here inside, are parallel texts that penetrate each other (cited in Busch 2003: 324).

As the abstract orientation towards something as identical, the attention required for sensation is related to a supposedly objective and independent being (to which attention is paid), but this is itself an abstract other-being. There is no other content than that of the intuited object, where intellect finds itself *apparently* determined from outside. In this way an initial knowledge of the thing is achieved. A complete active knowledge, however, has not yet been achieved, only a 'first sight' of the object, not yet an 'in-sight' (*Ein-Sicht*). The dimension of finding, of the given, entails that the subject treats as cause of an affection something existing outside of themselves. So intuition necessarily projects this content into space and time (*Werke* 8: 83) and intuits it as particular content in these forms: this spatio-temporality is the first abstract externalization. Intellect requires a formal milieu in which something is discretely and continuously contrasted with something else. These are indispensable coordinates for the epistemic determination of the contents of feeling.[2]

Schelling understands the present as something constantly driven back to a moment, to a point of time to which in reality we cannot return: "In order to be able to intuit the object in general as object, the I must posit a past moment as the ground of the present. The past thus originates ever anew only through the action of intellect, and the past is only necessary to the extent that this going back of the I is necessary" (Schelling 1985: 554). Here time and movement are given fundamental importance, for it is the intuition of an event that is being

---

[1] Cf. Schelling 1985: 528: "The *I* is in one and the same action formally free and formally compelled or passive".

[2] Rometsch 2006: 173. I hereby thank Mr Rometsch for letting me study his dissertation.

discussed. Space and time are, for Hegel, subjective as well as objective forms, he distinguishes his argument both from a one-sidedly objective view – space and time as forms of natural existence – as well as from the Kantian position – time and space as merely subjective forms of intuition. Reason thus has not only a regulative relation to knowledge, but also a constitutive one.

Attention requires a pure immersion in the object, the disregard of all other things and indeed of oneself. This embarking from the I towards the thing is indispensable for knowledge. It is a question of becoming wholly *absorbed* in the thing. By means of a sceptical suspension of our uniqueness and our vanity, we let the thing hold sway in us. Yet, at the same time, contra any Pyrrhonian-Buddhist quietude or total passivity, contra any total submission of self to the object, there remains the self-validation of subjectivity. The content of the object is also *mine*. Yet it is *not merely mine*, for subjectivity has become objective, just as objectivity has been made subjective. The form of internality is transformed into the form of externality and vice versa. In this inversion, in this oscillation, intellect has reached the first level of its self-determination: formal self-determinateness. This simple particularity implies a common subjective universality (Schelling 1985: 173ff), a sort of commonality of intuiting, and the finitude of intuition.

With the movement inwards, with 'remembering' (*Er-Innerung*), intuition becomes immediately sublated into representation – it is preserved, negated, and brought to a higher level – whereby its spatio-temporal determinateness is transformed. This border crossing is sketched by Hegel as follows: "The path of intellect in representations is to render immediacy inward, to intuitively posit itself in itself, and at the same time to sublate the subjectivity of inwardness and inwardly to divest itself of it; so as to be in itself in an externality of its own" (*Werke* 10: 257).

3 Representation

3.1 *Recollection*

In the first step – the immediacy of intuition – Being is changed, insofar as it is something finite, into *something past*. But at the same time the intellect preserves the intuition as *inner, unconscious presence*. "The intellect, as it at first recollects the intuition, posits the *content of the feeling* in its internality, in its *own space* and its *own time*" (*Werke* 10: 258). Hegel refers to this content as an 'image' or 'picture' (*Bild*) that is freed from its first immediacy, its abstract singularity, and taken up in the universality of the intellectual I. Speaking in a Kantian way, what is at issue is the capacity to represent an object without its presence in intuition. This unique space-time posited by intellect is valid as a universal spatio-temporality in which the content first gains permanence in distinction to past intuition (*Werke* 10: 259). The space and time of intuition, on the other hand, are particularities, bound to the immediate present of the object. This *external* space-time is resolved at the price of the original determinateness of the content which can experience arbitrary and contingent changes in the shape of my image.

At this level – recollection as *the first way of representing* – intellect appears as the unconscious, timeless place in which images are preserved. Indeed, in a play on Aristotle's ideas, Hegel uses the metaphor, so treasured by Derrida, of a "nocturnal, dark shaft (*nächtlichen, dunklen Schacht*)" in which a world of infinite images is stored (*Werke* 10: 260). Without being in consciousness, they sleep and are the inactive soul. A countless number of images and representations slumber in this well of internality, a powerful reservoir of images hidden by nocturnal darkness, a dark picture gallery of immeasurable expanse, comparable to the Parisian Louvre at night. These images are indeed the 'property' of the intellect, as Hegel puts it. They bear the legal title of inalienable opinions, but they are *not yet in my actual possession*. What is still lacking is the capacity to call up the sleeping images at will. There is a lack of will, lack of free control over the contents of this treasure chamber. All determinations exist in seed, but in an unconscious, dark spring, as generally existing but not yet posited as discrete (*Werke* 10: 260).[3] What is purely formless, chaotic, and indifferent, this shoreless ocean – *the dark side of intellect* – is a new form of universality. It is like a locked chest which I am certain contains treasure but I cannot work out which jewels are preserved there. In fact the images no longer exist, they are no longer there in consciousness but in the past. They exist as 'unconscious', since it is only with the distinction, with the positing of difference in the light of the present, that knowing can proceed.

Thus we reach the seam between remembrance and the faculty of imagination, the transition to the second stage of representation, to inner presencing, inner representation, by a positing of the inner presence of the image, the overcoming of the merely existent, the past. The inner is placed, pre-sented, before the intellect, thrust before the inner eye. The waking of the sleeping picture, intellect awakening to itself, enables the relating of the picture to an

---

3 Elsewhere, Hegel speaks of the I as a receptacle, a container and a refuge for everything and anything. Every human being is a whole world of ideas buried in the night of the ego" (*Werke* 8: 83). The ego is the universal, in which everything particular is abstracted, but in which everything is at the same time veiled, the abstract universal and the universality, which contains everything in itself.

intuition of similar content. The initial creations of the faculty of imagination also appear as a world of spatio-temporally unformed shapes, shapes without mass, positings by which one can be thoroughly displaced. In principle there follows a subsuming, for example, the sensation "blue" or "sorrow" is subsumed under a universal "the blue", "sorrow as such". Kant spoke of the active capacity of the synthesis of the manifold – "the faculty of imagination should bring the manifold of intuition into one image; so previously it must record the impressions in their activity, i.e. apprehend them" (Kant 1968 Bd. 3: 89). On the basis of the apprehension, the subsumption of the multiplicity under the unity of representation, intellect can *take internal possession of its property*, the images, externalize them, and *give them (internally) the seal of the external*. Intellect is able to place what is unique to it in an internal opposition to itself and thus to possess its existence (*Dasein*), to be by itself – an internal presencing (*Vergegenwärtigung*) as free subjectivity of internality.

Already with this subsuming or reflecting as a power of the universal, representation proves itself to be the middle between the immediate finding of oneself determined and thinking as intellect in its perfect freedom. The idea of a pure imagination without thought that is often hypostasized, especially by artists, is a deception. Any representation is essentially infected and determined by thought. It positions itself in the intermundane world of intuition and thinking as their hinge, as the universalization of the sensual, i.e., the particular, and the sensualisation, the particularization of the universal, the universality of intuition and the making-intuitive of the universal. In this process a special power resides in the deficiency of representing.

Following this long but necessary preamble, I come directly to our main theme, the faculty of imagination as the *determining of images*, the actual transition from finding to inventing, from finding to active finding. Here lie the cornerstones of Hegel's theory of symbolic forms, his logic of signs, and with which, according to Derrida, he became the founder of modern semiotics.

3.2   *Imagination*
3.2.1   First Stage: Reproductive Imagination
Images are (as already suggested) internally re-presented. Intellect places these before itself in a new space-time in which the original spatio-temporal concretion is dissolved. On the basis of this abstraction and the coming-to-be of universal representations, there occurs a contingent and arbitrary reproduction of the content. This supposed occurrence in succession, the attraction between similar images, remains the deed of intellect itself, which subordinates individual intuitions under the internally constituted picture and thus gives itself universality, presenting the universal as something common, re-presenting it

(*Werke* 10: 266). Intellect raises either a particular side of a thing into the status of the universal, or brings fixed form to a concrete universal.

3.2.2   Second Stage: Productive, Associative Imagination – Fantasy

With the activity of associating images, the relating of images to one another, the intellect climbs to the next step, that of fantasy. This involves the activity of free combining or synthesizing of images and representations, the inventive inner presentation of created representations, a freely willed production of new images. This creative imagination undertakes the uncreative sensualisation, the making of the content into an intuition without a concrete example. In consequence of the transition from an objective connection to an innovative subjective bond, internal-imaginative existence is conferred to a self-constituting content originating from the intellect itself, whereby the self-intuition of the intellect is perfected – the power of forming its own images. Taken in anticipation, the intellect emerges as a singular concrete subjectivity determined in itself with its own content, and it demonstrates here the already present universality of thinking, whose justification has been in play from the very beginning. The representations are anticipations of a concept yet to be constructed. The intellect demonstrates its sovereignty over the stock of images and representations belonging to it, *the imagination as a 'gentle force' over the self's images* (cf. Hume 1960: 10).

In fantasy we now have a new, second present, consciously posited in arbitrary freedom by the intellect, a higher identity of universal and individual. What is found and what belongs to the intellect are completely posited in a unity, with imagination being the capacity of fantasizing and the images of fantasy presenting the unification of what is inner or mental and what is intuitive. In this the intellect proves its power over images, seeking through them to give itself validity and objectivity, to manifest and preserve itself in its own creations. Hegel sees the identity of singularity and universality at this higher stage as consisting in the intellect, now constituted as a singularity in the form of a concrete subjectivity in which the self-relation – the basic structure of the mind – is determined as being and as universality by means of the intuition of the universal and the universalization of the intuition (*Werke* 10: 268).

The intellect creates novel inner worlds, a cosmos of the coming-to-be and passing away of possibilities, numerous inner word-images. It appears as unbridled image-giving power, as the untiring and active inner artist, as free play with possibilities. There is nothing more worthy of wonder than the openness with which the imagination assembles its representations: it "runs from one end of the universe to the other in collecting those ideas, which belong to any subject" (Hume 1960: 24). Kant sees here the disclosure of an "illimitable field of kindred representations" in which the content, a determined concept, could "be aesthetically extended in an infinite way" (Kant 1968 Bd. 5: 315). Thus the creative imagination is able to promulgate endlessly in its own products. According to Hegel, this play of fantasy constitutes the universal foundation of art, its formal aspect, presenting the true universal in the form of the singular image (*Werke* 10: 267).

But the play of fantasy has a double aspect: being restless and without rules, the form of representation implies an indifferent external arrangement of the manifold images with their many meanings. The attributes of 'creative', 'active', 'restless' always remain ambivalent and the opposite attributes of 'non-creative', 'tranquil', 'passive' and 'letting-be', are not to be denigrated, for they are the very foundation of the faculty of imagination. Fantasy is able to create the human und the inhuman, to build heaven and hell, and thus to demonstrate its power as well as its deficiency. It can darken the present with shadows cast back from the past and others from the future moved closer (Schelling). This play – similar to the understanding – is capable of showing the monstrous potential of all art. According to Hegel, in this synthesis of the faculty of imagination we are only concerned with formal reason, for it presents neither the highest capacity of free being nor a completely successful making-present.[4] The content as such is indifferent to fantasy, for thought has not yet attained the form appropriate to the content. It is *only in thought*, which conceptualizes, tests, and verifies, that universality and individuality are completely identical and content and conceptual form coincide.

The notion of *phainesthai* that is the root of 'fantasy' originally meant *appearing*. We thereby unintentionally fall into the domain of the Pyrrhonian sceptics, the genuine advocates of appearing. Pyrrhonism's criterion is what appears, the *phaenomenon*, which we are to understand as the image, *phantasia*, and the subjective aspect of my imagining, that is, appearing as subjectively holding something to be true. As core positions of sceptical philosophy, negativity, subjectivity, relativity, and *ataraxia* each operate with the language of appearance. Fantasy has the function of a necessary transition point on the path to knowing and, like scepticism, bears a Janus face: one free and the other unfree, one steadfast and the other negative, one tranquil and the other restless, one happy and the other unhappy, for the countenance of imagination is an amalgam of the phenomenal and the logical, of image and concept (see Vieweg 2007).

---

4   According to Hegel, Christianity's reconciliation of God and man happens in the past, while the reconciliation of man is futural. Cf. Vieweg 2008.

In aesthetic terms, the art that has its formal source in fantasy is considered to be *free play with appearance* or a world of appearance. Such activity is described by Schiller as an *idealization*. According to Humboldt, as a *facultas fingendi*, art creates a non-reality, a picture and appearance that surpasses all reality. Imagination or fantasy can thus also be understood as *ideation*. In its images, in its thoroughly ambivalent imaginings, fantasy is freer than nature. The sphere of the external and internal empirical world, the lights of the world and the firing of the neurons, are not a world of true reality, but rather, in the yet stronger sense used in art, they are the appearance of being, though they also bear the stamp of contingency and arbitrary will. Only art based on beautiful fantasy offers appearances a "higher reality born of Geist" (*Werke* 13: 22). So, far from being mere semblance (*Schein*), it is art's appearances – its inventions – that are to be characterized as the higher reality and the truer existence, for they are the ways the universal is made present. They are monograms of the absolute (Schelling), though not its highest way of being presented.

3.2.3 Third Stage: Sign-Making Fantasy

The creations of fantasy initially remain only internal and subjective, for their images are *particular and only subjectively capable of intuition*. Still missing is the moment of being, the externalization, *creating the present in the external*, a new external representation as a step towards objectification. What is perfected in inner self-intuition, the mere synthesis of concept and intuition, the merely internal and subjective, must be determined as being and be made into an external object. In this activity, in externalizing, the intellect produces new intuitions and so, at this higher level, we return to the point of departure of "intuition". In the sign (*Zeichen*) real clarity is added to the self-constituted representation. The intellect, as Hegel puts it, makes itself into a thing, into an object in which merely singularized subjectivity is transgressed. It becomes sign-making fantasy. In this movement we find the basic features of Hegel's semiotics, including his philosophical concept of language, of linguistic signs. Here Hegel appears as one of the founders of the modern philosophical understanding of language.

Since at the level of fantasy the intellect relates to itself in arbitrary freedom and identity, it has already turned back to immediacy and so must posit what it has itself created, the images and representations, as existing and objectified, and thus fulfil the mind-structure in a higher way. Sign-making fantasy constitutes a unity of self-created, independent representations and an intuition – again a higher identity of subjectivity and objectivity. To an arbitrarily chosen external object an alien meaning is attributed or offered. As a result of this arbitrary attribution, the immediate and characteristic content of intuition disappears and another content – meaning – is given to the intuition. Ernst Cassirer calls this a 'meaning content'. An intuition is radically transformed into the possession of the intellect, handed over to the full sovereignty of the subject, and a fulfilled space-time is created, culminating in *language*, in the time of the tone and the space of the letter. In this construction, in the invention of a sign-world, the intellect proves itself to be the sovereign of the sign and of meanings, the free-ruling semantic power that is able to preserve our knowledge and our wisdom, make them endure, and make them communicable. This is the *mnemosyne* that constitutes the formal foundation of history.

As metaphor for the sign Hegel uses the *pyramid* (which, along with the *pit* or *shaft* (*Schacht*), would later give Derrida the title of an essay – see Derrida 1988; Vieweg 2007b). The move from shaft to pyramid concludes thus: "The sign is any immediate intuition that presents a completely different content than what it has for itself – the pyramid into which an alien soul has been conveyed, and where it is preserved" (*Werke* 10: 270). A spirit-structure is again attained, this time at a higher level, a spirit-born language which, with its logos-constitution, its inner logic, indicates the transition to a thinking that has its appropriate form in language.

The imagination, for all its creativity, lies between intuition and thought and thus fails to achieve the perfect identity of self-relation and self-determination that is thought thinking itself. The true iconoclasm of conceptual thought as Hegel conceives it remains beyond imagination's reach.[5] But that would be another story.

---

5 "In thinking, I am free, because I am not in an other, but remain simply and solely in communion with myself" (*Werke* 3: 156).

CHAPTER 13

The World Turned Upside Down

Humour follows the *lex inversa*: "its descent to hell paves its way for an ascent to heaven.* It is like the bird Merops, which indeed turns its tail towards heaven but still flies in this position up to heaven. This juggler, while dancing on his head, drinks his nectar *upwards*" (Richter 1963: 129). Jean Paul, who once reported that the reason for his intellectual vitality lay in philosophy, coffee, and chess, thus aptly described the figure of *lex inversa, inversion, turning round*.[1] It is no accident that the poet often uses the term 'castling', which constitutes a favourite move in his literary chess games. It is well known that in the royal game, castling consists of the one-time, simultaneous repositioning of two pieces – a move that breaches all the rules that otherwise apply: it involves the inversion of the placement of the king and the rook in the form of short or long castling, either to the kingside or to the queenside.[2]

Jean Paul likewise uses the topos of *hysteron proteron*, the reversal of the usual order: the later (chronologically or logically) is suddenly the earlier, the last and foremost (*Hinterst-Zuvörderst*), as Goethe calls it in his *Farbenlehre*. World and consciousness are thus reversed, turned upside down. The descent into hell as the requirement for the ascent to heaven, Merops' backwards flight to heaven, dancing on its head, and drinking the nectar upwards; castling, or *hysteron proteron*: the inversion of given relations is expressed in various ways. This is inversion thoroughly in the spirit of Aristophanes, the Olympian of comedy and humour: in radical contrast to Euripedes, who lets the noble Bellerophon float away elegantly on proud Pegasus to the gods, the ingenious playwright sends the farmer Trygaeus off to heaven with an enormous dung beetle.

Before going any further, it is necessary to mention some connotations of the German word '*umkehren*' (to invert) which may aid our understanding of

---

* This chapter is based on the previous publication "Literary Castlings and Backward Flights to Heaven", in "Shandean Humour in English and German Literature and Philosophy", edited by Klaus Vieweg, James Vigus and Kathleen Wheeler, Legenda 2013.

1 With regard to the royal game, too, Jean Paul works with reversal: "The field of reality is a game board divided into squares" (1963: 37).

2 Jean Paul would have felt like he was in heaven in many cafes in Seattle, where the man of letters and the philosopher can enjoy a game of chess over a cup of good coffee. The author of this essay wishes to thank these cafes, where the logic-laden loneliness of life writing at a desk was 'inverted' by the conviviality of intellectual play.

this thought. The following reflections were developed in the context of Hegel's treatment of inversion in *the Phenomenology of Spirit*.[3]

1) To invert as to turn around, as the turning point in the sense of a re-turn; the beginning of a going back, which can involve the eschewal of reaching the destination.
2) Inversion as stop, the movement of proceeding proves one-sided, repose takes the place of movement, a holding-in (*'Inne-halten'*) or pause; the two-ness (*'Zwei-heit'*) of movement and repose emerges.
3) To invert in the sense of taking a new view on that which has to remain behind in going forward, also in the sense of re-membering the way from a new perspective, *re-vision* in terms of seeing and checking the travelled path from the perspective of the stopping place.
4) The eschewal of a particular goal, the transformation of the wayfarer into a vagabond, who supposedly sets off without resolution or purpose; the moment of contingency, personal will as intellectual chance – 'to trifle upon the road' (Sterne).
5) Inversion in the sense of inverting or turning the tables – 'arabesque of an arabesque' (Jean Paul) or 'irony of irony' (Hegel).
6) Inversion as reversal, as 'turning something on its head', or even falsification.
7) To invert as to upend, to upset, to change fundamentally, with no continuation of the previous pace; the continuation must occur in a completely different, new way, as the rebellious or revolutionary.
8) To head home, back to the starting point.

We may pursue the question of how to understand the figure of inversion in the context of the relationship between poetry and philosophy, between logic and fantasy; or, as Sterne puts it, in the area of creative tension between "the wit and the judgment" (Sterne 1985: 174). In self-consciousness, in the knowledge of oneself as a result, we have, according to Hegel, the identity of certainty and truth: "consciousness is to itself the truth" (*Werke* 3: 137). Self-consciousness is the truth of the preceding modes of consciousness. There follows, in the form of scepticism, *utter inversion*, the radical transformation of the object, and so *the appearance completely loses the status of being in the sense of the other, something external, 'standing-against'* (*Gegen-Stehend*). The object is exclusively now *my representation*, and so precisely what Sextus Empiricus means by 'the appearing'. In Hegel's words, "the criterion of scepticism [...] is what appears (*phainomenon*), by which we, in fact, understand

---

[3] See: 46–47. For further discussion, see Vieweg 2007: 85–108.

its appearance (*phantasian autou*), hence the subjective" (*Werke* 2: 224). The object has become completely my own, in the object I have only knowledge about myself. Following the spirit of Sterne, all stories are true because they are about me. The measure is the appearing, the *phainomenon*, by which is meant the representation in consciousness, that which is subjective in my representation, *phantasia*, representation as the involuntarily experienced or suffered, appearance as subjective belief that something is true (Vieweg 2007: 85–108; cf. Sextus Empiricus 1994: 46–47, 49). Here, we may note the affinity with the ancient view of *phainomenon* as way from the sensual, objective appearance (as thing) to the appearing as *subjective representation*, as fantasy.

The first turning point is the one point along the way at which a particular inversion, a radical transformation, occurs through all forms of the relations of the consciousness to the object. At this point, appearance loses the status of being in the sense of external objecthood; the object is now *my representation* as the product of imagination. The constitutive element of the consciousness, the appearance of the spirit, 'I' as *absolute negativity*, emerges itself as its own gestalt. At one point along this path, at one station, there occurs the "liberation from the opposition of consciousness" (*Werke* 5: 45), an 'inversion', an about-turn in consciousness itself. A basic condition of consciousness is indeed its necessary *inversion* into self-consciousness. Sterne expresses this inversion with the motto of Epictetus that serves as an epigraph on the cover page of *Tristram Shandy*: "It is not circumstances [*pragmata*] themselves that trouble people, but their judgements [*dogmata*] about those circumstances".

In what follows I will provide some evidence for the relevance of the figures of inversion and reversal (both of which touch upon poetic imagination) for Sternean humour as a form of literary scepticism in the work of the great German Shandeans Jean Paul and Theodor Gottlieb von Hippel (see also Vieweg 2007: 215–23; Vieweg 2005: 113–122). The focus is on an essential moment in Shandean humour as 'Über-Humor', as Friedrich Nietzsche aptly described the literary form employed by the "freest writer of all time" (Nietzsche 1982: §113). Interestingly, Sterne, Jean Paul, and Hegel all name the same heroes of early modern romantic humour: Shakespeare and Cervantes, whose representations of the idea of negativity are poetic, imaginative, and ingenious. The relevant archetype is the fool in *King Lear* and *Falstaff*,[4] as well as the incomparable knight from *Don Quixote de la Mancha* – a 'crazy misfit' in a topsy-turvy world, a constant adventurer who is at the same time fully confident in his mission

---

4 "How great does the noble spirit of Shakespeare appear when he uses the humorous Falstaff as commentator of his wild life of sin!" (Richter 1963: 135).

and exudes a Pyrrhonian peace of mind: "without this peaceful lack of reflection in regard to the object and outcome of his actions, he would not be genuinely romantic" (*Werke* 14: 218). With his "twin stars of folly" Cervantes is "above the entire human race" (Jean Paul 1963: 126).

The literary form of inversion proves to be an essential facet of Romantic subjectivity. It is this subjectivity which "with its feeling and insight, with the right and power of its wit, can rise to mastery of the whole of reality; it leaves nothing in its usual context and in the validity which it has for our usual way of looking at things" (*Werke* 14: 222). Humour as "comic world spirit" (*komische Weltgeist*) represents the inversion of the world, the reversal of life (Richter 1963 161, cf. 128f.). Shandean humour involves the inversion of the sublime; a fascinating, poetic game is played with the seemingly small and insignificant – a game that makes us "joyful and free" (Richter 1963: 115). According to Hegel, fleeting appearance is made stationary; appearance as such is inverted and becomes the actual content. Art itself is now marked by this inversion; it becomes free art (culminating in objective humour) and thus adequate to its concept. Art freely generates an unfamiliar, 'inverted' order (*Werke* 14: 227), the world of fantasy. In poetry we have "antipodes of life", a more human-like ascent to heaven; "heaven itself descends to us" (Richter 1963: 512ff). Humour is similar to a glance into a curved mirror; it resembles Hogarth's traveling comedian who dries his stockings on the clouds (Richter 1963: 77–8). What is aesthetically engaging is the – as far as the object is concerned – disinterested 'appearance' (*Scheinen*):

> The one thing certain about beauty is, as it were, appearance for its own sake, and art is mastery in the portrayal of all the secrets of this ever profounder pure appearance of external realities. Art consists especially in heeding with a sharp eye the momentary and ever changing traits of the present world in the details of its life, which yet harmonize with the universal laws of aesthetic appearance, and always faithfully and truly keeping hold of what is most fleeting (*Werke* 14: 227).

Romantic-modern art involves a double inversion; it is a kind of *double check*:[5] with true humour, art triumphs over transience (*vanitas*); it is primarily capable

---

[5] Two pieces attack the king with one move at the same time. Such a move is particularly effective because the attacking pieces are then 'safe'. If one of the two were taken, the king would be in check, which is against the rules. The only option open to the attacked monarch is escape.

of representing the substantial in the momentary and transitory, in supposed insignificance.

Goethe seizes upon Sterne's phrase 'trifle upon the road' and speaks of "meandering along undisturbed", of 'peculiarities' that are erroneous on the outside, but true on the inside. And as long as they actively express themselves, they are called *ruling passions*: "through them the universal is particularized and in the most peculiar there is still perceptible some understanding, reason, and good will that attracts and fascinates us" (Goethe 1960 Bd. 18: 350). The merely subjective appearance is promoted to the actual content: a deeper coherence can be illustrated through the supposedly disordered detail; the spiritual can be imaged in the detached; the highest concept appears in its sensual realization. Second, this substance is deprived of its power over coincidence and transitoriness, so to speak – *Vive la Bagatelle!*[6]

All reflections call continually for a Sternean virtue: representation should be digressive and progressive – that is, both at the same time (Sterne 1985: 64). Or, as Sterne puts it in his peerless metaphor of a long castling: "when my aunt Dinah and the coachman came across us, and led us a vagary some millions of miles into the very heart of the planetary system [...]" (Sterne 1985: 63).

1   Reversals as Fantasy Castlings

"But heavens!" – thus proclaims the chessplayer Jean Paul – "What games we might win if we could only castle with our hermetic ideas!" (Richter 1963: 200). The castling of propositions allows for the lightning to come after the thunder and is capable of overturning the usual world order (Richter 1963: 180). Shandean world-humour provides this chance; it is, for Jean Paul, the greatest antithesis to life itself. As an anagram of nature, it is by nature a denier of spirits and gods, an inverter, a rebel: "It reveres and scorns nothing; everything is the same to it" (Richter 1963: 201). It is situated between poesie and philosophy and "desires nothing but itself and plays for the sake of play" (1963: 201). It emerges as a liberator (1963: 116), as "true poetic art", humour grants mankind "emancipation" (1963: 469).

The Richterian *lex inversa* contains precisely these dimensions: Jean Paul describes the adventures of fantasy and language as a 'free hysteron proteron' – free in the sense of the desired inversion of the familiar and usual, free in

---

[6] "Uncle Toby's military campaigns do not make Toby himself or Louis XIV alone ridiculous; they are the allegory of human hobbyhorses. There is a child's head kept in every man's head as in a hatbox" (Richter 1963: 126).

the sense of the "fool's leap of fantasy" (Vischer 1837: 204). In volume three of *Tristram Shandy*, the author announces to the puzzled reader that the introduction to the novel will now follow. In this way everything has to be romantic, in the sense of upended. The lyrical spirit "always throws the humorists back at themselves as the concave mirror of the world" (Richter 1963: 470). Humour is fundamentally self-referential; it has no other goal but its own existence; it does not engage in dialogues with the world, but rather – just like Strepsiades in the Aristophenian clouds – only in conversation with itself. As Richter says, "who should not wish to be allowed to write like Montaigne and Sterne? Humour is always in flux; it never remains on one track; for, indifferent to the true relationships of things, it seems to lag behind and lose its way through the pursuit of its catch in all of its devious dealings" (Richter 1873: 1). According to Hegel, everything that strives to gain a concrete form in reality or in the outer world "destroys and dissolves itself by the power of subjective notions, flashes of thought, striking modes of interpretation" (Richter 1963: 229). The presentation becomes a "sporting with the topics, a derangement and perversion of the material, and a rambling to and fro, a criss-cross movement of subjective expressions, views, and attitudes whereby the author sacrifices himself and his topics alike" (ibid.) This self-relinquishing, self-reversing humorist appears in Richterian imagery as a self-parodist, his own court jester or quartet of masked Italian comedians (Vieweg 2005: 121; Richter 1963: 94). Therein lies the now decisive role of the literary 'I', the subjectivity of the poet, and the related inversion of the dominance of tragedy over comedy: the *soccus*, the lowly shoe of comedy, now stands higher than the *cothurnus*, the high shoe of tragedy. In terms of the development of subjectivity, Aristophanes is above Euripides, Trygaeus above Bellerophontes, and the dung beetle above Pegasus. At the same time, Sterne is able to change Shakespeare's "simple succession of the pathetic and the comic into a simultaneum of the two" (Richter 1963: 105). Now, too, folly – folly's freedom, and the fool's wisdom – are understood as necessarily intrinsic; negativity is immanent. The humorist posits himself as self-parodist and his own court jester; he carries on conversations with himself and represents only himself.

En passant,[7] a further kind of inversion related to chess playing, should be mentioned. The two pieces that start beside the king and the queen (one

---

7   Taking an opponent's pawn '*en passant*' is a special move in chess: a pawn standing on its fifth rank can capture a pawn that has just 'passed by' it by moving two squares forward (from the second to the fourth row) – that is, *as if* this latter pawn had only moved forward one square! Another exception consists of the fact that the opposing piece (the pawn that moved two squares forward) can only be taken from its present position on the next turn.

moving diagonally on the white squares, the other diagonally on the black squares)[8] have contrasting names in French and in English: in French, *fou*, the fool; in English, bishop. Jean Paul's comments on this contrast are spot on: first, the fool is the "court preacher reversed"; second, the "serious clerical estate" has produced the greatest comic writers – Rabelais, Swift, and Sterne (Richter 1963: 116, 82).

Even language tries to sublate itself: things should be thrown back into some kind of anonymity in which they had slept through the naming process (Richter 1963: 135). Jean Paul reminds us of the "pure grammatical inversion" which is absent from French and English but characteristic of German. This "grammatical suicide of the first person pronoun" expresses itself in the fact that monarchs, princes, or university principals can humbly use the *pluralis majestatis* 'we' instead of 'I'; and the addresses 'he' or 'she' may be used to exclude the reference to the self which 'thou' and 'you' imply. "There have been times when perhaps in all of Germany no letter passed through the mail containing the word 'I' " (Richter 1963: 135f). This peculiarity had advantages for Romantic humour.[9] First, because Romantic humour cannot abstain from using the first-person pronoun – 'I' must play first fiddle (the masters of humour must both poetically posit themselves as fools and refer to themselves) – the linguistic omission of the first-person pronoun sets up the comic punchline. Second, to refrain from using 'I' generates the humoristic "parody of parody": much like the "delightful Musäus, whose *Physiognomic Journeys* are true picturesque excursions of Comus and the reader" (Richter 1963: 135). A grandiose, comical resurrection of the displaced first-person pronoun can be found in the work of Johann Gottlieb von Hippel: his *Lebensläufe* begins provocatively and effectively with the single word 'I' (*Ich*), which is to convey the theme of the novel.

Sterne reasons long and deliberately about all kinds of matters, until he finally decides that there is not one word of truth in anything anyway. Jean Paul sees an extreme example of the constant whirl of upturning and reverse polarity in one of Ludwig Tieck's representations of inversion: a piece in which the "the *dramatis personae* finally believe themselves to be merely fictive nonentities" (Richter 1936: 131). In inversion, the true condition of art itself is articulated. In the following section, castling shall be more thoroughly explained

---

8 The *fianchetto*: Uncle Toby surely would have liked the effective positioning of the bishop or *fou* at the flank in his military exercise games.

9 Referring to the translation of *Tristram Shandy*: "The humor of the self extends even to small parts of speech [...] Bode often therefore translates 'myself' and 'himself' into German by 'Ich *selber*' or 'er *selber*' " (Richter 1963: 136).

and illustrated by looking at some characteristic examples and variations of the concept.

1.1 Heaven and Hell, or: the 'Sacraments of the Devil'

One of the fathers of comedy, Lucian, had suggested writing from the standpoint of Hades. Sterne explicitly references this forerunner.[10] As I mentioned at the beginning of this chapter, Jean Paul imagines Merops flying backwards to heaven and drinking nectar upside down. Instead of the noble, winged steed in Euripides, a stinking dung beetle flies to heaven in Aristophanes' *Peace*. In *Tristram Shandy* we find lengthy depictions of scholastic sophistry about Luther's descent to hell and its progress (Slawkenbergius's tale in Vol. IV). Jean Paul, probably also thinking of Sterne's references to the reformer, mentions Luther's calling our will a *lex inversa* in a bad sense – on which basis Luther scornfully hurled at Erasmus's *Praise of Folly* the comment "spiritus sanctus non est scepticus" (Richter 1963: 129).[11] It is well-known that the devil is a decisive literary figure for Jean Paul. Satan is, according to Friedrich Schlegel, a "favourite of German culture", for he embodies the "unconditioned wilfulness and purposefulness" that is evil and symbolises "enthusiasm for destruction, confusion and temptation" (Schlegel 1958 Bd. 2: 235). Jean Paul sees the devil as "the true *inverted* world of the divine world, the great world shadow ... the greatest humorist and whimsical man" (Richter 1963: 130, my emphasis). But he has a double identity: as the fallen Angel of God and bringer of light, the devil shows (already in Milton) strength of character, a free self-assertiveness, agility, acumen, and ingenuity – in a way he is indispensable, a court jester who speaks truth, the "court preacher reversed" in the Kingdom of God (Richter 1963: 160). Richter sees devils in this superlative form à la Milton as "inverted gods" (1963: 80). Satan's seductive power grows out of this brilliance of the negative, similar to the case of the naked and highly erotic ironist as she-devil (see Vieweg 2012b: 149–168). But at the same time, Satan is marked by his absolute vanity, total complacency, pure arbitrariness, indifference, and boredom with the merely negative. As just this figure, reduced to himself, as pure negativity without the positive, he remains an *isolani*[12] for both Jean Paul and Hegel: an

---

10   "By the tomb stone of Lucian –" (Sterne 1985: 173).

11   Richter says the following about Erasmus: "just as reprehensible as the pseudo-humorist is Erasmus's self-critic, Folly: first, she is an empty, abstract self, i.e., a non-self; and second, instead of lyric humour or strict irony she recites only from the primers of Wisdom, who shouts even louder from the prompter's box than Columbine herself" (Richter 1963: 135).

12   In chess, this refers to an entirely isolated pawn that does not have any more partner-pawns in the neighboring files and therefore often becomes a weakness. But even such

unaesthetic, boring person, "for his laugh would have too much pain; it would be like the colourful flowery garment of the – guillotined" (Richter 1963: 92). For Hegel, "the purely negative is in itself dull and flat and therefore leaves us empty or else repels us"; like the Furies of hatred, evil is "in general inherently cold and worthless, because nothing comes of it except what is purely negative, just destruction and misfortune"; it lacks "affirmative independence and stability" (*Werke* 13: 289). The only thing that remains, as in the case of the guillotine, is *la mort*. This "uniformity is highly tedious" (*Werke* 2: 547), in Hegel's words: "evil as such, envy, cowardice, and baseness are and remain purely repugnant. Thus the devil in himself is a bad figure, aesthetically impracticable; for he is nothing but the father of lies and therefore an extremely prosaic person" (*Werke* 13: 288–9). The devil can only play his role as the greatest humorist as the personification of the death of God, as the declaration of the indispensability of negativity, of the evil in life. "What you call evil, the negative, is indeed its own element, but the delusion, the misapprehension, evil are given to the good and the true as companions, as an instance of free will in which good and evil conceive of each other" (*Werke* 2: 556). The 'great world shadow', the prince of darkness, the 'shadow kingdom' can only be taken as the second moment (talk of the devil already signifies the second) and refers necessarily to the light of the first.[13]

In the concave mirror of humour, reversal makes no exception for the devil. Jean Paul describes this self-inversion aptly in the following passage: "About three weeks ago I, the devil, revealed on the parapet a few doubts about my own existence". The grandmaster of doubt is compelled to apply this doubt to himself, humour applied to the greatest humorist. And the poet caps it off with yet another inversion: that which he calls the 'counter-step' (*Gegenschritt*) or 'antidote' (*Gegengift*). It is the notorious turning of the tables, the humoresque of the humoresque, or the irony of irony: "against the newest anti-egotism of Satan, or the reasons why the devil in his own person had the audacity to deny his own existence in a public place". The devil possessed, similar to irony as divine impudence, the unbelievable impertinence to question his own

---

a pawn has the baton of a marshal in its knapsack: on the last row of the board it can undergo an 'inversion' to become the strongest figure: a queen.

13   All verification requires the acceptance of the possibility of at least a *second* case, a *second* variation, an otherness; it is therefore *two*fold, a *dua*lity – this is how Hegel initially uses the word 'doubt' ('Zwei-*fel*'). The Italian verb *dubitare* (to doubt) can arguably also be traced back to two: *duo, diversi generis*; *diversitas* expresses variety, difference. 'Zweifel' (doubt) thus includes the possibility of otherness, the differentiation, and implies the negation of the first.

being – which ought to be revealed in inverse as the anti-egoism of the absolute egoist (Richter 1974: 927).

We can find parallels in the work of Theodor von Hippel: "whoever needs to go to heaven must set a course for hell. Whoever wants to recognize God must first recognize himself" (Hippel 2013: 1). This sounds at least ambiguous, for we could also read: self-awareness is the descent to hell. The *nosce te ipsum*, the *gnothi seauton*, the inscription from the Temple of Apollo in Delphi, remains equally polyvalent itself – precisely through the use of the word 'I' (*Ich*), that begins von Hippel's *Lebensläufe*. In any case, heaven and hell are inverted, and the journey begins first in the opposite direction; only at the first destination, in the Kingdom of Lucifer, does the second inversion occur.

2 Narrating Lives and Journeys 'Downhill'

Von Hippel's novel, which was highly esteemed by Jean Paul, as well as by Hölderlin and Hegel, carries the title *Lebensläufe nach aufsteigender Linie*. On the first page, the author characterizes himself as a "writer from bottom up" (von Hippel 1828: 1). However, this statement is turned on its head just a few lines later: he wants to tell the lives "downhill" because "these days we are so used to climbing *upwards*." This habit should be upended, the course of life should be told from the grave to the cradle, from death to life. The grandfather should rather die as he is born. A noteworthy comparison suggests itself here to Deleuze's concept of the rhizome: roots, branches, and leaves, his plants all have the same structure: "bury the branches in the earth and let the roots look up to heaven in the free air" (von Hippel 1828: 1). Here, we are clearly going against the grain: the roots grow towards heaven, not into the earth. Similar ideas may be found in the work of Jean Paul: in the crossings and traversals of nature, it is not possible to differentiate between river and shore.

The similarities to Sterne are of course readily noticeable, in the central topic of birth and the course of life in *Tristram Shandy*. After the death of Tristram in Vol. 1 Ch. 12 and after the famous empty black page and the graveside speech 'Alas, poor YORICK!', Chapter 13 introduces an inversion with the midwife: "It is so long since the reader of this rhapsodical work has been parted from the midwife, that it is high time to mention her again to him" (Sterne 1985: 63). With this, we are cast back into the birth of Tristram Shandy, laden with problems, through the crux in which the name is inverted, right up to the actual act of procreation. The latter necessarily requires attention and caution, for in addition to the choice of name and the nature of the birth, it determines the abilities of the born child. In all three respects, there were considerable difficulties: first, babies are usually born head-first, that is, in reverse into the world. They are pulled out into the world by the upper halves of their bodies, which has the dangerous potential for causing bodily injury. In the case of Tristram Shandy, instead of a head-first birth, the appropriately inverse feet-first birth is recommended. The whole thing must be turned from its head to feet for the salvation of the soul. Second, the essential naming of the newest Shandy is based on a fatal error, a misunderstanding that not least of all brings with it a trail of theological problems. Third, the act of procreation was burdened in a bizarre manner: as we read right at the start in Vol. I Ch. 1, "*Pray, my dear*, quoth my mother, *have you not forgot to wind up the clock?-----Good G--*! cried my father, making an exclamation, but taking care to moderate his voice at the same time,-----*Did ever woman, since the creation of the world, interrupt a man with such a silly question?*" (ibid. 35-6). In any case, the three named 'mortgages' must have had dire effects on the life of Tristram, so that not even a Bishop's cap could fit his misshapen head – this is what the dying hero tells us in his final sentence.

The clock in the Shandy household plays an important role, that is to say, a reversing one: Through fantasy, proclaims Tristram, through "an unhappy association of ideas which have no connection in nature, it so fell out at length, that my poor mother could never hear the said clock wound up,—but the thoughts of some other things unavoidably popped into her head—*& vice versa*" (ibid. 39). The clock was an example for the "extreme exactness" and pedantry of Walter Shandy, who in the end becomes a "slave" to it (ibid.).

It is this general pedantry to which von Hippel's comedy *Der Mann nach der Uhr oder der ordentliche Mann* refers. This piece alludes to various matters of fact, as well as people: Sterne, Kant and his English friend Green. The erotic, sexual dimension of Sterne's work is difficult to miss. Indeed, Sterne opened many doors and broke many taboos in this area – a fact that was, however, clearly registered neither in the work of Jean Paul, nor in von Hippel's comedy. The representative of this radical pedantry is Orbil, who stands for the English merchant and Kant's friend, Joseph Green: a true *whimsical man*, as von Hippel notes in the introduction. The English clock is a symbol of pedantry. With this symbol, von Hippel also takes aim at Kant, who appears in the comedy as Magister Blasius and is presented as a character similar to Green. According to von Hippel, Kantian philosophy has taken a too studious approach to life. A reference to the young Kant would also be possible, however – one who knew *Tristram Shandy* and would have quite clearly understood the allusion to the clock in a letter he received from Maria Charlotta Jacobi: "good, then, I will expect you, and my clock will be wound as well" (Kuehn 2004: 199). The Kant biographer Manfred Kuehn recognizes the sexual references, but he considers them to be only a playful, literary comment. However, despite the absence of certain evidence, this interpretation seems implausible. As Kuehn's own biography shows, the young author from Königsberg might very well have written a *Critica della donna pura* next to his *Kritik der reinen Vernunft*.

In terms of travel, von Hippel plays with another form of inversion that derides the new style of travel literature: the travels are no longer those of Gulliver and Yorick; journeys are also imagined through one's own room, or during midday in the provinces of France. Since Laurence Sterne "engaged in a sentimental journey, half of Germany readies itself, and a good part is already on its way [...] the suitcase is closed and opened. People tell their own life story" (Hippel 1979: 56–7). Sterne pulled – as Jean Paul wrote acerbically about some German writers – "a long, watery comet tail of then famous (and now anonymous) humorists" (Richter 1963: 127). The author from Königsberg lapidarily counter-checks this general obsession with travelling and stylised adventuring (also perhaps an allusion to the stay-at-home friend, Kant) with a reference to the Romantic, Pyrrhonian principles of calm and composure: "I am invariably at home; since the world has been discovered, it has been a part of our birthplace" (Hippel 1828: 8).

3   Free *hystera protera*: Scepticism – Music – Carnival – Politics

For Jean Paul, certain forms of music and carnival, the humorous festivals of fools, are examples of the cheekiness of inverting, annihilating humour as the expression of 'contempt for the world' (*Welt-Verachtung*) – that is, very close to scepticism, as represented by the Leipzig pedagogue Ernst Platner. Jean Paul recognizes a fundamental law of humour in the idea of negativity: the "annihilating or infinite idea of humour" (Richter 1963: 91); humour stands for a form of aesthetic-poetic scepticism,[14] for the *advocatus diaboli* that belongs inextricably to modern art.[15] In the constitution of antithetics, Richter sees an essential instance of humour, and the resulting indecision reveals itself to be a basic concept of real scepticism: in the language of chess, the draw (see Vieweg 1999). Jean Paul characterizes hell in terms of negativity – it is the "pyre of the infinite" (Richter 1963: 93) where everything finite is sacrificed, a kind

---

14   Cf. Vieweg 2002.
15   Friedrich Theodor Vischer recognizes in comedy "the negative side of Hegelian method translated into the language of side-splitting humour" (Vischer 1837: 188).

of metaphysical gambit.[16] (Incidentally, the sceptic in Goethe's *Faust* jokingly confirms the affinity of scepticism with the devil thus: "Devil and doubt both start with D" ("*Auf Teufel reimt der Zweifel nur*") (Goethe 1960 Bd. 8: 290). Music such as Haydn's, writes Jean Paul, "destroys entire tonal sequences by introducing an extraneous key and storms alternately between pianissimo and fortissimo, presto and andante" (Richter 1963: 93). One speaks of humouresques and scherzinos, as well as counterpoint in music. Medieval festivals of fools also enter into this context, which involved a temporary, carnivelesque eversion and inversion of all existing order. With an "inner spiritual masquerade", the idea was to reverse "the worldly and the spiritual" and to invert "social ranks and moral values", to reduce all to "one great equality and freedom of joy" (Richter 1963: 94). Hegel clearly articulates the critical, upsetting dimension of comedy and humour, the "turn against the content that was alone valid hitherto," against all political and cultural hardenings and ossifications: Aristophanes turned against his own present, Lucian against the whole of the Greek past, Ariosto and Cervantes against medieval chivalry (*Werke* 14: 234). Sterne himself had more political force and clarity in this respect than his German successors Jean Paul and von Hippel, for example when he directly and humorously attacks the inversion of politics: "in the foreground of this picture, a *statesman* turning the political wheel, like a brute, the wrong way round – *against* the stream of corruption, – by heaven! – instead of *with* it" (Sterne 1985: 179). Humour, with its free *hystera protera*, proves itself to be a decisive component of Romanticism, as the *free dimension of modern art*, which is characterized by the *inclusion of true humour*. Modern subjectivity requires free humour, felicitous humour as an intrinsic moment – without this there can be no genuine representation of frankness and intellectual "robust goodness".[17] As Goethe puts it, "Yorick-Sterne was the most beautiful spirit that ever lived; who reads him immediately feels free and beautiful; his humour is inimitable, and not all humour frees the soul" (Goethe 1960 Bd. 18: 594).

4   Closing Remarks, or: Endgame

In twentieth-century literature, there is one author who explicitly draws a connection between Hegel and Sterne in terms of the motive of inversion: Robert

---

16   Gambit in chess: the sacrifice of material for an advantageous position. This word was probably first used by the Spanish chessmaster Ruy López de Segura (c. 1530 – c. 1580). Pascal's Gambit is well-known in the field of philosophy.
17   Cf. Vieweg 2007: 215–234.

Menasse, who like Hegel has a favourite book in *Tristram Shandy*. Menasse's character Judith Katz lectures on Tristram's narrative, which attempts to move towards his own birth, towards the cradle. For the Hegelian philosopher Leo Singer, in love with Judith, this is the opportunity to write a *Phenomenology of Dismay* (*Phänomenologie der Entgeisterung*), in other words, to invert Hegel's *Phenomenology*, to read backwards (Menasse 1994). Menasse entitles one of his novels with the terminology of modern aviation, in the truest sense of *lex inversa*: *Thrust Reversal* (*Schubumkehr*). Hegel might very well have enjoyed reading Menasse's work, with its educative and sentimental voyages to a Sternean world – he might have read with in-spiration (*Be-Geisterung*) the trilogy of dis-may (*Ent-Geisterung*).[18] It is well-known that Hegel favoured the imagery of the circle, ascent as descent into the ground, the return to the cradle.

In a dialogue with Leo Singer, Judith cries out, incredulously, "Leo, today no more about master Hegel?" Leo answers, "The starting point and the destination have become identical. We have returned to the beginning. This means that we are at the end" (Menasse 1996: 165). Or, in other words: we are in the singer's club in faraway Brazil with the ambiguous name Bar Every Hope ('*Bar jeder Hoffnung*'), a kind of Mecca for checkmated negativists. There, we might find Leo Singer at any given time, and he would point at us with his finger and yell, To hell with you, to hell with all Kantians, analytical philosophers and all other false prophets! Turn round! Mount Rosinante and ride on a flight of fantasy to the new Don Quixoteries! Set sail on the ship of fools! Follow William of Baskerville! Read the second book of Aristotle's *Poetics* that he found, the one about comedy! Find your way at last to Shandean humour and enjoy laughing! Read Hegel and Laurence Sterne!

---

18   The trilogy contains the novels *Selige Zeiten, brüchige Welt* (*Blessed Times, Brittle World*), *Sinnliche Gewißheit* (*Sense Certainty*) and *Schubumkehr* (*Thrust Reversal*).

CHAPTER 14

On Hegel's Humour

Humour was never absent from Tristram Shandy's life. As death knocked at his door he demanded him to come back another time, and in such a humorous tone of careless indifference that death came to doubt the correctness of his act and left Shandy Hall. Such humorous indifference resembles the Pyrrhonian *ataraxia* which grows out of sceptical antinomies. But, according to Tristram, his life was not the same after death's visit, since death now knew where he lived. Yorick's eulogy to humour, which also causes death to become sceptical, was enthusiastically read by such diverse minds as Jean Paul, Goethe, and Nietzsche. Above all, Hegel was a keen reader of Sterne. The choice of topic in this chapter, Hegel and Sterne's extreme humour, initially seems surprising. Study of Hegel's philosophy and aesthetic shows, however, that it is more astonishing that there is as yet no specific research on this topic.

The focal point of the following discussion is Hegel's interpretation of comedy and humour as forms of poetic and literary scepticism, the revelation of the sceptical potential of humour, as well as the relationship of sceptical acumen to humorous rashness. Essential here is Hegel's understanding of the Sternian type of novel as a paradigm of modern art. Drawing upon Jean Paul's *Propaedeutics to Aesthetics*, Hegel holds humour to be the form of comedy proper to romanticism and modernity, indeed, the culminating point of the romantic art form.

In looking at Hegel's texts there are, first of all, his two direct references to Sterne, and, secondly, his indirect statements in the various lectures on aesthetics that treat the modern novel and humour, where his discussions of Jean Paul and Goethe are important, and, thirdly, there are his remarks concerning the most important Sterne disciples, Jean Paul and especially Theodor Gottlieb von Hippel. Hippel's *Lebensläufe nach Aufsteigender Linie* (Life on an Ascending Course) was indeed the first German humoristic novel in the modern (that is Sternian) style and a favourite book of Hegel. Hegel knew the Sterne tradition in Germany well. He also knew the relevant novels of Hermes, Nicolai, Lafontaine and Friedrich Heinrich Jacobi. Fourthly, the *Phenomenology of Spirit* plays an essential role here. This was Hegel's first attempt at translating modern subjectivity from the representational form into the conceptual form, entailing a transformation of the sceptical and humorous metaphor into the concept of self-fulfilling scepticism which constitutes the key element of the *Phenomenology*.

In order to explore Hegel's understanding of humour, I will first discuss the two explicit references to Sterne. Both cases occur in the context of a treatment of authentic humour as the dénouement of the romantic art form, that is, in context of the thesis of the 'end of art' and the transition from the representational form to the conceptual. In Hotho's compilation of lecture notes – better known as Hegel's *Aesthetics* – Sterne and Hippel are held to be representative of true humour: "Much depth and richness of spirit is needed to render conspicuous the true expressiveness found in *merely subjective appearance* and to allow the substantial to emerge from its very *contingency*, from mere whims" (*Werke* 14: 231, my emphasis). Hegel describes humorous indifference as a literary 'sauntering forth', which immediately reminds one of Stern's expression "to trifle upon the road" (Sterne 1985: 41).[1] In this appearance of unimportance, however, Hegel finds "the highest concept of profundity" (*Werke* 14: 231). Hegel continues: "since there are singularities which bubble up irregularly, the inner connection must lie deep and produce the light of spirit in that which has been separated from it" (ibid.). In this way one arrives at the conclusion of romantic art, the standpoint of the art of the most recent time, modern art itself. Humour as self-portrayal of the artistic self, as the poetic model of modern subjectivity, stands for the dénouement of romantic art in its movement towards formalism, towards the dissolution of the objectivity of the work of art. In Hegel's words: "Yorik's *Sentimental Journeys* and Sterne's *Tristram Shandy* are the best works of humour" (Hegel 1995: 180).

In Hegel's talk of the 'conclusion' or 'dénouement' of romantic art, its marginalization, one of the essential dimensions of his theory of 'an end of art' is made explicit, namely, the systematic transition from literature to philosophy, from literary imagination to conceptual construction. With humorous literature, with the comical aspects of humour, the transition point is reached, and one steps into the border region between the world of the beautiful and the world of the concept, the bridge between two genres of writing, between two languages. Those spheres are abandoned where the beautiful as such is held to be the highest. Romantic art is "art's self-transcendence, but within its own domain and in the form of art itself" (*Werke* 13: 113). As the turn to the self, subjectivity triumphs over objectivity, over what is sensually external. Hegel holds literature to be the most universal, the most spiritual

---

1 "Let me go on, and tell my story my own way: – or, if I should seem now and then to trifle upon the road, or should sometimes put on a fool's cap with a bell to it, for a moment or two as we pass along, – don't fly off, – but rather courteously give me credit for a little more wisdom than appears upon my outside; – and as we jog on, either laugh with me, or at me, or in short do any thing, – only keep your temper" (Sterne 1985: 41).

art form, "which can express and put in any form any content which can be approached in phantasy, since its actual material is phantasy itself" (*Werke* 15: 233). In literature we have the most crucial treatment of the sensual. The connection between internal spirituality and external form is dissolved at the point where art begins to no longer correspond to its own principle. Literature can "lose itself in the realm of the spiritual" (*Werke* 15: 235). It transcends itself and becomes the prose of thought. Already in the *Phenomenology of Spirit,* in the *Aesthetics* and in his philosophy of subjective spirit, Hegel attempts what Derrida would later attempt: namely, to reconceive the traditional distinction between literature and philosophy and to rethink the complicated boundary between them. Here I can only sketch a few aspects of this issue. Neither type of text consists of pure form, since language itself is both metaphorical and conceptual. Both literature and philosophy are complexes of the metaphorical and conceptual; what distinguishes them is the respective predominance of one of these two forms of expression. According to Hegel, at the point of transition there are intermediate forms, which represent bridges. There are border crossers, thinkers who "philosophize in the form of literature and thus transgress the limits" (Hegel 1995: 303) and poets who go in the opposite direction, such as Jean Paul with his 'Fichtian Glossary' in his work *Titan*.

Within the sceptical tradition it is Timon, Sextus Empiricus and Lucian who serve as examples of this interdependence between speculative and literary scepticism. In his *Sillen,* Timon proves himself to be an astute thinker and biting cynic. Hegel holds Sextus and Lucian to be paradigm cases of the relation between wit and humour, between the sceptical world and the satirical world. Both Sterne and Hegel celebrated Lucian, who wrote with Aristophean wit and the linguistic skill of Greek comedy. Lucian himself questioned whether it might not be too audacious to combine two such alien genres as philosophical dialogue and comedy into a third genre. For this frivolous coupling he might reckon with the punishment of Zeus. In Lucian's biting joke about the philosophers, one alone is spared – Sextus Empiricus. However, neither the humorous satire of Lucian nor the Pyrrhonian tropes are pure forms. Tropes traditionally belong to the art of rhetoric and possess this connection to the literary world, while Lucian's histories also contain philosophical arguments.

After the 20th chapter of Volume II of *Tristram Shandy,* the author finally gives us the Preface, where a single theme is treated – the connection between wit and judgment. He claims to have combined both wit and judgment in his book and argues against those views which maintain that wit and judgment do not belong together. He likens wit and judgment to the ornamental finials on the back-rest of his chair; were one to be missing it would look like "a sow with one ear" (Sterne 1985: 209). In their opposition, the proponents of wit stand for the humorous retort, chaos, and the interplay of action and reaction, whereas people of judgment stand for order, reconciliation, and unity. The main advantage of comparative wit consists in its goal of purification: "to clarify the understanding, previous to the application of the argument itself, in order to free it from any little motes, or specks of opacular matter, which if left swimming therein, might hinder a conception and spoil all" (ibid. 203). These two skills are considered to be the highest adornments of the human spirit. They are the most highly valued, most unavoidable, and most difficult to acquire. Each has as much sense and symmetry as the other. If, as Sancho Panza, one is allowed to choose a kingdom, for Tristram it must be a kingdom of laughing subjects who are both funny and wise.

Hegel, however, insisted at the same time on the clear distinction between literature and philosophy as two forms of intellectual expression, as two different ways of spiritual self-conception – the self-reflection of metaphor and the self-reflection of thought. Crucial here are the considerations, already mentioned, concerning the difference between the form of representation and the form of the concept. Especially important for Hegel's characterization of this issue is the discussion of the nature of 'representation' (*Vorstellung*) as concerns the literary art form.

Hegel defines the comical as the unity of idea and form in the mode of its self-negation. Spirit becomes valid in its negative form. Everything not adequate to spirit, all of finitude, all which is in itself nothing, is negated. Only subjectivity remains aware of itself in this disintegration. In its self-certainty, subjectivity can endure the negation of its ends and their realization. For Aristophanes and Lucian the result of this subjectivity is at the same time the decline of the ancient world as the world of the beautiful. It is the principle of the end of art and the origin of a new world, the world of free subjectivity. In art's infinity, universality is expressed in a concrete, sensual form. In the classical art form of the ancient world this took the form of the thorough interpenetration of thought and sensual being: in this melding, however, spirit does not become manifest in its true concept. For this reason romanticism again negated that unseparated unity, for romanticism had attained a new content, namely that of a free subjectivity which goes beyond classical art forms and their modes of expression. In this sense the Aristophean / Lucian spirit reappears in modern art as the tension between content and form. For Hegel, indeed, this occurs by means of the more profound content and inwardness of humour, this being the form of the comical appropriate to the modern world. The modern style is influenced by the prominence of and preference for metaphor. In various ways, comedy, metaphor, wit, humour, and the symbolic each characterize romantic art, the very unity of idea and form in the mode of non-correspondence and indifference. The figurative writing of a Shakespeare or Jean Paul is the appropriate form of expression in modern art; metaphor is the very characteristic of romanticism (cf. *Werke* 14: 230).

In his considerations of representation as it is found in literature, Hegel investigates the power and limit of metaphor and wit. Located between an intuition and a concept, a representation (*Vorstellung*) is defined as a metaphor of thought. The metaphor makes the meaning accessible to intuition in a similar, external form. What is present is a picture whose actual meaning has been effaced. The representational meaning can only be inferred from the context. The unique strength of metaphor lies in its empowerment through sensual magnification as well as in the multiplicity of potential pictorial interpretations. This is the basis of free imagination, of the free thinking of fantasy. On the other hand, in its non-pictorial form the meaning must be re-written, 'translated' into a related picture, involving the transition from actual thought to a figurative mode of expression.

As an imaginative power of association, wit connects highly diverse representations and shows their relatedness. It relates images to one another, often on the basis of unexpected similarity, and so transforms them into universal representations. Through this linkage, the singular is reduced to the universal. Creative poetic imagination, characterized by originality and genius, is distinguished from shrewdness, which works with reflection and looks for more subtle relations and distinctions.

In romantic art we find the development of an indifferent, external form. The free linkage of representations leads to an adventure of fantasy. In humour the freedom of subjectivity is presented according to its inner contingency. Related connections are disclosed in the apparently most heterogeneous things. The most diverse things are combined. By means of humour's running here and there each material and each form is displaced, perverted, or obliterated. There emerges a self-dissolving world, a comical world. As opposed to the epic poetry of classical antiquity, where the poet's subject is never seen, where the epic 'sings itself', the modern humoristic novel is a radically individual project, an odyssey of the poetic self. Here too one finds the problems and dangers at the limit of metaphor. The many forms of representation exist independently of each other. They are known from context. They are not self-satisfying expressions or depictions of thought but are ambiguous. This uncertainty leads to a restless searching for new surprising pictures. Inner rest is transformed into permanent unrest. According to Nietzsche, Sterne is "the freest writer", his "squirrel-soul" jumps with insatiable unrest from branch to branch (Nietzsche 1982: §113). But the quick-fire of bizarre combinations and unrelenting digressions can just as easily lead to tediousness, to the opposite of originality, to boredom.

As the highest form of the metaphor of subjectivity and the apex of self-consciousness in the form of representation, humour constitutes the bridge towards a conceptual expression, 'from heart to head', 'from whim to insight', as von Hippel puts it. It is the destiny of form to lead philosophy to truth. This form, however, is not something external to the content. According to Hegel, the true content is first constituted in the translation from the form of representation to the form of the concept, that is, in the transformation of one language into the other. The unity of form and content is first established in the self-relation of thought. The concept is this very form which has itself as its own content.

This relation between the form of representation and the form of the concept can now be more closely defined in reference to selected aspects of philosophical and literary scepticism. From among several possible points of reference, such as negativity, subjectivity, autonomy, withholding of judgment, *ataraxia*, and indifference, I would like to concentrate on the first two, with a particular focus on Sterne and Jean Paul's description of the chief component of humour in his work *Propadeutic to Aesthetics* (Richter 1963).

1   Negativity and Humour

The Principle of negativity is a cornerstone of scepticism both in its philosophical as well as in its literary form. Hegel emphasized the self-conflict and self-annihilation of the finite – the finite is that which negates itself. With help of antinomies the negative and sceptical process reveals the nothingness of the finite and undermines any immediate or unmediated acceptance of world's existence. Scepticism casts into doubt the whole realm of reality and certainty. The sceptic's sober acumen, persistently questioning and avoiding unfounded assumptions, climbs logic's rope-ladder on the way to antinomy, to theoretical indifference. This leads to a withholding of judgment as the practical implications of the theoretical indifference. Indifference here constitutes a property of both discursive and literary scepticism. Walter Shandy "had a thousand little sceptical notions of the comic kind to defend" (Sterne 1985: 79). Two positions would hang "so equally in the balance before him, that they were absolutely indifferent to him" (ibid. 80). These positions negated each other "like equal forces acting against each other in contrary directions. For which reason, he would often declare, He would not give a cherry-stone to choose amongst them" (ibid. 81). Later in Sterne's narrative the possibility is raised of determining "the agreement or disagreement of two ideas by the intervention of a third, called the *medius terminus*" (ibid. 242). The fundaments of Pyrrhonian scepticism, in other words, correspond to those of modern humour.

The comical subjectivity of 'the art of humour' takes over the role of a fundamental opposition to everything fixed and stable. Everything supposedly objective or subjective is obliterated and all apparently certain value-claims are destroyed. For Hegel this is "the turn against all previously valid content" (*Werke* 14: 234). Yorick calls himself a sworn enemy of presumptuous and artificial seriousness, which he sees as nothing other than disguised stupidity and indecision. He declares war on pretence wherever he meets it and under whatever protection it stands. He exercises no caution in the use of his sceptical weapon, a crushing wit and humour, and consciously calls upon the sarcasm of Lucian, the seriousness of Cervantes, and the brilliant humour of Shakespeare. It is in these very authorities that Hegel perceives the forbidden principle of modern subjectivity. In Sterne's sarcasm we see vanity, stupidity, and superstition, dogmatists reasoning about Luther's trip to Hell, people left lying at the bottom of the inkwell, philosophers demonstrating with trumpets, prudishness, fads, whims, in short the whole foolishness of humanity. In the cheerful humour of a Lucian and a Sterne one becomes indifferent to the external world, which is revealed in its nullity. In the romantic subjectivity of humour the apparent world loses importance. Everything objective, everything which has (or appears to have) a fixed actual form in the external world is shattered by the power of subjective whim, flashes of thought, and fantastical notions. Humour reveals everything to be self-disintegrating and intuitively dissolved. Contemporary art, makes this thematic, becoming an art of mere appearance. It has a sceptical character in the sense that mere appearance is for Sextus Empiricus a principle of scepticism. In the laughter of the individuality which dissolves everything, the triumph of subjectivity is established. Every authentic philosophy also has this negative side, which is directed against everything finite and limited and brings to fulfilment the complete negation of the truth of finite knowledge.

From this perspective *Tristram Shandy* is a novelty of modern literature, the first novel of authentic, sceptical modernity. It represents the paradigm shift in art as diagnosed by Hegel. Whereas earlier art was essentially defined by time, culture, and explanations, the opposite standpoint arose in the modern period – freedom of art and artistic imagination. Jean Paul speaks of an "inverted law" (*lex inversa*)[2] where all prior connection to a specific matter

---

2 Richter 1963: 129. See also Vieweg, 'The World Turned Upside Down' (in this volume).

or a specific form is now broken and matter and form are freely chosen in the most extreme sense. Nothing but the subjectivity of the artist is presented, who now is indebted only to a single principle, that of humanity in general, the only principle immune to scepticism. Humanity is held to be the new, unique, and final sacred object. It is in this sense that Goethe speaks of Sterne's fundamental sympathy for eccentric and foolish individuals of "noble tolerance" (*edler Duldung*), individuals of "understanding, reason and goodwill for humanity" (Goethe 1960: 350). Similarly for Jean Paul, modern humour is characterised by "mildness and tolerance of individual foolishness", because in contrast to the common jester and the "cold, satirising man" the humorist "cannot deny his own kinship with humanity" (Richter 1963: 128). For Hegel, the new art can only be constituted by an indifference which perceives its own vanity.

As testament to the liberation of form, *Tristram* is, of course, a particularly suitable example. One need only mention the mixture of the most diverse types of text, the reflection of the author on his writing procedure, or the narrative in reverse that goes from maturity to birth. As in ancient scepticism, spirit here makes itself indifferent to everything which reality presents (*Werke* 12: 385). For Jean Paul "the audacity of destructive humour" converges with scepticism: both are directed at the deceptiveness of the world's existence, which is laughingly disrespected but with a philosophical purpose: "as reason dazzles and subdues the understanding, as a god dazzles and subdues a finite thing, so does humour" (Richter 1963: 131, 132). It is the devil in particular who incorporates this inverted world and is thus held to be the greatest humorist and trickster. We have to be diabolical humorists in order to send the world to the devil. Sterne's sceptical antirealism negates the thesis of the world as something given and thus shatters all objectivity. He narrates and ponders countless events and then shows that no word of it is true. The finite is annihilated in a firework of pictures, the nothingness is unmasked. Wit is the sceptical crusher of everything. For Jean Paul, "it respects and disrespects nothing; it is indifferent to everything" (Richter 1963: 201). Whoever wants to ascend to Heaven must first traverse Hell.

The rich metaphors of negativity are taken up by those philosophers who employ the sceptical method. Sextus and Kant talk of purifications, the protection against dogmatism; Kant and Hegel speak of throwing the finite into the empty abyss; Hegel compares total scepticism to the terror of the guillotine. True scepticism is characterized as a speculative Good Friday. Sharp-witted sceptics, proponents of the antinomy of pure wit, are the advocates of negativity, the celebrants of this philosophical and literary Good Friday – here the metaphysical knights, there the poetic fools.

2 The Victory of Subjectivity

For Hegel, ancient scepticism represents the new principle of free self-consciousness which causes the order to rupture. Every philosopher must also be a sceptic, unbiased, free from all unfounded assumptions and prophetic assurances. She must submit her thought to the inferno of the touchstone of scepticism. The positive side of Pyrrho is found in his character. The individuality of this character was his very philosophy and his philosophy was nothing other than the absolute freedom of his character. Here his affinity with modern humour is clear. The difficulty first begins when this subjectivity of character has to be transferred into a subjectivity of wisdom. This purely sceptical attitude which wants to remain mere subjectivity and appearance adds to each sentence the clause 'as it seems to me,' and thereby ceases to be relevant for knowledge.

The free subjectivity of the self, the subjective mood, is given free play in humour. Significant here is the liberation of the subject as regards her inner contingency, the absolute freedom of self-consciousness in the world of subjective amusement. In humorous self-negation, comic subjectivity remains peaceful and certain of itself. Aristophanes' heroes, Don Quixote, and Sterne's eccentrics embody this self-certainty, this unreflective quiet as regards success, this careless indifference, which is related to the sceptical *ataraxia*. Hegel's description of Don Quixote's "certainty of self, peace, firmness of mind in itself" (*Werke* 14: 218) mirrors that of the sceptic's *ataraxia* (*Werke* 19: 363). For Hegel, humour belongs to the highest form of the romantic depiction of character, of individual peculiarities, of particular destinies. The uniqueness of individuality is attributed to subjectivity. These novels are autobiographies, life journeys of rounded individuals – as in the title of Hippel's chief novel, which significantly begins with the word "I". As Sterne notes, the biographer could depict the character of a man especially well with the help of a "hobby horse" (Sterne 1985: 98, 132), the authentic expression of individuality. Humour means hopping around on a hobby horse and "playing the fool ... nineteen hours out of the twenty-four ... with all the burdens [of life] (except its cares) upon my back" (ibid. 459).

Sterne and Hippel are indebted to the credo of the sceptic Michel de Montaigne: who in the preface to his *Essays* wrote "I am myself the substance of my book". Yet Montaigne travelled as a vagabond "*pour mon plaisir*" (Montaigne 1965: 258) and thus completely rends asunder knowledge and narration. Dreams are higher than arguments. In *Tristram Shandy* and in the autobiographies we find cheerful poetic monologues, self-constructions full of fantasy and humour, in which the central focus is the witty dialogue that reveals the diverse dimensions and perspectives of the self and particularly the encounter between thought, representations, and feeling. Everyone must tell their own story in their own way. The stories told in *Tristram Shandy* "are all true; for they are about myself" (Sterne 1985: 533). The author must write as she herself is. Hippel's motto is: "I write for myself, I hold a monologue for my own pleasure and displeasure" (cited in Michelsen 1972: 271). As Jean Paul says, for each humorist it is the self which becomes protagonist; the humorist is "his own court jester and his own comical masquerade ball quintet, but also its sovereign and director" (Richter 1963: 132).

It is precisely in these terms that Hegel characterizes humour: the artist only reveals herself; the author's reflections and perceptions find their own expression; it is the person of the author's self which produces itself according to its particularity as well as its deeper sense. Novels are the journeys within the self, narratives of fate, of the education of individuals, of their years of learning and travel, poetic self-portraits as biographies, trips, and walks as journeys into the self. In other words, they depict the self's representations of itself, the highest expression of the metaphor of self-reference, the culminating point of self-consciousness in the form of representation. At the same time, it is a narrow bridge on which modern art travels, risking triviality, primitiveness, sentimentalism, and boredom. Goethe's notion of a 'daring deed' (*Wagstück*) is appropriate here. Only the noble character or the beautiful soul of the author provides a certain guarantee of success.

One must not only laugh at the world but also at the poetic self. As antinomy is applied to antinomy, so is humour applied to vanity, which is negated by humour. In addition to the world, the humoristic subject must surrender itself to the ridiculousness and foolishness of human nature. This self-surrender of the poet entails that objective humour can only exist as particularity, as a part or a dimension of the work. Ancient scepticism was the free aspect of philosophy, while its accommodation as a sceptical moment implicit and inherent in philosophy was the necessary development, whereby philosophy gained immunity against the sceptical tropes. In a similar way, humour is the free dimension of modern art, an intrinsic aspect of being modern.

In this sense modernity is a time of literary and philosophical scepticism, but equally a time of the 'incorporation' of the sceptical. Sterne's *Tristram Shandy* is a prototype of *representational* self-reference, of the self-fulfilment of humour as literary scepticism just as Hegel's *Phenomenology of Spirit* is a model of *conceptual* self-reference, a self-fulfilling scepticism. The subjectivities of humour and thought are the paradigms of modern literature and philosophy. Modern subjectivity requires scepticism; without it we have no concept of subjectivity and freedom. But it equally requires an amusing type of scepticism, a laughing, free humour.

CHAPTER 15

Religion and Absolute Knowing

In the *Phenomenology of Spirit*, where the transitions are of essential importance, the final of these, the ultimate *transitio*, must be accorded special significance. In his thesis that Hegel is the philosophical Dante, Karl Rosenkranz describes this final transfer in metaphorical manner: Hegel leads consciousness out of the Inferno of the natural via the Purgatorio of human ethical deeds to the Paradiso of religious reconciliation and scientific freedom.[1] This narrative corresponds to Hegel's hint in the declaration of his book: the ultimate truth is to be found in religion and then in science as the outcome of the whole. We are dealing here with the final change, the concluding transition from religion to absolute knowing. Spirit (*Geist*) is now compelled to change its shape (*Gestalt*), its imperfect design. Approaching the core of this trans-formation involves three steps.

1 Basic Determinations of the Transition

In Hegel's architectonic we find ourselves at the bridge between Chapter 7 and Chapter 8 where self-consciousness finds itself "at its last turning point" (Werke 3: 573), the sublation (*Aufhebung*) of religion in absolute knowing. Spirit is the starting point, the bridge-head, which now, after its movement through various shapes, arrives at an unavoidable pass, at 'true content' in the form of religion. In religion, spirit exists in the shape of *representation (Vorstellung)*.[2] The determinacy of this form is that of *being* and of *immediacy*. What is achieved here is the knowledge that the absolute is divine – that self-consciousness is necessarily divine consciousness.

Absolute religion can be understood as a shape in which the essence is known as spirit and which draws together all the preceding shapes of consciousness

---

[1] Rosenkranz 1998: 206–207. Elsewhere Rosenkranz points out that in his time in Jena, Hegel clearly recognized the deficit of the geometrical, poetic, organic, and mythologizing forms of expression, "the inadequacy of the form of representation of pure thought", the fact that the concept of spirit escapes all representation (Rosenkranz 'Bericht über das Fragment vom göttlichen Dreieck' in *Werke* 2, 534, 536).

[2] Cf. *Werke* 16 (esp. 'Der Begriff der Religion') and Hegel 2004: 33: "The form of religion then is the form of representation in general, where the absolute truth is given to representation in a subjective way".

with their general determinations into a new order which Hegel describes as the self-moving becoming of the totality, as *event*. The form in which this wholistic event is communicated is the mythical-logical, a story of divine happening, a divine history. The absolute is depicted in descriptive-representational form. Religion is regarded as the highest and final shape of the consciousness of spirit; it concludes the series of these shapes but does not yet have "the form of the concept" (*Werke* 3: 555). As religion, divine self-consciousness has a shape which is not yet adequate to its content, the truth.[3] To put it in terms of the journey which spirit has made in the *Phenomenology*: although an overcoming of the paradigm of consciousness has been underway from the beginning, the ultimate sublation of the structure of consciousness, the transition to the final form of spirit, can only now take place in its "spirit-shape" (*Werke* 3: 573, 582), that is, in the form of comprehensive knowledge.

The form of representation (*Vorstellung*) is the moment to be overcome, and from which spirit must pass into the concept. This will involve a *translation from the form or the language of representation into the form or language of the concept*, the "sublation of this mere form" (*Werke* 3: 574). Only with the sublation of the form of representation into comprehensive thinking, only in the pure form of the concept, does spirit gain its own existence, a form which is wholly adequate to it. Comprehensive thinking (*begreifenden Denken*) represents the "final shape of spirit, the conceptual shape which concludes the entire series of its shapes" (*Werke* 3: 584).

In this brief introduction to the topic I have already hinted at the key terms and problems to be unpacked – *representation, faith as immediate knowledge, event, divine self-consciousness and mytho-logical history*. These components indicate a necessary return to pure thought, to a confrontation with a form that, in its one-sidedness, has already been encountered in the *Phenomenology*, namely the pure free thinking of scepticism. In performing and perfecting scepticism, consciousness learns the inescapability of its own reversal, it is inverted. It learns that it is on its way to itself, to its essence and to its concept. This continuous structure of alternation between pure subjectivity and pure objectivity can be illustrated here only in selected examples. The way of pure thought typical of the understanding leads into the supersensible inverted world (*verkehrte Welt*), while the free, sceptical self-consciousness proves to be an un-free, self-less, inverted self-consciousness.

---

3 Cf. *Werke* 3: 503 and *Werke* 10: 410: "But as *religion*, this *divine self-consciousness* still has a shape which is not *adequate* to its content, its truth".

2   Core Determinations of the Turning Point of the Transition, the Final Return out of the Realm of Representation

The following reflections restrict themselves to one aspect of this transition – Hegel's talk of the '*form of representation*'.[4] In religion, the rift between insight and faith is overcome in such a way that spirit as religion has its immediate, pure self-consciousness, knows itself directly as spirit, it has the *certainty* of being spirit. Self-consciousness becomes substantial, the substantiality becomes 'self-like'. We are dealing with a shape of perfection of spirit, but only insofar as it succeeds in becoming the true *substance*, the true *content* of itself. However, at the outset of Hegel's original understanding of religion, we find, surprisingly, an apparently *non-religious* statement, a statement that recalls Pyrrho and Lucian: *the self is the absolute essence (Wesen)*. In absolute religion, the identity of human and divine nature, of being-in-itself and being-for-itself, the identity of substance and subject, is formulated in a complementary way: a) God exists immediately as self, as particular human; and b) the self represents the life of the divine spirit.

Spirit encompasses the preceding shapes in their general determinateness, it forms the simple totality of these moments; however, these appear only as predicates of a divine subjectivity. The particular moments have here gone back to their ground, and *in their movement they represent the becoming of the complete reality of spirit*. In spirit as a religion, we have the movement of these components, differentiated and returning to themselves. Religion, in this peculiar Hegelian sense, means an intellectual self-presentation and self-knowledge of spirit, one which combines a theoretical-representational and a cultic-practical dimension. Religion, alongside art and philosophy, forms the foundation of culture as such, the 'Sunday of life'. It is one of the three absolute forms (each necessary for the other yet irreducible to the other) by which humans express and 'represent' their general self-understanding, and are thus at one with themselves. The essential, by no means trivial, distinction between the three moments lies in their form of expression or communication, in their 'medial' status. It depends on "which determinateness spirit expresses itself in" (*Werke* 3: 501), in which medial mode spirit presents or communicates itself. On the basis of the distinction between *representational* and *comprehensive thinking*, Hegel gives the outlines of a concept of translation out of the language of the concept into that of the concept – the form of representation is

---

[4] Rolf-Peter Horstmann has drawn attention to the extraordinary relevance of this theme in Hegel (Horstmann 1993).

to be sublated so that the true content can receive its true form (*Werke* 3: 556, 574). Hegel will later make this understanding of representation explicit in his *Encyclopaedia* (the section on Subjective Spirit) as well as in his Lectures on the Philosophy of Art and on Religion. In the following, I reconstruct the decisive interrelated dimensions and categorial determinations of the 'form of representation' and the necessity of their sublation.

2.1 *Representation as Mean between Universality and Individuality*

Representation (*Vorstellung*) is situated between sensuous intuition and conceptual thought, it is the mere "synthetic connection of sensible immediacy and thinking", the combination of "universality and individuality" – the illustration of the universal or the universalization of intuition (*Werke* 10: 257–267). In the *Phenomenology of Spirit* one can also find a link between representation and the *image* of spirit, the idea of representation as a combination of the logical and the visual, the synthetic connection of the self-conscious and external existence (cf. *Werke* 3: 531). A content, a meaning, finds visual illustration in the form of a comparable and related externality. We are dealing with 'inner' images, with inner representations and their expression and, in their highest form, with the verbalization of what is represented. The imagination or fantasy (*Einbildungskraft*), which lies at the core of representation, involves an activity of productively connecting and combining images, the inner presentation of self-created ideas, the 'placing-forth' (*Hervor-Stellen*) of new images. In this illustrative content, an anticipated concept and an intuition are brought into unity, in which the intellect proves to be the determining force over the images.[5] The higher identity of individuality and the universal, the spiritual and intuitive, which has now been attained, nevertheless represents only formal reason, a formal knowledge and action, a combination of individuality in the form of imaginative-arbitrary subjectivity and universality in the form of essence (*Wesen*). In this formal universality, we have, in theoretical terms, a universality of essence, of reflection, of an imagined commonality, of 'representing what is common' in the sense of totality; in practical terms, we have the 'universality of reality' as the totality of selves, in the sense of a community of all.[6] Thus, the immediate is not completely overcome, spirit has not yet reached the appropriate formation: the identity of form and content, a complete being-at-one-with-itself. Individuality and universality remain in an inadequate symbiosis.

---

5 See Vieweg 2007 and (in this volume) 'Hegel's Concept of the Imagination'.
6 The more precise determinations are presented in the 'Doctrine of Essence' in Hegel's *Science of Logic*, *Werke* 6. See also *Werke* 3: 555 & 560.

Religion has its appropriate form of communication in mytho-poetic language, more precisely in mytho-logical scripture. In their main components, such religious narratives are characterized by a merely synthetic connection between the sensuous and the conceptual; the examples Hegel gives of such pure syntheses include the words 'God', 'Hell', 'Devil' and 'Creation'. This emphasis on the purely synthetic marks out both the capacity and the limits of the representative: there is a unity of intuition and concept, by no means irrational, but there is no closed, perfected unity. Representations or images oscillate continually between the two poles of *universality* and *individuality*; these have not yet been brought into a speculative unity, there is still a constant 'transfer' or 'carrying-over' (*Über-tragen*) – *metaphora* – between them.

The imagination (*Einbildungskraft*) is the creative force behind the realm of representation and forms the foundation and source of the infinite number of diverse images. But this also means that there can be no complete liberation from the objective, from isolated individual phenomenon. The notions of negativity and wickedness, for instance, find their depiction, their representation, in different versions of the 'devil', as they appear in different religions, and the same goes for conceptions of 'creation'. God appears in a variety of forms and, like the pantheon of Greek Gods, displays the comic self-forgetfulness of his own nature, namely, that he must be essentially *one* as well as *several*. The idea of God as the sun (ancient Egyptian religion) or as a father (Christianity), etc., is a random attribution, since no conclusive connection with the idea of an absolute can be established; with equal justification God could be imagined as the earth, as mother, etc. Hegel speaks explicitly of *religions* in the plural, of religions as particular representations, of religion existing necessarily in multiplicity. The shape of spirit consists in the form of *spirits* (*Geistern*), although one can only truly speak of spirit in the singular. Both positions equally claim validity and within the internal space of religion this *isothenia* can find no solution.

The representation of the universal, while embracing thought, pointing towards it, is not yet at the stage of comprehensive thinking; it has the content without its internal logical necessity, and instead of the form of the concept it brings forms of externality (cf. *Werke* 10: 410), for example natural relations such as father, son, etc., into the realm of pure consciousness. In every religion as a *specific* shape, one of the assembled shapes is dominant, and this determination or peculiarity affects every moment, giving them a common character. All the particular components have in common the same determinateness of the whole. In clear contrast to the previous 'linear' series of developments in the *Phenomenology*, what arises now is a completely new order of individual shapes. As a result of the fundamental multiplicity of representations (here the manifold of religions) the *series* or *path* of phenomenology now splits into *a variety of lines or paths*, expressing itself in the multiplicity of religions, in another type of 'polytheism'. Here, too, a circle of gods arises, which is not a system, not a logical whole, but a loose, accidental connection of manifold worlds of representation. This manifold could, however, be united or synthesized in a 'covenant' (*Bund*), in a circle of religions, on the basis of the status of the respective formative ideas, which represent the individual moments of the whole (*Werke* 3: 501). Herein lies, firstly, the justification for the necessary diversity of religious representations and, secondly, the indispensability of mutual respect between religions and the untenability of every claim to religious exclusivity and supremacy.

Important aspects of Hegel's understanding of religion indicate the modernity and topicality of his outlook and avoid the one-sidedness and reductionism present in much thinking about religion today. If we are talking of the representation of God, then we are dealing with a substantial knowledge of truth, not merely with feelings, sublime sensations or something neuropsychological. Excluding conceptual thought from religion, reducing religion to the sensual and to feelings leads to the notion that what is highest is incomprehensible or inaccessible. Limits are thereby placed on thinking, irreconcilable barriers and boundary fences are erected for the concept.[7] In this dogma which posits the inaccessibility of truth to comprehensive thought and which fundamentally curtails the reach of the concept or even disparages the conceptual, Hegel sees an essential misunderstanding and a threat to the modern world as such. It implies, says Hegel, that knowledge is bankrupt and the truth is unknowable, "it is this *vanity* which has become widespread in philosophy, and is still abroad in our times, doing all the talking". In modern times, according to Hegel, "no concept has had a harder time than the *concept itself*" (*Werke* 13: 127). Secondly, when one strives for a purely self-legitimating representation there arise untenable claims that one possesses *the sole and exclusive* representation. The extreme form of this is 'fanaticism', Hegel's word for fundamentalism. Yet whoever represents something only has the legitimacy of what they have found or created themselves, they have yet to undergo the test of argumentation, which cannot be avoided.

Thus Hegel recognizes the main reason for the decline of faith and for continuing secularization and disenchantment, namely *the rejection and repression of comprehensive thinking*. The so-called modern triumph of rationality

---

7   Alluding to a Kantian perspective, Hegel speaks of an absolute being who remains mere representation and who cannot be conceived. The divinity thereby lacks legitimation, proof, it is then a mere postulate (*Werke* 3: 450).

is only the problematic victory of the understanding, an understanding which is still essentially determined by representation, and whose reduction of everything to mathematical-scientific rationality is merely the flipside of the decline of faith. Both tendencies are one-sided, expressions of the turn away from comprehensive thinking.

For Hegel, representation's imaginary is liberated in modernity. Everyone can be free in one of the religions and thereby acquire a substantiality, find their own unique visualisation of the absolute, their reconnection to the world of representations. But no *individual* formation can *on its own* provide the unifying bond of modern society, no individual religion can claim to be binding upon every individual. Only an examination of the content of each religious idea can achieve this, only comprehensive thinking is able to justify the definite contents of representations. This clearly entails that certain religious images can also lack the necessary legitimation.

Hegel's understanding of religion as a form of substantial knowledge in the shape of certainty also counters a reductionist position of the understanding, according to which religion is mere fiction, merely alienated or enslaved consciousness.[8] Religion is no fossil or relic surviving in a totally secularizing world. Such an understanding, often found today, throws out the content with the form and fails to understand the essentials of the authentic religions, makes them into something knowledge-less, just as the pure religion of feeling with its claims to exclusivity fails to understand knowledge. In this talking-past-each-other of reason-less religion and reason-less understanding we find a fundamental problem of the modern world, a deficit which Hegel tries to counter with the idea of a true unity of both sides, with the concept of a mutual translation between the languages of representation and of the concept. The question of the possibility of sublating the form of representation in the form of the concept is thus no mere interesting history lesson but is of considerable relevance to modern culture.

2.2 The Form of Representationalism

In religion, we have the universal spirit that contains all beings and all reality.[9] With the presence of objectivity, of externality, of otherness, we still have a moment of the structure of consciousness, of being distinguished from something to which one is at the same time related. It involves an object, as is did in

---

[8] Here lies a significant difference from Marxist, Nietzschean, and Freudian positions on religion, which gained considerable influence in the 20th century.

[9] If this condition is not fulfilled, we are dealing not with religion but with superstition, with pseudo-religion or the perversion of religion, all of which are now on the rise.

the shape of consciousness (*Werke* 3: 576).[10] The form of objectivity has not yet been completely transcended, although the other has been completely transferred into subjectivity. This other cannot yet fully assume the form of free reality, the form of free objectivity. The spirit, enclosed within itself, cannot be the free creator of nature, its creations are shapes as *spirits*, its determinateness is only a predication of the highest subjectivity.

In religion the authentic consciousness of spirit does not yet have the form of free otherness. Spirit, caught in itself, implies the reality enclosed in religion, which is only the "shape or the clothing of representation" (*Werke* 3: 497). Thus the idea is essentially lacking in objectivity, in the determinateness which conceptual thought has achieved. In this way, reality is disallowed its full right, namely to be *not just clothing or external form* but *independent, free existence*. Religion thus fails to fully reach what it wants to represent.

2.3 *Immediacy and Being*

A fundamental determination of representation is *immediacy*,[11] the immediate certainty of faith. In absolute religion, the self of the existing spirit has the form of complete immediacy, the immediate self-consciousness is consciousness of the existence of God. The determinateness of the shape in which spirit appears in this immediate form is that of *being*, and specifically, as a mere relation of the eternal being (*Wesen*) to its being-for-self (*Fürsichsein*), in the manner of immediate, simple, pure thought. Therein the Spirit appears or is revealed. In faith, consciousness has the positivity, the content, but the object is pure thought, something which, in its immediacy, leaves no distinction, whose other cannot be something opposed to it, something real.

To the extent that this idea persists, the eternal being decays into an empty word, and the true reality of spirit falls away from religion, resulting in a separation between this world and a beyond. Truth is then constituted by an externally posited authority, and revelation remains *a fundamentally concealed, self-less Being*, which is diametrically opposed to the demands of self-consciousness. As such an individual, self-consciousness is still opposed to the universal, and spirit, as such an exclusive individual, has the form of a sensible other for consciousness. Spirit has thus *not yet* reached the true unity of individuality and universality. The shape does *not yet* have the form of the concept,

---

10   Cf. *Werke* 3: 576. "In each of these forms, representation is something alien, external". Spirit cannot permeate or comprehend these external representations and so is unable to halt in the shape of religion (*Werke* 10: 411).

11   "Immediacy is the principal category of representation, where the content is known in its simple relation to itself" (*Werke* 16: 155).

i.e. "of the universal self, that in its immediate reality is also sublated, thinking, universal" (*Werke* 3: 555).

As is well known, one of Hegel's key ideas is that immediacy is just as much pure mediation or thinking, and therefore it must represent this in itself as such. In religion, however, this only happens in the form of representations, in the finding and production of representations, a process ultimately devoid of critical examination. Against faith, as *the advocate of the immediate*, Hegel employs *the lawyer of the mediate*, the consistent representative of relativity, the sceptic, whose cross-examination destroys all preconceptions, all supposedly pure immediate certainties – he employs free, independent, investigative thought, the thought of absolute negativity. Determinate negation must also be carried out upon religion.

Only this radical resumption of the freedom of thought and volition can lead to the actual formation of spirit as something autonomous and self-determining, the mind in its conceptual formation: "The represented, the shaped, the existent, has to take a different form than consciousness. To *thought*, the object does not move in representations or shapes, but in *concepts*". In conceptual thought I am free, because I am no longer in the other, but solely by myself; and the object maintains the form of free reality, free otherness (*Werke* 3: 156).

2.4 *Representation and Event – Divine History*

Spirit includes all previous shapes in their universal determinations as moments of itself, and Hegel describes religion as *simple, particular* totality in its becoming. Individual moments return to spirit as to *their ground*. This self-moving totality, which brings together all previous forms as moments of itself, is construed and expressed in the form of a series of independent shapes and their movement, as an *event* (*Werke* 3: 420), as a *definite narrative* in the sense of a combination and composition of representations, linguistically composed in the manner of an amalgam of the logical and the figurative, as a mythological text. This becoming as a circling movement is not yet fully logically constituted, it is *no conceptual genesis* but a *divine history*, no complete self-determination of the concept but a composite of images and representations, a mytho-logy. In these representations, images and narrative forms, the necessity of the concept is construed as an event (*Werke* 3: 559).

Narrative (*Erzählung*) combines calm immediacy with the representation of becoming other and the return from otherness, thus presenting a kind of reconciliation. Spirit is thus the movement of distinguishing and returning to self of its sides, its moments. The religions express basic structures and fundamental contents, they assemble decisive determinations of human existence in the manner of a grand narrative, a composed sequence of episodes, a thought-based, holistic history in the manner of metaphors and allegories. In terms of fundamental types, Hegel reveals the basic logical structure (and at the same time exposes the limits of) the framework of representation. These two dimensions are demonstrated using selected components of the type "absolute religion".

Just as the individual moments themselves occur in the form of representation, so the connection between the moments and the scenario of the images take the same deficient form, an arc of exposition which stretches from the creation of the world to its reconciliation. The independent moments are gathered into a single whole, placed on the foundation of imagination and reflection, and, through a list of predicates, juxtapositions and successive groupings, are linked by means of mere conjunctions (words such as "and" or "also"). This is similar to the form taken by the *hypotypesis* favoured by the Pyrrhonians: a tableau is created which presents the phenomena in outlines, to the naked eye, in the sense of the 'Evidentia'. A mytho-poetic life of the divine being is created, the essential events of the human being are expressed, history appears as a logo-mythical biography. Again, we are dealing with a purely synthetic, amalgamating connection, which has no strictly logical necessity. In this 'vividness', this pictoriality, this 'sensualising of concepts' (to use Hölderlin's expression) lies a major advantage of such representation-dominated texts. The connections follow the form only outwardly, randomly, and arbitrarily; as with poetic texts, their unfolding involves no logical connection. The individual moments are not related to each other by a concept; the connection lacks the determinateness of the category. However, the linkages can point beyond representation towards the concept, such as in the representation of the triad. It shows that in religion's images and representations, thought is implicitly present, but not yet in its own authentic form of expression (cf. *Werke* 16: 139–151).

Hegel begins with the image of divine work in the form of the creation of the world: "this Creation is representation's word for the concept itself, its absolute movement" (*Werke* 3: 561), a metaphoric that suggests a before and an after, a sequence. But the Absolute is precisely "not before or after time, not before the creation of the world, nor when it perishes [. ...] The world is created, is created now, and has been created forever" – as Hegel's translating of this representational event puts it (*Werke* 9: 26).[12] Neither are representations such

---

12   In the following passage a translating from the language of representation into the language of the concept is clear: "God has revealed that his nature consists in having a Son, i.e. in making a distinction within himself, making himself finite, but in his difference he remains in communion with himself, beholding and revealing himself in the Son, and

as Paradise, Father and Son, the eating of the Tree of Knowledge forms which relate necessarily to the concept. A key difficulty for religion is the question of how evil comes into the world, to which there are the various answers, ranging from the wrath of God to the appearing of the Devil, to talk of a Fall – in each case the divine Being is attributed a purely alien moment that does not emanate consistently or logically from itself. Here Hegel sees representation's greatest struggle with itself. Yet lacking the concept, the struggle is to no avail – representations remain incoherent in themselves and lead only to equivocations (*Werke* 3: 564). The negative arrives here only from the outside and is in no way logically necessary to the positive; in such terms it is impossible to *conceive* the origin of evil. Eating of the Tree of Knowledge is a merely accidental event, in no way necessary. In the case of Father and Son, religion produces inadequate analogies with natural life: the Son has a spiritual Father and a real Mother (*Werke* 3: 550, 574).

A second example consists in the specific connection between divine and temporal events. The divine story arises from the imagination, yet it is not an empty fiction but is regarded as a '*real event*'. Against the view of history as a chaotic, incoherent series of happenings, against the inadequate concepts of the 'as if' and 'regulative ideas', against the thesis of the death of grand narratives, a *universal is already to be found*, it involves the constitution of a thought founded on thought, a meaningful story. But these representations which are proffered in the narrative form of providence and theodicy are at the same time regarded as incomprehensible, and thus the true, concrete universality is missed.

Finally Hegel discusses the representation of *reconciliation* (*Versöhnung*), the creation of a real, complete, present contentful unity of the individual with the universal. At this key point, Hegel's key argument can be clarified: in the very immediacy of representation, mediation emerges; thus the reference to (or foreshadowing of) the necessity of translating into comprehensive knowledge, of taking the path from *grasping* (*Ergreifen*) to *comprehension* (*Begreifen*). The reconciliation of spirit with itself expresses an event in which the divine being, the universal, *particularises itself, individualizes itself,* and from its death arises the unification of this individual and the universal. The death of the divine individual and the becoming-spirit of the mediator – the God-man – has two aspects: this death loses its *immediate*, natural meaning. Individuality dies in the universality of the spirit that *lives, dies and rises again*. As a result of this

---

by this unity with the Son, by this being-for-himself in the Other, he is absolute mind or spirit" (*Werke* 10: 29).

mediation of the immediacy of representation, the "element of representation is posited as sublated and thereby returns to its concept" (*Werke* 3: 571). On the other hand, this overcoming of the isolated individual, which is already indicative of the concept, also affects the pure negativity of mere thinking: the pure subjectivity of scepticism, which is concerned only with the individual, must pass on to objective, substantial subjectivity. The final victory of Pyrrhus proves to be a pyrrhic victory and scepticism's 'speculative Good Friday' implies its own sublation on the 'Sunday of Thought'.

Here we find two unlikely bedfellows: scepticism and religion, pure insight and faith.[13] In the death of the man-God on Good Friday we see too the destruction of the *abstraction* of divine being, the second moment of the grasping (*Ergreifen*) of representation. The actual self had not previously had the same value as the universal; God was still the higher, the unequal. Yet even having the *same value* does not mean a *complete identity* of individuality and universality has been achieved. Through the death of the mediator – *God himself is dead* – the divine becomes something spiritual, something known, and only in this knowledge, that is, in the *death of representation* on the 'Sunday of thought' does the single self-consciousness become a universal self-consciousness. *In thought* (and *only* in thought) the self now has the same value as the universal being. In the limited sphere of representation, however, reconciliation takes place only externally, for this reconciliation is afflicted with the contradictions of the hereafter. The reconciliation of the mediator lies in the distant past, the reconciliation of individual humans is postponed to the future, to the Day of Judgment (*Werke* 3: 574). The *present* thus remains by definition unreconciled, and the individual's path to true being-for-self, to self-determination and freedom, remains partially closed.

3   Freedom and Comprehensive Thought

With the concept of freedom we have arrived at the nerve-centre of Hegelian thinking. The syntheses, construction and amalgams of representation must transform into the immanence of the concept, the logo-mythical event into the self-determination of the concept. The distinction between the representational and the conceptual is that between, on the one hand, the event based

---

13   Already in the final passage of *Faith and Knowledge*, Hegel treats both positions in parallel, which agree in the idea of negativity – here "formal abstraction" and "the speculative Good Friday", there "infinite pain" and "absolute suffering" (*Werke* 2: 432). Here Hegel also mentions Pascal, a thinker who represents a peculiar symbiosis of scepticism and faith.

on substantive ideas, narrated and illustrated, and on the other hand, the self-movement of the concept; it is a distinction between pictorial and conceptual modes of communication. In religion, spirit finds a new expression: on the one hand, the essence, the substantial content of the human event, is visualized in the manner of the pictorial-representative and so returns to its ground; on the other hand, this necessarily gives rise to the variety of religious stories, to the multiplicity of religions.

Spirit, as the principle of evolving self-determination, emerges in religion and philosophy in various forms. Translation from the language of representation into the language of the concept, the sublation of the form of religion, occurs solely for the purpose of justifying its content, the divine, *the absolute*. Only in *comprehensive thinking* is the transition which Hegel articulates at the end of the *Phenomenology*, from *mytho-logical event* to *comprehended history*, completed. Only in comprehensive thinking can the difference between subjectivity and objectivity be *fully* overcome, the paradigm of consciousness fully sublated. Free thought has proved itself to be divine, as absolute content – the absolute, divine content in the conceptual form appropriate to it, as comprehensive thought.[14] The misfit between form and content changes into their identity, analogy and mythology into the logic of the concept. Spirit conquers its imperfect forms, its inadequate formations. Spirit now gives "its complete and true content the form of the self, and thereby realizes its concept, and in this realization remains in its concept" (*Werke* 3: 582). That the content preserves a 'self-like' form shows the authentic basic structure of a single spirit, of a single knowledge, of pure self-relation as the thinking of thought. The moments of the movement of spirit are no longer forms of consciousness or representations but determinate concepts, moments in the self-determination of the concept.[15] In place of the multiplicity of religions there comes a unified knowledge, a unity of dynamic conceptual determinations. This is the principle of wholism, a wholism and monism of thought and freedom, which Hegel terms absolute idealism.

---

14   On the task of philosophy, Hegel remarks in his *Lectures on the Philosophy of Religion*, that it is "the determination of the form to which philosophy adds the truth" (*Werke* 16: 150). Cf. *Werke* 10: 29: "That which representation provides, and which essentially involves the grasping of the concept, is the task of philosophy, which has not been solved truly and immanently as long the concept and freedom are not its object and soul".

15   In this sense, Hegel understands the concept as an "absolute form, the content in its own form," as the "pure form itself, which becomes the content" (*Werke* 10: 235; *Werke* 11: 357). Philosophy must sublate the content "given in the manner of representation into the form of the concept or that of absolute knowledge" (*Werke* 10: 32).

The idea of modern freedom, the complex nexus of the modern world, very much needs artistic and religious representation; but the modern world *cannot be adequately articulated* by the diverse, vivid and colourful worlds of representation. It requires too – and this is decisive – the *gray phalanx of the concept*, through whose power the forms of representation first find their justification and legitimation. It requires *conceptual knowledge*, in which the self gains its true being-in-itself, its freedom. All of which goes to say that it should not surprise us that a contemporary of Hegel's celebrated his once-in-a-millennium masterpiece *the Phenomenology of Spirit* as "the elementary book of liberation" (Rosenkranz 1998: 276).

CHAPTER 16

The East and Buddhism from Hegel's Perspective

Against the background of the relationship between East and West, a selected facet of Hegel's understanding of Buddhism will be illuminated: according to Hegel, the West forms a *sublation* of the East in the triple sense this word carries – preservation, overcoming and elevation. This 'translation', this transformation or replication, takes place in two basic steps:

1) The first sublation of the East is carried out in the transition to antiquity, represented in the myth of the Zeus, who steals the daughter of the Phoenician king Europa and takes her to Greece.
2) The second sublation takes place beginning with the Renaissance, in the modern period, constituting a unity of ancient classicism and the East.

1   The First 'Translation': That of Antiquity

With regard to this first 'translation,' the origin of Greek culture, a few aspects will be mentioned regarding the marriage of Zeus with the Asian daughter:

(a) The beginnings of Greek culture came from outside, its actual establishment beginning with the arrival of foreigners. Hegel sees in the Asian world the land of 'morning', of the rising (of the sun), of the beginning, of inception in the widest sense. But this beginning was "transformed by the independent spirit of the Greeks" (*Werke* 12: 292) Hegel speaks of a mixture of introduced culture – Indian, Persian, Egyptian, Jewish – and the indigenous. The Greeks were "transforming creators" who led an amphibian existence, living on land and sea, they could "float freely on the waves" (*Werke* 12: 294, 280). This was an essential source of the thought of freedom, of subjectivity. As in the case of their Asiatic predecessors, the cosmopolitan, sea-travelling Phoenicians, everything, according to Hegel, was now left up to human activity, to human prudence, courage, skill, rationality. This liberation from the traditional relationship to nature was cultivated by the Greeks, but inspired by Easterners. In Greek mythology, the Eastern marriage gift has been preserved with gratitude – especially mentioned are the Phoenician letters Cadmus brought, the iron and the oil tree of the Scythians, and the introduction of agriculture by Triptolemos under the instruction of Ceres (*Werke* 12: 280). Hegel thus addresses the two strata of Greek culture that Nietzsche later describes as the 'Apollonian' and the 'Dionysian'. In a well-known line, Hegel refers to the ancient

Eleusinian mysteries, to the relationship between cults of Demeter (Ceres) and Dionysus (Bacchus) (*Werke* 12: 91). Both were of Eastern origin and not popular with the Ionian nobility; Dionysus was probably only later granted hospitality at Delphi. Hegel construes both cults in terms of the principle of negativity, of nothingness, of the "absolute certainty of the nothingness of sensual things" (*Werke* 3: 91). These cultural patterns have thus been present since the origin of European culture, not dominant but influential undercurrents.

b) Eastern, especially Indian, Persian, Phoenician, and Egyptian ideas had played a considerable part in the origin of Greek philosophy. The early Ionic philosophers of nature, in particular, whose opinions were articulated against the background of Middle Eastern and Eastern thought,[1] along with Plotinus and Pyrrho, represent the linking of the foreign and the indigenous. Diogenes and others report numerous travels by Greek thinkers and their contacts in the East: Thales associated with the Egyptians, Solon travelled to Egypt, Cyprus, Libya and Lydia, Pythagoras visited Egypt and learned the language while Democritus travelled as far as Persia and the Red Sea and may even have visited India, where he is associated with the Gymnosophists. Everard Flintoff adds that many of the Greek philosophers were very much in search of knowledge in other regions, and long before the time of Pyrrho; they were in an intense conversation with Eastern thinkers (Flintoff 1980: 89). According to Antigonus of Carystos and Diogenes, Pyrrho, as a companion of Alexander the Great, had the doctrines of the Indian Magi brought with him to Greece and then amalgamated with Greek views of happiness. According to Flintoff, Pyrrho fundamentally altered both his way of life and his thinking as a result of Hindu, Jainist, and pre-Buddhist ideas. Flintoff emphasizes the Indian provenance of significant elements of Pyrrhonism: a) calm or "the tranquil consciousness" (*ataraxia, adiaphoria, aphasia*); b) the antinomic-isosthenic argumentation; c) the form of argumentation of the quadrillemma, d) the *apominosyne*, and e) the peripatetic form of life (ibid. 91–100).

Nietzsche puts this point emphatically: Pyrrho was "a Buddhist although a Greek, a Buddha himself" (Nietzsche 1988 Bd. 13: 347, 265). But Lukian of Samosata, a Pyrrhonian from Syria, had already expressed this in ancient times: the goddess of Philosophy, he says, first appeared to the Indians. From Hegel's point of view, on the other hand, the resulting tension between the principles of Pyrrho and Parmenides represents the beginning of philosophy in the strict sense.[2] Actual philosophy as the 'thinking of thinking' thus begins

---

1   See Graeser 2000: 1–2. See also the work of U. Hölscher and W. Burkert.
2   "Thinking must be for itself, must come to existence in its freedom, break away from the natural and step out of being submerged into contemplation [...] The actual beginning of

in the Greek world, freedom of thought is the condition of philosophy's inception (*Werke* 18: 116–117). The first two concepts of Hegel's *Science of Logic*, as is well known, have their prototypes in Parmenidean being and Buddhist-Pyrrhonian nothingness.

c) Just as in Aeschylus' *Lycurgeia* Lycurgus begins the struggle with Dionysus, so Western philosophy in its authentic founding act begins by taking a strong position against the East, which is indispensable for the structure of independence.

But in the very act of repelling the other, this other must be taken into consideration. In the violent attacks by Parmenides against the protagonists of nothingness we read that to hold nothingness for truth is the path of "error" on which "mortals knowing naught wander two-faced" like "confused blind men" (Parmenides cited in Burnet 1930: 174). Being, on the other hand, is unchangeable, it is "the same, and it rests in the self-same place, abiding in itself" (ibid. 175). But Being in this sense is merely indeterminate, says Hegel, while Nothingness turns itself around and is a being as soon as it is thought (*Werke* 18: 288). Thus, at the very dawn of philosophy, the principles and protagonists of Being and Nothingness, East and West are systematically juxtaposed in a surprising way. At the origin of European thought, Parmenides attempted the exclusion of the other and Hegel, in the modern period, its inclusion.

Again, Nietzsche was the one who pointed out the philosophical difference between East and West: Parmenides' thought "bears no relation to the intoxicating dark fragrance of the Indian, which is perhaps not wholly imperceptible in Pythagoras and Empedocles" (Nietzsche 1988 Bd.1: 835). Parmenides's being could be the most pure and "completely bloodless abstraction," "the rigid death-repose of the coldest concept", "the odourless, the colourless, the soulless" – a philosophy "poured from ice," the "coldest piercing light". Nietzsche sees the contrast both with regard to the content, the thought of fixed, immovable being, the "audacious insight into the identity of thought and being", the "terrifying energy of striving for certainty", and with regard to the form of communication, the expression of thoughts (ibid. 835ff). This Greek "truth, ascending the rope-ladder of logic", this icy coldness of the concept, turns against the Eastern, which is vivid, mythical, colourful, full of fantasy. The new form of Greek philosophy lacks the form of the intuitive, of the symbol, of allegory, Nietzsche deems this logos to be the "horror of all fantasy" (ibid. 844). Hegel

---

philosophy is to be made where the absolute is no longer an idea, where free thought does not merely think the absolute but grasps the idea of it" (*Werke* 18: 116).

too speaks in this sense of European philosophy as the "painter of grey in grey" (*Werke* 7: 28).

2 The Second 'Translation': Modernity

a) Descartes is typically taken to stand for the origins of modern European philosophy, while on the other side, bearing the stamp of the East, stand Bruno and Spinoza, along with the Pyrrhonist Montaigne. In the pantheism of the Spinozists, according to Hegel, one finds "the general view of Eastern poets, historians, and philosophers" (*Werke* 19. 519). Since both Descartes and Montaigne were strongly influenced by sceptical thought, Pierre Bayle sees in Sextus Empiricus the true father of modern European philosophy. Thus, the origin of modern European philosophy was accompanied by the Eastern-coloured traditions of Pyrrhonism and Pantheism, that is, by a reception and transformation of the East.

b) Hegel finds in modern art a marked presence of Eastern thinking. To explore this one must go back to Hegel's interpretation of the modern novel with respect to Goethe.

On this basis a promising assessment of Hegel's interpretation of Buddhism might proceed. As is well known, the focus of his discussion is so-called Indian Buddhism, especially Lamaism. Here, the basic pillars of the Hegelian point of view ought to be elaborated, including some that have often been overlooked in previous accounts. Here I will largely dispense with the question of the validity of Hegel's understanding of Buddhism, for this would require profound investigations into the distinct variations of Buddhist teaching. I will limit myself to elaborating the central lines of Hegel's interpretation – this perhaps has the advantage of indicating, first of all, the exact places in Hegel's thought where Buddhism is the theme.

3 Religion and Philosophy – Imagination and Concept

Central to Hegel's picture of Buddhism is that it involves a specific combination of philosophical thought and religious imagination (*Vorstellung*), it is a religious conception of the world that can be taken up by philosophy (*Werke* 18: 138). The universal principles found in the Buddhist worldview are related to philosophy: the Buddhist melding of imagination and conceptualizing is a "pantheism in the form of religion" (*Werke* 18: 147–170). Oriental philosophy "is religious philosophy; and this is the reason why it is more natural to consider the oriental conception of religion as philosophy as well" (*Werke* 18: 138). In this amalgam of philosophy and religion there exists one of the essential forms of expression of the Asian: a natural spirituality. Profound thoughts are made present, imagined, pictorialized in a particular religious form.[3] Dominant in the East is the pictorial (even a pictorial script), the combination of picture and writing, features typical of what Hegel calls the imagination – "we think in pictures".[4]

Hegel speaks of the East as a world of the symbolic, whereas the European is marked by the trend towards the iconoclastic, the word, literary language (with a script in which the pictorial is transcended). The imagination (as strictly pictorial) is the decisive term for illuminating this situation; it is about the relation between imagination and concept, about a sublation of imagination in the concept, about the relation between art, religion, and philosophy in the strict sense. Representations (*Vorstellungen*) are something pictorial-metaphorical, they are situated between the concept and what is immediately sensuous or intuitive; they oscillate between these, represent the middle, the between, the transition from the immediately singular of the sensual intuition and the universality of the concept. The pictorial is in turn made into universals, the universal made into pictures, meanings made into intuitions. Hegel understands not only Buddhism but religion in general in this sense, as the making present of the absolute content, as representation or imagining of the Absolute.

4   Buddhism as a Religion of Silent Being-in-itself

Famously, Hegel calls the practice of Buddhism a "silent being-in-itself". Yet only a very precise interpretation of the connotations of this phrase illuminates Hegel's meaning. According to the well-known beginning of Hegel's *Logic*, being-in-itself means initial, abstract negativity, the principal negation of everything other, a setting free of consciousness from everything external, the overlooking of or abstraction from any determinateness (*Werke* 5: 65–81). Being-in-itself is immaculate as regards the determinate, it is pure immediacy, an

---

3   "In the Persian and Indian religions very profound, sublime, speculative thoughts are expressed" (*Werke* 18: 84).

4   The words of Teruaki Takahashi. Interesting in this context is a certain unity of text and image in traditional Japanese books and in the *bunjinga*. As a result of the growing influence of the Europeans, a dividing line between image and writing was later drawn. In today's *manga* culture, the old tradition continues. Takahashi even claims "It would be easier to understand Japan if one read its mangas" (Takahashi 2005: 11).

in-itself-being of consciousness as being-sunk-in-itself, complete emptiness, lack of distinction, mere and simple self-identity, relationless negation as being-closed-in-itself, lack of determination, negation of all particulars, the one as pure nothing, the absolute as nothingness. All these characteristics return in his description of Buddhism, whose principle expresses this same nothingness. Thus, we can say that Buddhism is assigned a prominent place in Hegel's systematic thinking. The dissolution of definite thought is a property of the Asian spirit, determinations are simply transitory, vanishing, all determination disappears.

With regard to the historical situation of Indian religions, Hegel sees a fundamental advance in terms of the principle just mentioned. The concrete determinations of the religious conception are freed from their wild, unbridled breakup, from their natural disintegration, and brought together, put into inner relation, their oscillating frenzy brought to stillness (*Werke* 16: 374). It leads "to the idea of the pure unity of thought in itself", to being-in-itself, "wherein the empirical all of the world, as well as those highest substantialities called gods, disappear" (*Werke* 10: 385). The death of traditional gods lies in this "collapse of difference into the category of unity". The previous relationship of unity and distinction induced the infinite process, the permanent alternation of negation and positing, now this – as with the Pyrrhonians – becomes cut off, any relationship, any connection to another is truncated (*Werke* 16: 374). Although this being-in-itself is merely the overcoming of the independent differences, the fury of disappearing, and not yet the being-for-itself as the highest stage of the being-in-itself, it behaves in the most abstract way as regards the soul's being-for-itself. This being-in-itself implies the ever-quiet, unchanging, tarrying that does not step into the stream of time, the transitory. With this intellectual substantiality, all subjective vanity is thrown away and solid ground can be trod; it is nothing less than the essential foundation of all philosophy, idealism as the being-for-itself of thought (*Werke* 18: 167). (In its Greek adaptation, this thought is called *ataraxia*, stillness of the soul – "the surface of a sea not moved by any wind", as Sextus Empiricus describes it. According to Hegel, this is the beginning and the free side of every philosophy.)

Hegel's Buddhist-Pyrrhonian-idealist credo can be expressed in the following combination of impressive pictures, all of which emphasize the form of being-in-itself: "In the still spaces of a thought come to itself and existing only in itself the interests that move the life of peoples and individuals are silent" (*Werke* 5: 23) – "The resolve to philosophize throws itself purely into thinking – this thinking is alone in itself, it throws itself into nothingness as into a boundless ocean" (*Werke* 10: 416). The intellectual substantiality that Hegel understood as an advantage of the Asian standpoint forms the opposite of reflection, of Western understanding (*Verstand*). While in Asia the universal is held to be what is truly and uniquely independent, and the subjectivity of spirituality is lacking, the European is marked by the ideas of singularity and subjectivity as ground.

After Descartes launched a new, modern philosophy with a principle of free, abstract thought, there appeared the Jewish-inspired thinking of Spinoza as "an echo of the East". Hegel notes: "Eastern intuition has been brought immediately closer to the European way of thinking and more so to European, Cartesian philosophizing, and introduced into it" (*Werke* 20: 158). Within Spinoza's unity of substance "absolute pantheism and monotheism is raised to thought" (*Werke* 20: 164), an Eastern intuition expresses itself clearly at the beginning of the modern age.

In this annihilation of all determinateness lies the "essential beginning of all philosophizing". Every philosopher must pass through this ether of the one substance, through this ocean of the negative. But it was only the beginning, only the abstract, rigid unity from which no development, no subjectivity, no spirituality could be derived (*Werke* 20: 165–166). This negative, stripped of all determinateness, is abstract negativity, naked, pure nothingness. In Spinoza's system, "everything is tossed into this abyss of annihilation . … The particular he speaks of is only discovered, taken from the representation, without being justified" (*Werke* 20: 166). All determination is subordinate or subsequent, it falls outside of substance. This determination Spinoza calls modus or mode, understanding it as a way of being or property of substance. According to Hegel, mode as such is completely untrue, all determinateness is only transient. Inessential determinateness is not preserved, not sublated, the unity is only brought into a formal, contentless identity (in the form of all content sinking into emptiness), not brought to the concrete unity. In contrast to substance, to the one, to the first, to the infinite, everything coming second, every determinateness can only be contingent, only finite, unessential and outside of the essential. So the mode is what is simply non-essential, what can only be grasped by another (*Werke* 5: 388–9). No accident can last two moments. As in scepticism, we have only the here-and-now, the instant, connections and relations are dissolved, the particular and the singular is without necessity, a matter of pure accident. In Spinoza's pantheism, "the highest goal for the human being who is completely displaced into the sphere of origin and passing away, of modality, the sinking into unconsciousness is […] destruction" (*Werke* 5: 389). The individual human finds themselves excluded from substantiality, they have no value, are merely contingent, without justification, merely finite (*Werke* 18: 120). The general determinateness that exists only in finiteness is to be avoided. All determinateness is to be discarded, determinateness is seen as a stain, something merely transient. So self-consciousness seems to be destroyed in the universal, falling into the depths of nothingness. According to Hegel, the only activity consists in throwing everything into this empty abyss of substance where everything disappears. In this way one comes to a rest, to immobility, the sublime, without self, without subjectivity. Shizutera Ueda speaks of the "unconditional selflessness", where one has to be "completely detached both from himself and from the Buddha and once and for all spring into pure nothingness" (cited in Pöggeler 2003: 224). Eastern substance thus takes the path towards the indeterminate, lacking conceptualizing thinking as self-determining objectivity (*Werke* 16: 168).

Hegel considers such thinking to be the universal that is at the same time the basis of substantiality and subjectivity. Hegel sees the core of the Eastern way of presenting things in the negativity of tarrying (*Werke* 19: 521). This leads to a difficulty (one also characteristic of Neoplatonic models of 'emanation'), namely that of visualizing, clarifying, and legitimating the emergence from the peaceful and empty unity. The transition to the finite seems to be possible only via fantasy and imagination and so is presented pictorially (e.g., as creation or shaping the world). Yet the question arises as to the status of the execution of this transmission: with which capacity of consciousness is this to be accomplished?

In regard to Plotinus, Hegel speaks of the key difficulty of how the One decides to determine itself, how it emerges from something without defect and stain. This necessary transition to the second "is not made by Plotinus philosophically or dialectically" but rather "is expressed in representations and pictures" (*Werke* 19: 447). We know that Plotinus used the metaphors of flowing from the source, of overflowing and of illumination from the light of the sun. Around 1800, this facet of Plotinian philosophy was described as 'Oriental enthusiasm', as ecstasy in the sense of a sort of extraordinary effort of the imagination, as 'intellectual intuition'.

We also find this topic at the beginning of Hegel's theory of Objective Spirit, where criticism of the East and Buddhism reappears, and this is of considerable importance, especially in the field of practical, of action. The first, initial characteristic of the will is that of pure indeterminacy, every peculiarity, every content is annihilated, the boundless infinity of absolute abstraction as negative freedom, the freedom of emptiness. A human can destroy all differences, tear loose from all that is external, give up all goals, let everything collapse, they have the power to give themselves universality, that is, to extinguish all peculiarity, all determinateness (*Werke* 7: 51). This is a necessary but one-sided moment. If it remains merely theoretical it amounts to Indian pure intuition, absolute calm, the knowledge of simple identity with oneself, remaining in the empty space of inwardness, renunciation of any activity.

Hegel proceeds to argue that this abstraction from all determinateness is not in fact without determination; *the lack of determination is precisely a determination*, being abstract, deficient, it is inescapably afflicted with this stain of determinateness. The assumption of a pure immediacy is proved untenable, and the inverse of Spinozan *determinatio est negatio – negatio est determinatio –* also holds. If calm being-in-itself is held to be the highest for humans then it is a being "without passion, without inclination, without action", one that amounts to "destruction" and "silence" (*Werke* 16: 386). Silence and Pyrrhonic judgment are undeniably possible, but they amount to an *attitude* and an *activity*. A position that renounces any formative, determining action, and chooses only letting-be or refraining-from, proves in principle to be impossible.

5 Freedom from Oneself and the Beautiful Soul

Consciousness has its own essence affirmatively before it, since it knows this essence as its own essence, but at the same time – and this is the shadow-side – it represents it as an object, it still distinguishes between being-in-itself and empirical consciousness. Thus it cannot reach the end of the path from consciousness to self-consciousness; it is indeed self-consciousness – willing or not – but does not yet know itself as such, and tries to overcome such a self-consciousness. The Buddhist being-in-itself is thus pure freedom from itself, not yet being-in-itself as freedom for itself, the highest form of being-in-itself. This consciousness does not want to be a will, is not resolved, it does not want to renounce unity and purity, and it sees in fixed determination the fundamental stain, the stain of determinateness.

The version of this thought translated into European thinking is the beautiful soul that does not want to be determined, does not want to be polluted with the finite. It purifies itself and sees in its poverty, in its disappearance, its only wealth. It lives in fear of staining the perfection of its inner life by action, and therefore flees contact with reality; it glimmers and sinks into the stillness of the seas; in part it appears as mute consciousness, in part it has its deed in speaking, in conversation (*Werke* 3: 479, 483). The romantic Indian enthusiasm of Novalis, which Hegel regarded as just such a beautiful soul, is well-known. Novalis (in the essay 'Christianity or Europe') called poetry "a decorated India, a star-filled, warm heaven in which the infinitely creative music of the universe resounds", whereas rational philosophy is the "monotonous rattling of an immense mill, a cold sea with dead cliffs" (Novalis 1999: 746). Even before Nietzsche, the East was associated with vivid fantasy and the West with icy cold rigidity, dead rationality; there the music full of fantasy, here the desolate clanging.

6 The East and Modern Poetry

A special affinity exists between the East (the symbolic world) and modern art. An essential side of the sublation of the East is achieved as the sublation of classical antiquity and the East in modern, romantic art. The Eastern pattern of non-correspondence, the lack of fit between content and form, is found at a higher stage in modern art, which is understood as the art of absolute being-in-itself, as the art of absolute internality. The human descends into what is deepest inside them, into the inner world of the soul. Meaning and formation are divided, subjectivity existing in itself and objectivity are separated, fall apart, become counterpoints. Inwardness appears only in externality, as contingency in respect to meaning. Romantic art, then, is a "hovering and sounding over a world that, in its heterogeneous appearances, can record and reflect only a glimpse (*Gegenschein*) of the being-in-itself of the soul" (*Werke* 14: 140–141). Objectivity, the world in general, becomes a mere glimpse, it is dissolved. Actual, direct expression loses its dominance, meaning is formed and de-formed in, alienated, in the work. Indirect, inauthentic talk, metaphor, symbolism, allegory are the focus. In his West-East Divan, Goethe achieves this fantasy-filled internalizing, the synthesis of intellectual freedom and subjective-inner fantasy. With freedom of spirit, he also regains the symbolism, the cheerfulness and parrhesia of the imagination, the free, cheerful spirit of the East.

7 Brief Resumé

These reflections outline a Hegelian proposal for a West-East divan – an attempt at a union of Western rationality with Eastern imagination and wisdom. The core of Hegel's thought consists in a concept of sublation in two stages, first the sublation of the East into classical antiquity and then the shaping of a unity of classical and Eastern in the modern West. The core argument in Hegel's attempt to bring West and East into a successful unity lies in overcoming the isostheny of determinateness and indeterminacy, of immediacy and mediation, of infinity and finiteness of thinking self-relation, or put programmatically, Substance must be thought of as Subject.

If Asians and Europeans, Easterners and Westerners, were to build a new Hellespont, they should allow Buddha and Hegel a seat on the divan – there an intriguing conversation would surely transpire. Such a seat on the West-East divan seems a vital challenge for the twenty-first century. If we do not learn a way to cross bridges, then as Hegel tells us, it is all the worse for humankind.

Bibliography

Hegel's Works Cited

Werke = Georg Wilhelm Friedrich Hegel *Werke in zwanzig Bänden*. Theorie Werkausgabe. Neu edierte Ausgabe. Redaktion Eva Moldenhauer und Karl Markus Michel. Frankfurt am Main: Suhrkamp, 1969–1971. The volumes contents are:
Band 1: Frühe Schriften
Band 2: Jenaer Schriften 1801–1807
Band 3: Phänomenologie des Geistes
Band 4: Nürnberger und Heidelberger Schriften 1808–1817
Band 5: Wissenschaft der Logik I
Band 6: Wissenschaft der Logik II
Band 7: Grundlinien der Philosophie des Rechts
Band 8: Enzyklopädie der philosophischen Band Wissenschaften I
Band 9: Enzyklopädie der philosophischen Wissenschaften II
Band 10: Enzyklopädie der philosophischen Wissenschaften III
Band 11: Berliner Schriften 1818–1831
Band 12: Vorlesungen über die Philosophie der Geschichte
Band 13: Vorlesungen über die Ästhetik I
Band 14: Vorlesungen über die Ästhetik II
Band 15: Vorlesungen über die Ästhetik III
Band 16: Vorlesungen über die Philosophie der Religion I
Band 17: Vorlesungen über die Philosophie der Religion II
Band 18: Vorlesungen über die Geschichte der Philosophie I
Band 19: Vorlesungen über die Geschichte der Philosophie II
Band 20: Vorlesungen über die Geschichte der Philosophie III

Other Hegel Works Cited

Hegel, Georg Wilhelm Friedrich. 1968– . *Gesammelte Werke*. In Verbindung mit der Hegel-Kommission der Rheinisch-Westfälischen Akademie der Wissenschaften und dem Hegel-Archiv der Ruhr – Universität Bochum. Hamburg: Meiner.
   Hegel, Georg Wilhelm Friedrich. Bd. 1. *Frühe Schriften*.
   Hegel, Georg Wilhelm Friedrich. Bd. 5. *Schriften und Entwürfe (1799–1808)*.
   Hegel, Georg Wilhelm Friedrich. Bd. 8. *Jenaer Systementwürfe III*.
   Hegel, Georg Wilhelm Friedrich. Bd. 13: *Enzyklopädie der philosophischen Wissenschaften im Grundrisse 1817*.

Hegel, Georg Wilhelm Friedrich. Bd. 26.1: *Vorlesungen über die Philosophie des Rechts I*.

Hegel, Georg Wilhelm Friedrich. 1973. *Vorlesungen über Rechtsphilosophie 1818–1831*, ed. Karl-Heinz Ilting, 4 Bände. Stuttgart-Bad Cannstatt: Frommann-Holzboog.

Hegel, Georg Wilhelm Friedrich. 1983a. *Philosophie des Rechts: Die Vorlesung von 1819/20 in einer Nachschrift*, ed. Dieter Henrich. Frankfurt: Suhrkamp.

Hegel, Georg Wilhelm Friedrich. 1983b. *Vorlesungen über Naturrecht und Staatswissenschaft Heidelberg 1817/18 mit Nachträgen aus der Vorlesung 1818/19, Nachgeschrieben von P. Wannemann*, ed. C. Becker et al., Hamburg: Meiner.

Hegel, Georg Wilhelm Friedrich. 1995. *Vorlesungen über Ästhetik: Berlin 1820/21* (Nachschrift Ascheberg), ed. H. Schneider. Frankfurt: Suhrkamp.

Hegel, Georg Wilhelm Friedrich. 1999. *Philosophie des Rechts: Nachschrift der Vorlesung von 1822/23 von K.L. Heyse*, ed. E. Schilbach. Frankfurt: Suhrkamp.

Hegel, Georg Wilhelm Friedrich. 2000. *Vorlesungen über die Philosophie des Rechts, Berlin 1819/1820, Nachgeschrieben von J.R. Ringier*. ed. E. Angehrn, M. Bondeli & H.N. Seelmann. Hamburg: Meiner.

Hegel, Georg Wilhelm Friedrich. 2004. *Die Philosophie der Geschichte: Vorlesungsmitschrift Heimann (Winter 1830–1831)*, ed. K. Vieweg. München: Fink.

Hegel, Georg Wilhelm Friedrich. 2005. *Philosophie des Rechts, Vorlesung von 1821/22*, ed. H. Hoppe (ed.) Frankfurt: Suhrkamp.

Secondary Texts

Agamben, Georgio. 2005. *State of Exception*. Chicago: University of Chicago Press.

Allgemeines Landrecht für die Preußischen Staaten (ALR). [1794]. Online at https://opinioiuris.de/quelle/1622 (accessed 2.10.19).

Becker, Jurek. 1969. *Jakob der Lügner*. Frankfurt: Suhrkamp.

Bernstein, Jay. 2010. 'Hegel on Wall Street', *The New York Times*, 3.10.2010.

Bockelmann, Paul. 1935. *Hegels Notstandslehre*. Berlin: De Gruyter.

Böhme, Jacob. 1958. *Mysterium Magnum* in *Sämtliche Schriften*, Bd. 7. Stuttgart-Bad Cannstatt: Frommann-Holzboog.

Bundesverfassungsgericht. 2010. Urteil 1 BvF 2/05, 24.11.2010. Online at https://www.bundesverfassungsgericht.de/SharedDocs/Entscheidungen/DE/2010/11/fs20101124_1bvf000205.html (accessed 2.10.19).

Burnet, John. 1930. *Early Greek Philosophy*. London: Adam & Charles Black.

Busch, Werner. 2003. *Geschichte der klassischen Bildgattungen in Quellentexten und Kommentaren*. Bd. 3. Darmstadt: Wissenschaftliche Buchgesellschaft.

Cesa, Claudio. 1982. ‚Entscheidung und Schicksal'. In: Henrich & Horstmann (eds.) *Hegels Philosophie des Rechts. Die Theorie der Rechtsformen und ihre Logik*.

BIBLIOGRAPHY

Derrida, J. 1998. ‚Der Schacht und die Pyramide. Einführung in die Hegelsche Semiologie' in: Randgänge der Philosophie, ed. Peter Engelmann, Wien: Passagen Verlag.

Dolan, Kerry. 2016. 'The World's Billionaires', *Forbes Magazine*, 1.3.2016.

Düsing, Klaus. 1991. ‚Hegels Theorie der Einbildungskraft' in *Psychologie und Anthropologie oder Philosophie des Geistes. Beiträge zu einer Hegel-Tagung in Marburg 1989*, Hrsg. v. Franz Hespe u. Burkhard Tuschling. Stuttgart: Fromann-Holzboog.

Euchner, Walter. 1996. *John Locke zur Einführung*. Hamburg: Junius.

Ferguson, Adam. 1966. *An Essay on the History of Civil Society*, Edinburgh University Press.

Fichte, Johann Gottlieb. 1991. *Grundlage des Naturrechts nach Prinzipien der Wissenschaftslehre*. Hamburg: Meiner 1991.

Fichte, Johann Gottlieb. 2000. *Foundations of Natural Right*, trans. Michael Bauer. Cambridge: Cambridge University Press.

Flintoff, Everard. 1980. 'Pyrrho and India', *Phronesis*, 25 (1):88–108.

Fulda, Hans Friedrich. 1991 ‚Vom Gedächtnis zum Denken' in Hespe, Franz & Tuschling, Burkhard (eds.): *Psychologie und Anthropologie oder Philosophie des Geistes. Beiträge zu einer Hegel-Tagung in Marburg 1989*. Stuttgart-Bad Cannstatt Frommann-Holzboog, 321–360.

Fulda, Hans Friedrich. 1996. ‚Einleitung' in *Skeptizismus und spekulatives Denken in der Philosophie Hegels*, ed. Hans Friedrich Fulda & Rolf-Peter Horstmann. Stuttgart: Klett-Cotta.

Fulda, Hans Friedrich. 2003. *Georg Wilhelm Friedrich Hegel*. München: Beck.

Gans, Eduard. 1981. *Vorrede zu den Grundlinien der Philosophie des Rechts*, Stuttgart-Bad Constatt: Frommann.

Goethe, Johann Wolfgang von. 1960. *Werke*, ed. Siegfried Seidel (Berliner Ausgabe). Berlin: Aufbau Verlag.

Goethe, Johann Wolfgang von. Bd. 8. *Faust* Teil 1.

Goethe, Johann Wolfgang von. Bd. 18. *Kunsttheoretische Schriften und Übersetzungen*.

Graeser, Andreas. 2000. ‚Einleitung' in Erler & Graeser (eds.) *Philosophen des Altertums*. Darmstadt: Primus.

Grober, Ulrich. 2010. *Die Entdeckung der Nachhaltigkeit*. München: Kunstmann.

Grundgesetz für die Bundesrepublik Deutschland. Online at http://www.gesetze-im-internet.de/gg/ (accessed 2.10.19).

Hartmann, Klaus. 1982. 'Linearität und Koordination in Hegels Rechtsphilosohie', in *Hegels Philosophie des Rechts: Die Theorie der Rechtsformen und ihre Logik*. ed. Dieter Henrich and Rolf-Peter Horstmann. Stuttgart: Klett-Cotta.

Henrich, Dieter. 1976. 'Hegels Grundoperation: Eine Einleitung in die Wissenschaft der Logik' in *Der Idealismus und seine Gegenwart*, ed. Ute Guzzoni, Bernhard Rang and Ludwig Siep. Hamburg: Meiner.

Henrich, Dieter. 1982. ‚Logische Form und reale Totalität. Über die Begriffsform von Hegels eigentlichem Staatsbegriff' in Henrich and Horstmann, eds. *Hegels Philosophie des Rechts. Die Theorie der Rechtsformen und ihre Logik.*

Henrich, Dieter & Horstmann, Rolf-Peter, eds. 1982. *Hegels Philosophie des Rechts: Die Theorie der Rechtsformen und ihre Logik.* Stuttgart: Klett-Cotta.

Hippel, Theodor Gottlieb von. 2013. *Lebensläufe nach Aufsteigender Linie.* Berlin: Contumax-Hofenberg.

Hippel, Theodor Gottlieb von. 1979. *Über die Ehe*, ed. Günter de Bruyn. Berlin: Buchverlag Der Morgen.

Honneth, Axel. 2007. 'G.W.F. Hegel, Grundlinien der Philosophie des Rechts (1821)', in *Geschichte des politischen Denkens: Ein Handbuch*, ed. Manfred Brocker. Frankfurt: Suhrkamp.

Horstmann, Rolf-Peter. 1993. 'Metaphysikkritik bei Hegel und Nietzsche', *Hegel-Studien* 28: 287–292.

Horstmann, Rolf-Peter. 2005. 'Hegels Theorie der bürgerlichen Gesellschaft', in: *G.W.F. Hegel. Grundlinien der Philosophie des Rechts*, ed. Ludwig Siep.

Hösle, Vittorio. 1987. ‚Das abstrakte Recht' in *Anspruch und Leistung von Hegels Rechtsphilosophie*, ed. Christoph Jermann. Stuttgart-Bad Cannstatt: Frommann-Holzboog.

Hösle, Vittorio 1988. *Hegels System, Vol. 2: Philosophie der Natur und des Geistes.* Hamburg: Meiner.

Hume, David. 1960. *A Treatise of Human Nature*, ed. L.A. Selby-Bigge. Oxford: Clarendon Press.

Hüning, D. and Tuschling, D. 1998. *Recht, Staat und Völkerrecht bei Immanuel Kant.* Berlin: Duncker & Humblot.

Kant, Immanuel. 1968. *Werke* (Akademie-Ausgabe), Berlin: de Gruyter.
    Kant, Immanuel. Bd. 3. *Kritik der reinen Vernunft.*
    Kant, Immanuel. Bd. 5. *Kritik der Urteilskraft.*
    Kant, Immanuel. Bd. 6. *Metaphysik der Sitten.*

Kervégan, Jean-François. 2009. *L'effectif et le rationnel: Hegel et l'esprit objectif.* Paris: Vrin.

Kierkegaard, Sören. 2004. ‚Über den Begriff der Ironie' in *Gesammelte Werke* ed. Emanuel Hirsch, Hayo Gerdes und Hans Martin Junghans. Bd. 31, Simmerath: Grevenberg.

Knowles, Dudley. 2002. *Hegel's Philosophy of Right.* London and New York: Routledge.

Koch, Anton Friedrich. 2014. *Die Evolution des logischen Raumes: Aufsätze zu Hegels Nichtstandard-Metaphysik.* Tübingen: Mohr Siebeck.

Köstler, Josef. 1967. *Wald, Mensch, Kultur: Ausgewählte Vorträge u. Aufsätze zur Kulturgeschichte, zur Ökonomie des Forstwesens und zur Technik der Waldpflege.* Berlin: Pary.

Koselleck, Reinhard. 1989. *Preußen zwischen Reform und Revolution: Allgemeines Landrecht, Verwaltung und soziale Bewegung von 1791 bis 1848.* München, dtv/Klett-Cotta.

Kuehn, Manfred. 2004. *Kant: Eine Biographie*. München: C.H. Beck.

Locke, John. 2003. *Two Treatises of Government and A Letter Concerning Toleration*. New Haven: Yale.

Locke, John. 2007. *Zweite Abhandlung über die Regierung* [Second Treatise on Government], ed. Ludwig Siep. Frankfurt: Suhrkamp.

Losurdo, Domenico. 2000. *Hegel und die Freiheit der Modernen*. Frankfurt: Suhrkamp.

Lübbe-Wolff, Gertrude. 1986. 'Über das Fehlen von Grundrechten in Hegels Rechtsphilosophie', in *Hegels Rechtsphilosophie im Zusammenhang der europäischen Verfassungsgeschichte*, ed. Otto Pöggeler and Hans-Christian Lucas. Stuttgart-Bad Cannstatt: Frommann-Holzboog, 421–46.

Menasse, Robert. 1994. *Phänomenologie der Entgeisterung*. Frankfurt: Suhrkamp.

Menasse, Robert.1996. *Sinnliche Gewissheit*. Frankfurt: Suhrkamp.

Michelet, Carl Ludwig. 1970. *Naturrecht oder Rechtsphilosophie*, Bd. 2. Leipzig: Zentralantiquariat.

Michelsen, Peter. 1972. *Laurence Sterne und der deutsche Roman des 18. Jahrhunderts*. Göttingen: Vandenhoeck & Ruprecht.

Mohr, Georg. 2005. 'Unrecht und Strafe (§§82–104)', in Siep (ed.), *G.W.F. Hegel: Grundlinien der Philosophie des Rechts*.

Montaigne, Michel de. 1965. *Essais, tome III*. Paris: Gallimard.

Niethammer, Friedrich Immanuel. 1792. ‚Probe einer Übersetzung aus des Sextus Empricus drei Büchern von den Grundlehren der Pyrrhoniker' in Fülleborn, G. (ed.), *Beyträge zur Geschichte der Philosophie*, Heft 2. Züllichau, Freystadt: Fromannn.

Nietzsche, Friedrich. 1982. *Menschliches, Allzumenschliches*, in: *Werke in drei Bänden*, ed. Karl Schlechta, V.1. München: Carl Hanser Verlag.

Nietzsche, Friedrich. 1988. *Kritische Studienausgabe*. Berlin: de Gruyter.

Nietzsche, Friedrich. Bd. 1. *Die Philosophen im tragischen Zeitalter der Griechen*.

Nietzsche, Friedrich. Bd. 13. *Aus dem Nachlaß der Achtziger Jahre*.

Novalis. 1999. *Werke, Tagebücher und Briefe*, ed. Hans Joachim Mähl and Richard Samuel, vol. 2. Darmstadt: Wissenschaftliche Buchgesellschaft.

Nuzzo, Angelica. 2001. 'Freedom in the Body: The Body as Subject of Rights and Object of Property in Hegel's 'Abstract Right,"' in Robert R. Williams, ed., *Beyond Liberalism and Communitarianism: Studies in Hegel's Philosophy of Right*. Albany: SUNY.

Pawlik, Michael. 2004. *Person, Subjekt, Bürger: Zur Legitimation der Strafe*. Berlin: Duncker & Humblot.

Petersen, Thomas. 1996. "Widerstandsrecht Und Recht Auf Revolution in Hegels Rechtsphilosophie." *ARSP: Archiv Für Rechts – Und Sozialphilosophie / Archives for Philosophy of Law and Social Philosophy* Vol. 82, no. 4: 472–84.

Pippin, Robert. 2008. *Hegel's Practical Philosophy*. Cambridge: Cambridge University Press.

Platzeck, Matthias. 2009. *Zukunft braucht Herkunft: Deutsche Fragen, Ostdeutsche Antworten*. Hamburg: Hoffmann und Campe.

Pöggeler, Otto. 2003. ‚West-Ostende Todeserfahrungen' in *Zukünftiges Menschsein: Ethik zwischen Ost und West*, eds. Ralf Elm and Mamoru Takayama. Baden-Baden: Nomos.

Pöggeler, Otto & Lucas, Hans-Christian, eds. 1986. *Hegels Rechtsphilosophie im Zusammenhang der europäischen Verfassungsgeschichte*. Stuttgart-Bad Cannstatt: Frommann-Holzboog.

Quante, Michael. 1993. *Hegels Begriff der Handlung*. Stuttgart-Bad Canstatt: Frommann-Holzboog.

Quante, Michael. 2005. 'Die Persönlichkeit des Willens als Prinzip des abstrakten Rechts' in *G.W.F. Hegel. Grundlinien der Philosophie des Rechts*, ed. L. Siep.

Quante, Michael. 2011. 'Hegel's Planning Theory of Agency', in Arto Laitinen and Constantine Sandis, eds., *Hegel on Action*. Basingstoke: Palgrave-Macmillan.

Richter, Jean Paul. 1963. *Vorschule der Ästhetik*, ed. Norbert Miller. München: Carl Hanser.

Richter, Jean Paul. 1974. ‚Unpartheiische Beleuchtung und Abfertigung ...' in *Sämtliche Werke*, Abt. II. Bd. 1. München: Carl Hanser.

Richter, Jean Paul. 1873 [1782], 'Ueber Mich' in *Jean Pauls Sämmtliche Werke*, LXII, Dreizehnte Lieferung, Zweiter Band (Berlin: G. Reimer, 1837): *Bemerkungen über uns närrische Menschen 1782–1792*.

Ricken, Friedo. 1994. *Antike Skepsis*. München: Beck.

Ritter, Joachim. 2005. 'Person und Eigentum' in Siep, ed. *G.W.F. Hegel: Grundlinien der Philosophie des Rechts*.

Rometsch, Jens. 2006. *Hegels Theorie des erkennenden Subjekts* (Dissertation Universität Heidelberg).

Rosenkranz, Karl. 1998. *Hegels Leben*. Darmstadt: Wissenschaftliche Buchgesellschaft.

Rosenzweig, Franz. 2010. *Hegel und der Staat*. Frankfurt: Suhrkamp.

Roubini, Nouriel & Mihm, Stephen. 2010. *Das Ende der Weltwirtschaft: Crisis Economics*. Frankfurt: Campus Verlag.

Rousseau, Jean-Jacques, 1999. *Discourse on Political Economy and the Social Contract*. Oxford: Oxford University Press.

Sans, Georg, 2011. ‚Hegels Begriff der Offenbarung als Schluss von drei Schlüssen' in *L'assoluto e il divino. La teologia cristiana di Hegel*. ed. V. Tommaso Pierini, Georg Sans, Klaus Vieweg and Pierluigi Valenza. Pisa: Biblioteca dell'Archivio di filosofia.

Schelling, Friedrich Wilhelm Joseph. 1985. *System des transzendentalen Idealismus* in *Ausgewählte Schriften* Bd. 1, hrsg. v. Manfred Frank. Frankfurt: Suhrkamp.

Schlegel, Friedrich. 1958-. *Kritische Ausgabe seiner Werke*, ed. E. Behler. Paderborn: Schöningh.

Schlegel, Friedrich. Bd. 2. *Charakteristiken und Kritiken I. 1796–1801*.

Schlegel, Friedrich. Bd. 18: *Philosophische Lehrjahre. 1796–1828*.

Schellnhuber, Hans Joachim. 2009. ‚Manchmal könnte ich schreien' *Die Zeit* 26th March.
Schnädelbach, Herbert. 2000. *Hegels Philosophie*, 3 Bände. Frankfurt: Suhrkamp, 2000.
Sextus Empiricus. 1985. *Grundriss der pyrrhonischen Skepsis*, ed. M. Hossenfelder. Frankfurt: Suhrkamp.
Sextus Empiricus. 1994. *Outlines of Scepticism*, trans. Julia Annas and Jonathan Barnes. Cambridge: Cambridge University Press.
Sextus Empiricus. 1998. *Gegen die Dogmatiker*, ed. H. Flueckiger. Baden-Baden: Academia Verlag.
Siep, Ludwig. 1982. 'Intersubjektivität, Recht und Staat in *Hegels Grundlinien der Philosophie des Rechts*' in *Hegels Philosophie des Rechts. Die Theorie der Rechtsformen und ihre Logik*, ed. Dieter Henrich & Rolf Peter Horstmann.
Siep, Ludwig. 1992. *Praktische Philosophie im Deutschen Idealismus*. Frankfurt: Suhrkamp.
Siep, Ludwig. 2005. (ed.). *G.W.F. Hegel: Grundlinien der Philosophie des Rechts*. Berlin: Akademie Verlag.
Siep, Ludwig. 2010. *Aktualität und Grenzen der praktischen Philosophie Hegels*. München: Fink Verlag.
Smith, Adam. 1981. *An Inquiry into the Nature and Causes of the Wealth of Nations*. Indianapolis: Liberty Classics.
Sokel, Walter. 1963. 'Vorwort' in *Orest*, ed. J. Schondorff. München: Langen-Mueller.
Sterne, Laurence 1985. *The Life and Opinions of Tristram Shandy, Gentleman*, ed. G. Petrie. London: Penguin.
Stiglitz, Joseph. 2010. *Im freien Fall: Vom Versagen der Märkte zur Neuordnung der Weltwirtschaft*. München: Siedler.
Takahashi, Teruaki. 2005. ‚We Think in Pictures', *Humboldt Kosmos* 86, online at https://www.humboldt-foundation.de/kosmos/doc/kosmos86.pdf.
Vieweg, Klaus, 1999. *Philosophie des Remis. Der junge Hegel und das 'Gespenst des Skepticismus'*. München: Fink.
Vieweg, Klaus, 2002. ‚Heiterer Leichtsinn und fröhlicher Scharfsinn: Komik und Humor als Formen ästhetisch-poetischer Skepsis' in *Die geschichtliche Bedeutung der Kunst und die Bestimmung der Künste*. ed. A. Gethmann-Siefert. München: Fink.
Vieweg, Klaus, 2003. ‚Der Anfang der Philosophie – Hegels Aufhebung des Pyrrhonismus' in *Das Interesse des Denkens: Hegel aus heutiger Sicht*, ed. Wolfgang Welsch & Klaus Vieweg. München: Fink.
Vieweg, Klaus, 2004.'Selbstbewußtsein, Skeptizismus und Solipsismus in Hegels 'Jenaer Systementwürfen I bis II,': in *Die Eigenbedeutung der Jenaer Systemkonzeptionen Hegels*, ed. H. Kimmerle. Berlin: Akademie.
Vieweg, Klaus, 2005. 'Humor als ver-sinnlichte Skepsis – Hegel und Jean Paul', in *Das Geistige und das Sinnliche in der Kunst*, ed. Dieter Wandschneider. Würzburg: Verlag Königshausen und Neumann.

Vieweg, Klaus, 2007. *Skepsis und Freiheit*. München: Fink.

Vieweg, Klaus, 2007b. ‚Das Bildliche und der Begriff: Hegel zur Aufhebung der Sprache der Vorstellung in die Sprache des Begriffs', in: Klaus Vieweg & Richard T. Gray: *Hegel und Nietzsche. Eine literarisch-philosophische Begegnung*. Weimar: Bauhaus-Universitäts Verlag.

Vieweg, Klaus, 2008. ‚Religion und absolutes Wissen: Der Übergang von der Vorstellung in den Begriff' in Klaus Vieweg & Wolfgang Welsch (Hrsg.): *Hegels Phänomenologie des Geistes*. Frankfurt: Suhrkamp.

Vieweg, Klaus, 2012a. *Das Denken der Freiheit*. München: Wilhelm Fink.

Vieweg, Klaus, 2012b. 'Moralität, Ironie, Skeptizismus, in Skeptizismus und Philosophie. Kant, Fichte, Hegel, ed. Elena Ficara (*Fichte-Studien* vol. 39). Amsterdam & New York: Rodopi.

Vieweg, Klaus, 2012c. 'Hegels Handlungsbegriff in der praktischen Philosophie und in der Ästhetik' in A. Gethmann-Siefert, H. Nagl-Docekal, E. Rozsa, E. Weisser-Lohmann (eds.), *Hegels Ästhetik als Theorie der Moderne*. Berlin: Akademie.

Vischer, Friedrich Theodor. 1837. *Ueber das Erhabene und Komische: ein Beitrag zu der Philosophie des Schönen*. Stuttgart: Imle & Krauß.

Welsch, Wolfgang. 1987. *Aisthesis: Grundzüge und Perspektiven der Aristotleischen Sinnenlehre*. Stuttgart: Klett-Cotta.

Welsch, Wolfgang. 2012. *Homo Mundanus: Jenseits der anthropischen Denkform der Moderne*. Weilerswist: Velbrück.

Westphal, Kenneth. 1998. 'Metaphysische und pragmatische Prinzipien in Kants Lehre von der Gehorsamspflicht gegen den Staat', in D. Hüning and B. Tuschling, eds. *Recht, Staat und Völkerrecht bei Immanuel Kant*. Berlin: Duncker & Humblot.

Williams, Robert R. ed., 2001. *Beyond Liberalism and Communitarianism: Studies in Hegel's Philosophy of Right*. Albany: SUNY.

Wood, Allen. 2005. 'Hegel's Critique of Morality', in Siep (ed.), *G.F.W. Hegel: Grundlinien der Philosophie des Rechts*.

Wolff, Michael. 1985. ‚Hegels staatstheoretischer Organizismus. Zum Begriff und zur Methode der Hegelschen Staatswissenschaft' in *Hegel-Studien* 19: 147–177.

Wolff, Michael. 1992. *Das Körper-Seele Problem: Kommentar zu Hegel, Enzyklopädie (1830)*. Frankfurt: Klostermann.

Printed in the United States
By Bookmasters